Juridicum – Schriftenreihe zum Wirtschafts-, Unternehmens- und Bankrecht / Series on Business, Corporate and Banking Law

Die Schriftenreihe zum **Wirtschafts-, Unternehmens- und Bankrecht / Series on Business, Corporate and Banking Law** bietet ein Forum für aktuelle und herausragende wissenschaftliche Beiträge aus den genannten Rechtsgebieten. Veröffentlicht werden vor allem Dissertationsschriften, daneben auch ausgewählte Sammelbände zu aktuellen und rechtswissenschaftlich interessanten Fragestellungen. Der Fokus liegt vor allem auf dem deutschen und deutschsprachigen Recht, typischerweise jedoch mit europäischen und internationalen Bezügen. Die Reihe zeichnet sich auch ansonsten durch ihre internationale Ausrichtung aus: Publikationen sind sowohl in deutscher als auch in englischer Sprache möglich. Herausgegeben wird sie von renommierten Wissenschaftlerinnen und Wissenschaftlern aus Deutschland, der Schweiz und Italien, die damit einen grenzüberschreitenden wissenschaftlichen Dialog im Wirtschafts-, Unternehmens- und Bankrecht fördern möchten.

Lejla Hasanovic

Piercing the Corporate Veil: Shareholder Liability

Springer

Dr. iur. Lejla Hasanovic
University of Sarajevo—Faculty of Law
Sarajevo, Bosnia and Herzegovina

ISSN 3091-5384 ISSN 3091-5392 (electronic)
Juridicum – Schriftenreihe zum Wirtschafts-, Unternehmens- und Bankrecht / Series on Business, Corporate and Banking Law
ISBN 978-3-658-52986-4 ISBN 978-3-658-52987-1 (eBook)
https://doi.org/10.1007/978-3-658-52987-1

This Springer imprint is published by the registered company Springer Fachmedien Wiesbaden GmbH, part of Springer Nature.
The registered company address is: Abraham-Lincoln-Str. 46, 65189 Wiesbaden, Germany

It is one of those stories that takes us back to our childhood, a world populated with myths and marvelous creatures, a world where you can hide behind your hands and pretend not to be seen. Judge Pisani, (ECtHR, 2025)

For Haris, Ela, Noa & Kai

Foreword

The present dissertation was accepted by the Faculty of Law of Heinrich Heine University Düsseldorf in the Summer Semester 2025/2026. For the purposes of publication, more recent case law and literature could be taken into account up to March of 2026.

I would like to express my sincere gratitude to my esteemed supervisors, my Doktorvater Professor Dr. Till Zimmermann and my mentor Professor Dr. Zinka Grbo, for their invaluable guidance and exceptional supervision of this work. I have always been able to rely on their professional expertise and personal support. Their doors were always open, their support selfless, and their kindness inspiring. Thank you. Appreciation and thanks are due to Professor Dr. Anne Schneider and Professor Dr. Thilo Kuntz for their support as members of the disputation committee.

The thematic refinement of this dissertation greatly benefited from the insights gained through lectures, discussions, and conversations held within the academic activities and research seminars held both at the Faculty of Law of Heinrich Heine University Düsseldorf and the Faculty of Law – University of Sarajevo. Special thanks are due to the Max Planck Institute for Comparative and Private International Law, that granted me a scholarship to conduct research from March to May 2026. I would like to thank my parents and sisters for inspiring the love for knowledge, my husband and children for their love and my friends and colleagues for their support. Many thanks to my professors and lecturers from the University of Sarajevo – Faculty of Law, judges and attorneys, for their selfless delivery of case law and expertise.

Competing Interests The author has no competing interests to declare that are relevant to the content of this manuscript.

Contents

Abbreviations

AG	Stock Corporation (Germany)
AI	Artificial Intelligence
AktG	German Stock Corporation Act (Aktiengesetz)
ALLPC	Act on the Liability of Legal Persons for Criminal Offences of Croatia
AML Regulation	Regulation (EU) 2024/1624
AML/CFT	Anti-money laundering and countering the financing of terrorism
AMLA	Authority for anti-money laundering and countering the financing of terrorism
AMLBiH	Anti-money laundering and countering the financing of terrorism Law in BiH
AMLD Consolidated	Consolidated Anti-Money Laundering Directive
ATAD	Anti-Tax Avoidance Directive
BAM	Bosnian Convertible Mark
BD	Brčko Distrikt
BGB	German Civil Code (Bürgerliches Gesetzbuch)
BGH	German Federal Court of Justice
BGHSt	Decisions of the German Federal Court of Justice in Criminal Matters
BiH	Bosnia and Herzegovina
BRIS	Business Registers Interconnection System
CCBD	Criminal Code of Brčko District (Krivični zakon BD)

CCBiH	Criminal Code of Bosnia and Herzegovina (Krivični zakon BiH)
CCFBiH	Criminal Code of Federation of Bosnia and Herzegovina (Krivični zakon FBiH)
CCRS	Criminal Code of Republika Srpska (Krivični zakon RS)
CERCLA	Comprehensive Environmental Response, Compensation, and Liability Act
CJEU	Court of Justice of the European Union
CoE	Council of Europe
Company Law Directive	Directive (EU) 2017/1132
CPI	Corruption Perceptions Index
CRO AML Law	The Act on the Prevention of Money Laundering and Terrorist Financing of Croatia
Digitalization Directive	Directive (EU) 2019/1151
EC	European Commission
ECHR	European Convention on Human Rights
ECJ	European Court of Justice
ECtHR	European Court of Human Rights
EPPO	European Public Prosecutor's Office
EPRS	Directorate-General for Parliamentary Research Services
EU	European Union
EUROPOL	EU Agency for Law Enforcement Cooperation
FATF	The Financial Action Task Force
FBiH	Federation of Bosnia and Herzegovina
FDI	Foreign Direct Investments
FIU	Financial Intelligence Units
GmbH	Limited Liability Company (Germany)
GmbHG	German Act on Limited Liability Companies (Gesetz betreffend die Gesellschaften mit beschränkter Haftung)
GTA CRO	Croatia General Tax Act (Opći porezni zakon)
GwG	German Money Laundering Act (Geldwäschegesetz)
HGB	German Commercial Code (Handelsgesetzbuch)
HJPC	High Judicial and Prosecutorial Council of BiH
HRK	Croatian Kuna
ICSID	International Centre for Settlement of Investment Disputes Convention

JSC	Joint Stock Company
KBA	German Federal Motor Transport Authority
LBC/LBCs	Letterbox Company/Letterbox Companies
LLC	Limited Liability Company
LTAFBiH	Law on the Tax Administration of the Federation of Bosnia and Herzegovina (Zakon o poreznoj upravi FBiH)
OLAF	European Anti-Fraud Office
OLG Stuttgart	Higher Regional Court Stuttgart
OWiG	German Act on Regulatory Offences (Ordnungswidrigkeitengesetz)
PIF Directive	Directive (EU) 2017/1371
RS	Republika Srpska
SFRY	Socialist Federal Republic of Yugoslavia
SIENA	Secure Information Exchange Network Application (Europol)
SME/SMEs	Small and Medium-Sized Enterprise/Enterprises
SPEs	Special Purpose Entities
StGB	German Criminal Code (Strafgesetzbuch)
StPO	German Code of Criminal Procedure (Strafprozeßordnung)
TAFBiH	Tax Administration of the Federation of BiH
TEU	Treaty on European Union
UG	Entrepreneurial Company (Limited Liability)
UNCTAD	United Nations Conference on Trade and Development
VAT	Value-Added Tax
ZOOCRO	Croatian Law on Obligations (Zakon o obligacionim odnosima)
ZOOFBiH	Law on Obligations FBiH (Zakon o obligacionim odnosima FBiH)
ZOORS	Law on Obligations RS (Zakon o obligacionim odnosima RS)
ZPDBD	Company Law of Brčko Distrikt (Zakon o privrednim društvima BD)
ZPDFBiH	Company Law of Federation of Bosnia and Herzegovina (Zakon o privrednim društvima FBiH)

ZPDRS	Company Law of Republika Srpska (Zakon o privrednim društvima RS)
ZSR	Court Register Act of Croatia (Zakon o sudskom registru)
ZTD	Croatian Law on Companies (Zakon o trgovačkim društvima)

Introduction

1

In 2021, the European Commission (EC) conducted research on letterbox companies (LBC), which are entities established in jurisdictions where they conduct little or no real economic activity, often used for tax avoidance or regulatory arbitrage. In the study, EC concluded that the phenomenon of LBCs is linked to efforts of the European Union (EU) to develop the Single European Market through one of its cornerstones, the freedom of establishment.[1] While this freedom removes cross-border barriers for legitimate business formation, it has simultaneously encouraged "jurisdiction shopping"[2], the exploitation of corporate law loopholes to evade regulatory oversight. The increasing digitalization of company registration within the EU, coupled with the freedom of establishment, has made it considerably easier to create and manage companies across borders. While this development fosters market integration, it simultaneously intensifies conflicts of jurisdiction in corporate criminal matters, as companies can be incorporated in one state, operate in another, and cause harm in a third.[3]

The purpose of a company is to raise profits for its shareholders[4] so if a company has no economic activity, the use of such a company is always artificial.[5] This view, famously associated with the Chicago School of Economics,

---

[1] Morel et al. (2021), p. 1.

[2] Ibid., p. 246.

[3] Schneider (2014), p. 250.

[4] Friedman (2016), p. 112.; Friedman (2007), p. 1–6.

[5] Kärki (2020), p. 195.

L. Hasanovic, *Piercing the Corporate Veil: Shareholder Liability*,
Juridicum – Schriftenreihe zum Wirtschafts-, Unternehmens- und Bankrecht / Series on Business, Corporate and Banking Law,
https://doi.org/10.1007/978-3-658-52987-1_1

has been widely debated in recent decades, with critics arguing that it overlooks broader corporate responsibilities toward employees, the environment, and society at large.[6] When companies are established with no genuine business activity, their use becomes artificial and potentially fraudulent, raising concerns about shareholder accountability and triggering the application of the doctrine of piercing the corporate veil. Assessing whether a company lacks genuine business activity requires both legal and empirical indicators. International and EU instruments now provide important benchmarks for identifying artificial corporate structures. The OECD[7] outlines red flags such as absence of physical presence, no employees, or opaque ownership as typical signs of "shell"[8] or letterbox entities. At the EU level, the Business Registers Interconnection System (BRIS) improves transparency by linking national registries and helping identify companies with no substantive operations.[9] Additionally, Directive 2018/822 (DAC6) requires mandatory disclosure of cross-border arrangements that may be used for tax avoidance or evasion, especially where entities lack economic substance.[10] These tools serve both preventive and evidentiary roles and support judicial findings that the corporate veil should be pierced when formal separateness masks fraudulent, abusive, or evasive conduct.

Bosnia and Herzegovina is a candidate country seeking to join the European Union[11]. In terms of company law, it is required to integrate its existing legislation into the relevant national law. The company law acquis comprises regulations pertaining to the establishment, registration, merger, and division of companies. It includes a harmonized set of directives and regulations that govern legal forms, transparency obligations, digital registration, cross-border mobility, and shareholder protections. Notable instruments include Directive (EU) 2017/1132, which consolidates rules on company formation and restructuring; Directive (EU) 2019/1151, which promotes the digitalization of company law; and Directive 2007/36/

---

[6] Stout (2012), p. 2.; Freeman et al. (2004), p. 368.

[7] Morel et al. (2021), p. 23.

[8] Ibid., p. 6

[9] European Parliament and Council (2017), art. 16.

[10] Council of the EU (2018), para. 4.

[11] Directorate-General for Neighborhood and Enlargement Negotiations. (2024) Bosnia and Herzegovina Report 2024. https://enlargement.ec.europa.eu/bosnia-and-herzegovina-report-2024_en#details, accessed March 18, 2025.

EC on the exercise of shareholders' rights in listed companies. Additionally, regulations such as Regulation (EC) No 2157/2001 on the European Company (SE) and Regulation (EU) 2015/848 on insolvency proceedings extend harmonized legal frameworks across borders. For candidate countries like Bosnia and Herzegovina, the transposition of this acquis is essential for aligning national company law with the internal market principles of the EU, particularly regarding corporate transparency, governance, and digital access.[12] Consequently, it is of paramount importance to comprehend the challenges confronting Member States due to the fraudulent activities of companies and their ramifications across the spectrum of relevant disciplines, including company law, taxation law, labor and social security law, and criminal law. The EU has enabled some gatekeepers to avoid abuse

[12] The sources of EU law are divided into primary and secondary law. Primary sources include the founding treaties, protocols, and the Charter of Fundamental Rights, as well as unwritten general principles of EU law developed by the Court of Justice of the European Union (CJEU), such as proportionality, legal certainty, and procedural fairness. These primary sources occupy the highest position in the EU's hierarchy of norms, providing both interpretative standards and the basis for judicial review of secondary law. Secondary law, adopted by EU institutions under the authority of the Treaties, comprises legislative acts, delegated acts, and implementing acts, ranked hierarchically under the Treaty on the Functioning of the European Union (TFEU). Legislative acts include regulations and directives passed by the European Parliament and Council through the ordinary or special legislative procedure. Delegated acts, adopted by the Commission, supplement or amend non-essential elements of legislative acts. Implementing acts execute legislative or delegated acts but do not alter their content. The form of a legal act—regulation, directive, or decision—does not vary based on its classification (legislative, delegated, or implementing), but its legal effect and binding force are defined accordingly. Regulations have general application and are directly applicable in all Member States without requiring national transposition. For example, Regulation (EC) No 2157/2001 on the Statute for a European Company (Societas Europaea, SE) establishes EU-wide rules on company formation and governance but also relies on national implementing provisions. By contrast, directives are binding only as to the result to be achieved and must be implemented into national law by Member States, allowing for flexibility in form and methods. This two-step legislative process reflects a compromise between EU integration and respect for national legal systems. This legal architecture is essential when analyzing how candidate countries such as Bosnia and Herzegovina must harmonize their legal systems with the EU acquis, particularly in areas such as company law, digitalization of company procedures, and shareholder rights. (Gerner-Beuerle & Schillig (2019), p. 97–111).

of corporate forms, such as the rules on disqualification of directors[13], or preventive administrative or judicial supervision of incorporation.[14] These gatekeepers are unknown to legal system of Bosnia and Herzegovina, that in turn harmonizes its company law with the acquis enabling full online establishment of companies leaning into the abyss of the unknown. The fundamental principle underpinning the legal structure of limited liability companies is that shareholders are not held personally liable for any financial obligations or legal liabilities incurred by the company. This concept is further reinforced by the principle of limited liability, which serves to protect the personal assets of shareholders from any potential financial losses or legal claims arising from the company's activities.[15]

This dissertation seeks to address the question of how courts determine when to pierce the corporate veil and hold shareholders individually accountable for the corporation's actions, particularly in cases of fraud or abuse of the corporate form. The central research question guiding this study is whether there is a connection between criminal liability for corporate crimes (e.g. tax evasion) and shareholder liability in civil procedures. Furthermore, it investigates whether the criminal liability of corporate entities can be a determining factor for piercing the corporate veil in the civil procedure. This dissertation adopts a comparative approach that focuses on Croatia and Germany as reference jurisdictions in analyzing shareholder liability and the doctrine of piercing the corporate veil. The motivation for selecting these two legal systems is rooted in both regional relevance and legal functionality. Croatia serves as a natural comparator due to its shared legal heritage, language, and institutional traditions with Bosnia and Herzegovina. Both countries emerged from the same socialist legal tradition and experienced parallel transitions toward market-oriented legal systems and democratic governance following the dissolution of Yugoslavia. Importantly, Croatia

---

[13] Directive (EU) 2019/1151, art. 13. i. In 2023, Croatia adopted the Regulation on the Content, Manner of Keeping, and Conditions for Using the Register of Persons Who Cannot Be Members of the Management Board of a Company, which established a register and defined the grounds for director disqualification. The control mechanism prescribed by Directive 2019/1151 involves: (a) Statements that directors must provide when establishing a company, disclosing any circumstances that could lead to disqualification in a Member State, and (b) Information exchange through the e-Justice portal between Member States concerning director disqualifications. This regime is crucial for preventing the abuse of cross-border mobility. Without it, a disqualified director could continue illegal activities in another EU Member State. According to Croatian Company Law, illegal activities that can lead to director disqualification include money laundering, terrorist financing, abuse of trust in business operations, fraud in business operations, intentional bankruptcy, etc.

[14] European Commission (2023), art. 13.i.

[15] Bainbridge (2005), p. 78.

has recently completed the process of EU accession, including the full transposition of the company law acquis, making its experience directly relevant to Bosnia and Herzegovina's current path of legal harmonization. Studying Croatia provides insight into the challenges and strategies of integrating post-socialist legal structures with EU corporate governance standards, particularly in contexts where legal culture and administrative capacity closely resemble those of Bosnia and Herzegovina. In contrast, Germany does not share the same historical or political legacy but represents a model jurisdiction within the European Union due to its systematic, well-developed, and jurisprudentially rich approach to company law. Germany offers functional and doctrinal benchmarks, particularly in areas such as legal certainty, corporate accountability, and judicial tests for piercing the corporate veil. Moreover, Germany played a central role in shaping much of the EU's legal architecture and offers an example of optimal legal solutions grounded in civil law methodology and proportionality principles. Including Germany allows for a critical comparison between institutional adaptation in transitional jurisdictions (like Croatia) and structural design in a stable, long-established EU Member State. Together, the comparative analysis of Croatia and Germany enables this dissertation to contrast experiences of post-socialist legal integration, one as a newly harmonized EU Member State, the other as a founding architect of EU legal norms. This approach highlights both the procedural evolution and substantive alignment of national company law systems with EU requirements, providing Bosnia and Herzegovina with doctrinal, institutional, and policy lessons as it continues its path toward EU membership. Their experiences provide insightful information about how to address these issues in various legal and socioeconomic contexts. The use of companies as conduits for illicit activities is appealing because it allows perpetrators to disguise their malfeasance behind the veil of a separate legal entity.[16] This is why it is important to address the doctrine of piercing the corporate veil and identify situations in which the law holds additional persons liable for corporate obligations.

Considering the prevailing regulatory framework governing the doctrine of piercing the corporate veil in Bosnia and Herzegovina, this subject is of paramount importance, as the findings of this research will significantly enhance our comprehension of this doctrine. Furthermore, a more comprehensive grasp of the concept will assist in the detection of potential exploitation within the commercial domain, such as instances where individuals may seek to evade accountability for a company's financial obligations. By elucidating this institute through the presentation of a theoretical framework and comparative practices, it

[16] Stiglitz & Pieth (2016), p. 6; Pieth (1997), p. 119.

is possible to formulate recommendations that will prevent the abuse of corporate entities, thereby preserving market integrity and ensuring fairness in business relations. Conversely, effective regulatory measures concerning the piercing of the corporate veil enhance legal certainty by delineating the circumstances under which the corporate veil will be pierced and stipulating the rights and obligations of the parties involved. This simultaneously curtails the capacity of corporate entities to exploit the legal personality of a company as a shield to evade liability, deterring potential abuses and mitigating the risk of fraudulent actions that harm creditors and other affected parties.

Clearly regulated rules provide mechanisms for the accountability of capital owners and shareholders, thereby reducing the incentive to engage in illegal activities, such as tax evasion, money laundering, or asset misappropriation. An understanding of, and proper regulation of, this institute has an impact on the development of corporate culture and ethics. By establishing explicit criteria for the circumstances under which the corporate veil may be pierced, organizations are motivated to align their business practices with the prevailing legislation.[17] This, in turn, fosters the development of corporate ethics based on respect for the law, social responsibility, and long-term business sustainability. This, in turn, not only creates a favorable business environment but also strengthens the trust of investors, employees, and the broader public in the integrity and responsibility of organizations.

[17] Thompson (1990), p. 1073.

Research Methodology 2

2.1 Subject of the Research

- EU legal instruments regulating corporate and criminal liability, shareholder accountability, and the prevention of abuse of corporate structures, including directives relating to company law, anti-money laundering, taxation, and corporate governance.
- Jurisprudence from selected EU Member States, specifically Croatia and Germany, in comparison with Bosnia and Herzegovina's legal framework, with the aim of identifying best practices and transferable lessons concerning corporate liability and shareholder accountability.
- The legal criteria and circumstances under which shareholders are held liable for the misuse or abuse of the corporate form, such as fraudulent behavior, siphoning of assets, and evasion of legal obligations.
- Court decisions across the EU and in Bosnia and Herzegovina where the corporate veil was pierced, with the aim of identifying recurring judicial patterns, evidentiary thresholds, and the legal reasoning applied in such rulings.

2.2 Research Problem

The absence of explicit, coherent legal standards and judicial practices concerning the doctrine of piercing the corporate veil, presents a significant challenge for the legal system of Bosnia and Herzegovina. While the principle of separate legal personality is foundational to corporate law, its misuse allows individuals to hide

L. Hasanovic, *Piercing the Corporate Veil: Shareholder Liability*,
Juridicum – Schriftenreihe zum Wirtschafts-, Unternehmens- und Bankrecht / Series on Business, Corporate and Banking Law,
https://doi.org/10.1007/978-3-658-52987-1_2

behind the corporate form to evade legal obligations, conceal illicit activities, and defraud creditors. This legal gap not only undermines justice and enforcement but also has serious economic implications. In a transitional economy such as Bosnia and Herzegovina's, still navigating the legacies of post-socialist legal reforms and seeking to harmonize its laws with the EU acquis, the absence of clear legal and judicial standards on shareholder liability contributes to market uncertainty, deters foreign direct investment, and weakens creditor protection. It also erodes trust in the rule of law and creates a permissive environment for economic crime and regulatory arbitrage. Given the country's ongoing EU accession process, addressing this issue is not merely a matter of legal refinement, but a strategic necessity to strengthen the investment climate, improve institutional integrity, and foster sustainable economic development.

2.3 Research Hypothesis

The effectiveness of legal frameworks in combating corporate abuse, fraud, and financial crimes is significantly enhanced when clear, consistent, and well-defined legal criteria for piercing the corporate veil are established and consistently applied by courts, particularly in cases involving criminal liability such as tax evasion and money laundering.

Auxiliary Hypotheses

H1: There is a direct correlation between the clarity of legal standards for piercing the corporate veil and the accountability of shareholders in both civil and criminal cases, especially when corporate structures are used to facilitate fraudulent activities.

H2: The absence of harmonized legal provisions and judicial practices in Bosnia and Herzegovina regarding the piercing of the corporate veil increases the risk of corporate abuse, particularly in cross-border business activities aligned with EU market freedoms.

H3: The implementation of EU legal instruments, such as Directive (EU) 2019/1151, alongside robust national regulations, can significantly reduce the misuse of corporate entities for illicit purposes, including tax evasion, money laundering, and asset misappropriation.

H4: A comprehensive regulatory framework that connects criminal liability for corporate crimes with shareholder liability in civil procedures serves as a strong deterrent against the abuse of corporate forms, fostering greater corporate transparency and ethical business practices.

2.4 Research Methods

To prove the main thesis and auxiliary hypotheses, the following methods will be applied:

- **Historical Method:** The historical method is applied to trace the evolution of key concepts in company law, with particular focus on the doctrine of limited liability and the subsequent development of the piercing the corporate veil doctrine as a corrective mechanism. This analysis begins in the 17th and 18th centuries, throughout the emergence of modern limited liability in the mid-19th century. As limited liability became widespread, concerns grew about its potential misuse by shareholders to shield themselves from responsibility, even in cases of fraud, insolvency abuse, or evasion of obligations. This led courts, particularly in common law jurisdictions, to develop judicial doctrines that would allow the "corporate veil" to be pierced in exceptional circumstances.
- **Comparative Method:** To identify similarities, differences, and best practices in how different jurisdictions address the piercing of the corporate veil. The comparative method is employed to analyze how different legal systems, particularly Germany, Croatia, approach the doctrine of piercing the corporate veil, shareholder liability, and abuse of legal personality. This method enables the identification of shared principles, jurisdiction-specific approaches, and best practices in doctrinal development and judicial application. The comparison serves both a theoretical and normative function, providing Bosnia and Herzegovina with applicable legal models for reform and harmonization with the EU acquis.
- **Case Law Analysis:** Analyze judgments: 1) Corporate fraud cases in Bosnia and Herzegovina to assess how often corporate structures are abused and how the legal system responds. 2) Piercing the corporate veil cases in EU and Bosnia and Herzegovina, to analyze patterns, legal tests, and criteria courts use when deciding to pierce the corporate veil.
- **Deductive Method:** To derive unknown conclusions from known premises. (e.g., principles of corporate law and shareholder liability) to analyze specific cases and judicial decisions.
- **Inductive Method:** To infer general principles from specific observations to identify patterns and propose legal reforms.

2.5 Research Objective

The objective of this dissertation is twofold; first, to critically examine the doctrine of piercing the corporate veil as a legal mechanism to hold shareholders accountable for corporate misconduct, particularly in cases involving fraud, abuse, and misuse of the corporate structure; second, to identify and evaluate the circumstances and legal standards under which this doctrine is applied in Bosnia and Herzegovina, as well as in comparative jurisdictions such as Germany and Croatia, with the aim of formulating actionable legal and policy recommendations relevant to Bosnia and Herzegovina's process of legal harmonization with the EU *acquis communautaire.*

This dissertation situates its analysis in the broader context of Bosnia and Herzegovina's ongoing efforts to strengthen the rule of law, improve the business environment, and fulfil its obligations under the EU accession process. The misuse of corporate entities for fraudulent and illicit purposes, is both widespread and institutionally tolerated.[1] A notable example is the underreporting of employee wages, where employers use "envelope" salaries[2] to evade tax and social security contributions. This practice, while informally accepted by employees seeking higher net income, results in significant loss of public revenue, creates unfair market competition, and fosters shareholder impunity by insulating individual actors behind the corporate veil. Against this backdrop, the dissertation seeks to explore whether the doctrine of veil piercing can function as an effective legal and normative response to such systemic abuse.

To achieve its overarching aim, the research pursues the following specific objectives:

- To assess the effectiveness of existing legal frameworks, both in Bosnia and Herzegovina and in selected EU Member States, in preventing the misuse of corporate entities for illicit purposes, including jurisdiction shopping, the creation of letterbox companies, and other forms of fraudulent conduct.
- To develop legal and policy recommendations aimed at enhancing legal certainty, protecting creditors and minority shareholders, and strengthening Bosnia and Herzegovina's alignment with EU company law, with a particular focus on Directive (EU) 2017/1132, Directive (EU) 2019/1151, and relevant anti-money laundering instruments.

---

[1] Morel, Mathonet, Gounev, De Wispelaere, De Smedt & Schuster (2021), p. 159.

[2] Williams (2015), p. 284.

- To contribute to the theoretical and practical understanding of whether the doctrine of piercing the corporate veil can serve as an effective legal tool in combating financial crime, regulatory evasion, and corruption, thereby supporting broader efforts to strengthen institutional trust, rule of law, and the integrity of the market economy.
- To examine the interrelation between criminal and civil liability by investigating how criminal acts committed through companies (e.g., tax fraud, money laundering, or asset concealment) can establish grounds for civil shareholder liability, and to explore the mechanisms, both legal and evidentiary, through which this connection is established in different jurisdictions.

2.6 Significance and Potential Beneficiaries

The findings will make a substantial contribution to the advancement of the discipline of corporate law by deepening the understanding of how the doctrine of piercing the corporate veil can be effectively utilized to address fraudulent corporate practices. Furthermore, the research will contribute towards identifying any gaps that may exist within Bosnia and Herzegovina's current legal framework (criminal and corporate). In addition to this, it will propose solutions with a view to strengthening corporate accountability and reducing levels of corruption, which is necessary since companies often fail to report corrupt activity because of the stigma attached to admitting control and governance failures.[3] The proposed solutions will align with relevant EU directives. The research will benefit a wide range of stakeholders, including policymakers, legal practitioners, businesses, and academics. It will provide regulators with the tools to deter corporate abuse, promote fair competition, and enhance trust in the business environment, ultimately fostering a more sustainable and transparent economic system.

[3] Zimmermann & Riegner (2023), p. 57.

State of the Art

3

This Chapter will examine the concept of corporate personhood and with it the limited liability of companies, exploring the historical evolution that culminated in the conferral of legal personae on corporations. The acquisition of legal personality entails the assumption of liability for obligations and misconduct towards creditors. The historical underpinnings of this concept are pivotal, as they represent a critical juncture in the genesis of limited liability. The principle of limited liability, central to modern corporate law, protects shareholders from personal liability for corporate debts. Historically, this legal shield evolved from early theories of corporate personhood, such as Blackstone's notion of "artificial persons"[1], to contemporary views where corporations are seen as entities with legal rights and obligations distinct from their owners.[2] However, in contrast to the limitation of the liability of shareholders, the doctrine of piercing the corporate veil stands as an oxymoron within company law, defiantly demonstrating that the impossible is indeed possible, that the shareholder, rather than the legal entity, will bear unlimited personal liability for the obligations of the limited liability company in certain circumstances. To comprehend the circumstances in which personal shareholder liability comes into effect, this chapter will undertake an analysis of the various theories of legal personhood. Those legal theories have influenced the law and how it treats corporate activity and corporate actors. The central question to be addressed is whether legal entities are to be considered mere fiction or whether

[1] Blackstone (1809), p. 455.

[2] Easterbrook & Fischel (1985), p. 90; Hamill (1998), p. 1461.

L. Hasanovic, *Piercing the Corporate Veil: Shareholder Liability*,
Juridicum – Schriftenreihe zum Wirtschafts-, Unternehmens- und Bankrecht / Series on Business, Corporate and Banking Law,
https://doi.org/10.1007/978-3-658-52987-1_3

they are genuine constructs of law, endowed with rights (including human rights) and subject to criminal liability before the law? The chapter will also examine the tests and doctrines applied by courts when determining whether to pierce or lift the corporate veil to ascertain the applicability of personal shareholder liability in such cases. With the methodological roadmap in place, the dissertation now turns to existing scholarship and jurisprudence to situate the inquiry. The following 'State of the Art' chapter demonstrates why the theoretical foundations of corporate personality and limited liability are indispensable to understanding when that personality may legitimately be disregarded.

3.1 The Foundation of Legal Personality

In Europe, a company[3] acquires legal personality upon incorporation, thus becoming a separate legal entity with its own rights and obligations, distinct from those of its shareholders.[4] Historically, as Blackstone noted, legal persons were created to maintain "perpetual succession".[5] While early legal theorists viewed the corporation as a "legal fiction", modern scholars like Kuntz argue that corporate personhood serves as an essential tool for enforcing corporate liability, especially in cases of shareholder abuse.[6] Despite the absence of consensus among legal scholars on where legal personality emerged first[7], Blackstone was certain that the honor of originally inventing these political constitutions entirely belongs to the Romans.[8] The limited liability can also be traced back to ancient Rome where the concept of the Roman *peculium* was recognized as a precursor to limited liability and the organization of funds.[9] While scholars like Bainbridge

[3] For the purpose of this dissertation, I will focus on closed limited liability companies.

[4] Grbo (2017), p. 25.

[5] Blackstone (1809) p. 467.

[6] Kuntz (2018), p. 446.

[7] Von Gierke (1873), p. 32, advanced the argument that the concept of corporate personhood had emerged in German law long before the influence of Roman legal traditions. Bainbridge and Henderson (2016), p. 20 on the other hand, state that the concept of separating corporate and shareholder liability emerged in the common law, as early as in the fifteenth century.

[8] They were introduced, as Plutarch says, by Numa; who finding, upon his accession, the city torn to pieces by the two rival factions of Sabines and Romans, thought it a prudent and politic measure to subdivide these two into many smaller ones, by instituting separate societies of every manual trade and profession.

[9] Bainbridge & Henderson (2016), p. 23. The pater familias (when dedicating estate to his son), or the dominus (when dedicating estate to his slave) could transfer his assets to them even though they were *personae alieno iuri subiectae* (persons under the authority of

and Henderson argue that the corporation is a legal fiction, this view has direct implications in legal practice.[10] For example, in Salomon v. A. Salomon & Co Ltd, the fiction of corporate personhood was crucial in upholding the company's separate identity, reinforcing the importance of maintaining this legal separation unless abused.[11] Harari offers a compelling sociological parallel in his book Sapiens, where he argues that much of modern civilization is built on social constructs or intersubjective constructs such as money, nations, and corporations. According to Harari, the power of such constructs lies not in their physical existence, but in the collective belief in their legitimacy. From this perspective, the legal fiction of corporate personality is sustainable only as long as it serves a legitimate social and economic function. When the corporation is used to shield wrongful conduct or to manipulate legal boundaries, it loses its justificatory power as a shared fiction. This insight supports the idea that veil piercing is not an attack on corporate form per se, but a necessary corrective when that form is abused and the social contract underpinning it, is breached. The debate between fictionalists and entity theorists has practical consequences for veil piercing decisions.[12] Courts following entity theory are more likely to pierce the veil when the corporation is used as a 'sham' to defraud creditors, while fictionalist courts may place greater emphasis on corporate governance structures that protect the 'fiction' of corporate personality, as seen in Re F.G. (Films) Ltd (1953), where the court pierced the veil due to a lack of independent corporate function.[13] The fiction theory was formulated by Friedrich Carl Savigny and Roman scholars who claimed that legal persons are artificial constructs, created by law and dependent on the individuals composing them. The corporate legal personality protects the (private) assets of the shareholders by separating them from the assets of the company.[14] Shareholders of the company are not liable for more than the amount they invest. Several other authors have claimed that the company is a legal fiction, even pointing out

another). Any business activities or obligations entered into by the son or slave were considered limited to that peculium. The pater familias had control over the assets, but in business transactions done by the son or the slave, his liability, even if the son or the slave would own debt based on the peculium, the creditor could not go after the personal assets of the pater familias.

[10] Bainbridge & Henderson (2016), p. 6. The authors go so far as explicitly stating that corporations such as Microsoft or ExxonMobil are legal persons, but in reality, they are just a fiction.

[11] Salomon v. A. Salomon & Co Ltd (1897), p. 32.

[12] Gindis (2009), p. 25.

[13] Re F.G. (Films) Ltd (1953).

[14] Kuntz (2018), p. 446.

that the personalization of the company is misleading, because it is not real.[15] They stressed that the company has no individual will (companies cannot appear before court, they cannot sign contracts) and that their will is shown through humans (managers, workers, and contributors of capital). Therefore, only humans can have responsibilities and act responsibly (or not). This argument crumbles under today's criminal liability of companies. A company can be held criminally liable for its actions. Most European countries[16] have moved away from the legal principle *societas delinquere non potest*[17], and established criminal liability of legal entities. This in mind, the legal entity is individually liable and shows the capacity for action (*actus reus*) and culpability (*mens rea*). Even though the act itself is done through the management of the company or the lack of supervision thereof, criminal liability of companies proves that, at least in Europe, the fiction theory was abandoned. One exception to the rule is Germany. It formally adheres to the principle of individual culpability (*Schuldprinzip*) and therefore does not recognize criminal liability of legal persons in the strict sense. Legislative attempts to introduce corporate criminal liability have repeatedly failed, and the prevailing justification refers to the incompatibility of criminal punishment with the guilt principle, which presupposes personal blameworthiness.[18] This position, however, is only partially consistent. While legal entities cannot be subjected to criminal sanctions under the German Criminal Code (StGB), art. 30 of the German Administrative Offences Act (OWiG) provides for the imposition of substantial monetary fines on legal persons for offences committed by their managers or representatives. According to the dominant view, the principle of guilt also applies within administrative offence law, which is often characterized

[15] Meckling & Jensen (1976), p. 305; Easterbrook & Fischel (1985), p. 89.

[16] EU Legal Framework Encourages Corporate Criminal Liability. Several EU directives and international conventions require member states to establish corporate criminal liability, particularly in areas such as corruption, money laundering, environmental crimes, and corporate fraud. Example: Directive 2008/99/EC on Environmental Crime requires states to ensure companies can be held criminally or otherwise liable.

Countries That Recognize Corporate Criminal Liability:

France—Recognized since 1994 (Article 121–2 of the French Penal Code).

Italy—Legislative Decree No. 231/2001 establishes corporate liability for specific offenses.

Netherlands, Belgium, Spain, Portugal—All have corporate criminal liability frameworks.

Central and Eastern Europe (Croatia, Slovenia, Bosnia and Herzegovina, Poland, Czech Republic, etc.), have enacted laws explicitly recognizing corporate criminal liability.

[17] A legal entity cannot commit crimes.

[18] Kindhäuser & Zimmermann (2024), art. 7 margin number 1.

in the literature as "small criminal law" (*kleines Strafrecht*).[19] The coexistence of a formal rejection of corporate criminal liability and a sanctioning regime functionally equivalent to criminal punishment has therefore been widely criticized as doctrinally contradictory.[20] In Croatia, the criminal liability of the company is legally proven through the criminal liability of the person responsible for managing the company. According to the Law on Criminal Liability of Legal Entities of the Republic of Croatia[21] the establishment of corporate criminal liability is contingent upon the court's determination of two key elements: the commission of a criminal offence by a designated responsible person, and the presence of a causal relationship between the offence and the legal entity, thereby substantiating the attribution of the responsible person's criminal act to the corporation.[22] Without the person responsible for the criminal offence, the legal entity cannot be criminally charged. Which brings us back to the fictionalists and their arguments that corporations are artificial constructs existing through laws.[23] Contrary to those arguments, Maitland and Gierke[24] stated that companies are "…as real and natural as is the personality of man".[25] The theory they advocated is called entity theory and dominated legal discussions from roughly 1900 to 1930. According to entity theorists, companies have a will and its will is a group-will.[26] This view was significantly diluted by second generation entity theorists such as Dewey, who emphasized that Gierkes "person" signifies a right and duty bearing unit. In order for this unit to be given the rights and obligations of a legal person it must

---

[19] Rengier (2025), Section 2, margin number 14.

[20] Achenbach (2012); Zimmermann (2020), p. 306.

[21] Law on Criminal Liability of Legal Entities of the Republic of Croatia (*Zakon o odgovornosti pravnih osoba za kaznena djela)*, Official Gazette nr. 151/03, 110/07, 45/11, 143/12, 114/22, 114/23).

[22] Article 124 of the Criminal Code of BiH ("Official Gazette", nr. 3/2003, 32/2003, 37/2003, 54/2004, 61/2004, 30/2005, 53/2006, 55/2006, 8/2010, 47/2014, 22/2015, 40/2015, 35/2018, 46/2021, 31/2023 i 47/2023);

[23] Meckling & Jensen (1976), p. 308; Fama & Jensen (1983), p. 301.

[24] Gierke's four-volume: Das deutsche Genossenschaftsrecht and Maitland's translation thereof as „The German Law of Fellowship". The three relevant volumes were published between 1868 and 1881. The entity view can be traced back to Gierke's mentor, Beseler, who first introduced the term genossenschaft („fellowship") in 1843 (Harris, 2006, p. 1428). Within the German Historical School of Law, Beseler and Gierke were leading Germanist figures who opposed the Romanist followers of Savigny in the context of the drafting of the German Civil Code.

[25] Maitland (1900), p. 335–336.

[26] Gierke (1887), p. 613.

produce consequences.[27] Dewey states that the reason that molecules or trees are not juridical "subjects" is because they do not display the specified consequences. His stance was that the decision whether something is a legal person or not should be governed by the consequences of so doing. This view has been substantially reexamined in modern legal and philosophical discourse. For example, the Whanganui River in New Zealand is recognized as a legal person, even though it does not display consequences per se. This however can still be an argument for the fiction theorists, since it confirms that the legal person is a legal fiction and because of that, its principles can be applied to nonhuman beings.[28] Second generation of realist, or entity theorists depart from the argument that the company has "morals"[29], and they recognize the argument that the legal personality of a company is legal fiction, since the company has no personality, it is not human, but it is real and does exist distinct from its shareholders or members.[30] Authors such as Horwitz and Millon, emphasized that entity theory legitimated the rise of big business in the early 20th century.[31] This holds much truth if we look back on what the entity theory promotes. If the entity is a person of itself with its own rights and obligations, then it also is liable for its actions. Meaning that its shareholders, like the *pater familias* in Roman times, limit their liability to the amount of their stake. Due to the emergence of big businesses, it was harder to identify the management within the corporation pertaining to the will of the company, which was an additional push towards the entity theory and the recognition of the company as an autonomous entity.[32] By limiting shareholders liability, it enabled them to spread risk over several investments, and that paved the road to economic growth.[33] Even though entity theorists differed among themselves in their views on the corporate entity and its corporate personality, with some going so far as to describing it as an "organism"[34], many regarded it as a system of „human and nonhuman" components created to coexist as a network. This is particularly interesting from the standpoint of human rights of companies in modern times. The fictionalists would have been surprised that companies are granted victim status

27 Dewey (1925), p. 665.

28 Hutchison (2014), p. 179.

29 Maitland (1905), p. 199.

30 Machen (1911), p. 565; Dicey (1905), p. 154.

31 Horwitz (1992); Millon (1990), p. 201.

32 Mark (1987), p. 1441; Phillips (1993), p. 1061.

33 Kuntz (2018), p. 440.

34 Deiser (1908), p. 310.

before the European Court of Human Rights (ECtHR). All States that are signatories to the European Convention of Human Rights (ECHR)[35] have recognized the fact that companies' human rights are protected under its Charter. Emberland was among the first to introduce the conditions for granting the status of "victim"[36] to companies, but also to their founders and shareholders in proceedings before the ECtHR. Article 34 of the ECHR stipulates that the court may receive applications from any person, non-governmental organization or group of persons claiming to be victims of a violation of the rights established by the ECHR or the protocols thereto, committed by a High Contracting Party. Non-governmental organizations are not a pseudonym for non-profit organizations, but they include for profit companies.[37] The first version of the ECHR listed any natural or legal person as possible applicants. Later versions changed the terminology to legal person, with the final choice being "non-governmental organizations", however, there is nothing to indicate that this final formulation excluded companies from the protective scope of the Convention.[38] This view is supported by the jurisprudence of the ECtHR, which has consistently extended the protection of ECHR to commercial companies in areas such as property rights (Article 1, Protocol 1), fair trial (Article 6), and respect for correspondence (Article 8). However, some cases illustrate the limits and complexities of locus standi for companies, particularly in interstate disputes involving politically sensitive matters. In Ljubljanska banka v. Croatia and Slovenia v. Croatia[39], the ECtHR declined to rule on the

---

[35] For the purpose of this dissertation, statements made are always referenced to the States that are relevant for the comparative analysis conducted through this research. These countries are Bosnia and Herzegovina, Croatia and Germany.

[36] Emberland (2006), p. 206.

[37] Dignam (2000), p. 151; Dhooge (2006), p. 197; Van den Muijsenbergh & Rezai (2012), p. 43.

[38] Emberland (2006), p. 220.

[39] In Ljubljanska banka v. Croatia (2015) and the related interstate case Slovenia v. Croatia (2020), the European Court of Human Rights declined to recognize Ljubljanska banka, a commercial bank, as having locus standi under Article 34 ECHR. This position was not based on a denial of the general principle that companies are legal persons protected by the ECHR, but rather on an exception grounded in the bank's inseparability from the State of Slovenia. The key exception applied by the Court is what may be called the "state-controlled entity exception" or "instrumentality of the State" doctrine. According to this reasoning, an entity that is effectively indistinguishable from the State, or closely tied to its political or institutional apparatus, cannot qualify as a "non-governmental organization" under Article 34. The ECtHR maintained that Article 34 is intended to protect individuals and organizations independent from State power, not entities through which the State itself exercises rights or influence. In both cases, the Court found that Ljubljanska banka did not act with sufficient institutional or commercial autonomy from the Slovenian government: The ownership and

admissibility of claims brought by or on behalf of a bank, raising doubts about whether a company can independently invoke the ECHR when its legal standing is intertwined with unresolved issues of state succession and international diplomatic relations. These exceptions highlight the tension between the theoretical inclusion of companies within the protective scope of the ECHR and the pragmatic constraints imposed by specific legal and political contexts. Contrary to this standing the ECtHR has granted and acknowledged intangible damages to companies.[40] The ECtHR, in its judgements, protected right to freedom of expression and the prohibition of discrimination of companies, rights that have

operational control of the bank were tied to post-Yugoslav state succession. Slovenia had direct political and diplomatic interests in the outcome of the claims, as evidenced by its attempt to litigate through an interstate application under Article 33. Instead of piercing the corporate veil and allowing the bank to proceed as a private applicant, the ECtHR essentially respected the corporate veil in reverse—treating the bank not as a distinct corporate entity, but as a state instrument, thereby excluding it from the category of protected non-governmental organizations under the ECHR. The ECtHR regarded them as a governmental organization and thus stated that they have no standing to lodge an individual application with the Court.

[40] For example: case of *Comingersoll S.A. v. Portugal*, the key issue was whether Portugal had violated the rights of a public enterprise under Article 6 of the Convention and Article 1 of Protocol No. 1 to the Convention, as well as whether *Comingersoll S.A.* was entitled to compensation for non-material damage under Article 41 of the Convention. The European Court of Human Rights (ECtHR) ruled that Portugal had breached Articles 6 and 1 of Protocol No. 1, as *Comingersoll S.A.* had been denied the right to a fair trial (Art. 6 of the Convention) due to the excessive length of proceedings. Pursuant to Article 41, the Court awarded just satisfaction for the non-material damage suffered by the public enterprise, which was reflected in reputational harm, business losses, and stress caused by the prolonged litigation. (*Comingersoll S.A. v. Portugal*, 2000, p. 9).

In the case of *Centro Europa 7 S.R.L. v. Italy*, the commercial entity *Centro Europa 7 S.R.L.* sued Italy for violations of Articles 10 and 14 of the Convention, as well as Article 1 of Protocol No. 1. The applicant argued that it had been deprived of its right to freedom of expression, including the right to receive and impart information, due to its inability to use broadcasting licenses, despite having been granted the necessary permits. The Court found that, due to bureaucratic shortcomings and legal uncertainty, the Italian authorities had denied the company access to broadcasting frequencies, thereby preventing it from carrying out its activities. This constituted a violation of the right to freedom of expression and the prohibition of discrimination. Consequently, Italy was ordered to pay the applicant EUR 10 million as compensation for material and non-material damage.

Legal entities, just like natural persons, enjoy the protection guaranteed under Article 2 of the Constitution of Bosnia and Herzegovina. The phrase "All persons on the territory of Bosnia and Herzegovina" (Art. 2(3) of the Constitution of Bosnia and Herzegovina) applies to companies as well, to whom the Convention, as an integral part of Article 2, guarantees the right to non-discrimination, the right to a fair trial, the right to just satisfaction, and the right to freedom of expression.

been linked with human beings, rather than legal entities. In a dissenting opinion, Judge Rozakis and others, emphasized that companies can indeed suffer intangible damage due to, albeit to a lesser extent, the concerns and distress experienced by their management members.[41] In the United States, in 1886, the U.S. Supreme Court confirmed that corporations have legal personality for purposes of the Fourteenth Amendment[42] and in 2010 for the purposes of the First Amendment (free speech).[43] Connections between human rights and legal personality have been addressed by Machen[44], who stated that the essence of legal personhood are not the rights a company possesses, but rather the company's subjection to liability. Theories of corporate personhood are therefore important because they provide frameworks on how companies are treated and protected under the law, but also how they are liable. By understanding who is liable and when, and how this liability is implemented in practice, we can understand under which circumstances the liability of a company can be removed or expanded to the company's shareholders. What is certain is that both theories, the fiction theory and the entity theory, hold some truth. It is correct that companies cannot exist without any individuals (yet).[45] However, the company can "outlive" its owners and shareholders, it is independent of them. From the moment the company is established (through natural or legal persons) it continues to exist and can exist without those who established it, through legal regulations that built its framework. This "nexus of contracts" theory, further elaborated by authors such as Easterbrook & Fischel, predominantly relied on the fictionalist argument that companies are not real entities, since they represent a set of contracts, legal rules, provided by the state to regulate business among natural and legal persons.[46] Without the creation of legal entity status through formal incorporation, a company cannot exist in the legal realm. However, this principle is nuanced by transitional structures such as the pre-incorporation company or pre-GmbH

---

[41] ECtHR (2000), p. 9.

[42] Santa Clara Cnty. v. S. Pac. R.R. Co., 118 U.S. 394 (1886).

[43] Macey (2019), p. 1202. Free speech: Citizens United v. FEC, 130 S. Ct. 876 (2010).

[44] Machen (1911), p. 565.

[45] Hasanovic & Muftic (2024), p. 57. Currently, no fully autonomous AI system performs the role of a company director or board member, nor is there a company fully operated by AI. While this represents the least realistic application of AI in corporate governance, scholars note significant legal and practical challenges to such use. Nevertheless, future developments may allow AI to be introduced as a member of corporate boards, or even fully autonomous AI driven companies, reflecting growing interest in AI's potential role in company law and governance.

[46] Easterbrook & Fischel (1989), p. 1426.

under German law. Upon the notarized signing of the articles of association, but prior to registration in the commercial register, the company exists in the form of a pre-GmbH, a transitional construct that reflects a collective legal commitment rather than full legal personhood.[47] The pre-GmbH has no separate legal personality, yet it possesses an internal organizational structure and can enter limited legal relationships. This illustrates that legal personality is not an automatic consequence of social or economic coordination, but a status granted by the legal order, a point that strongly supports the fictionalist theory of corporate personality. The incorporation process is completed only upon registration, at which point the GmbH emerges as a legal person with full juridical capacity and limited liability. Before this stage, even a pre-formation association of promoters may exist, but unless their agreement is notarized, no binding obligation exists to continue the incorporation.[48] These stages highlight that corporate existence is not rooted in empirical function, but in formal recognition by law, further validating the fictionalist position that corporate entities are creatures of legal imagination, contingent on the will of the state rather than organic emergence. Companies cannot be established informally; there is a set of rules and regulations to be conducted before a company can receive legal personhood. In the EU for example, Directive (EU) 2017/1132 on certain aspects of company law and Directive (EU) 2019/1151 on the use of digital tools and procedures in company law have created a legal and administrative framework that allows citizens of the European Union to establish a limited liability company entirely online.[49] Which brings us back to the second generation fictionalists that either stressed the importance of law[50] or defined the company as a collection of assets, reducing the company to a collection of its parts (contracts, shareholders, etc.)[51] In both cases however, the company is an artificial creation, dependent on the humans who run it and the law that established it. Easterbrook & Fischel further emphasize that the founders and managers of the company make decisions on how the company will be organized, from payments, business decisions to decisions on the location of the incorporation.[52] The law enables those actors, to pursue goals for themselves, and as such they are to be held responsible for the decisions they make. Courts

[47] Kersting (2000), p. 112.

[48] Gerner-Beuerle & Schillig (2019), p. 188.

[49] Hasanović (2024), p. 210.

[50] Meckling & Jensen (1976), p. 310.

[51] Grossman and Hart (1986), p. 717.

[52] Easterbrook & Fischel (1989), p. 1426.

apply the „business judgment doctrine“ when looking at the system of governance of a company.[53] The Business Judgement Rule has also been codified in German law, namely Article 93 (1) sentence 2 of the German Stock Corporation Act (AktG). It applies accordingly to limited liability companies (GmbHs). All that is permissible by law in relation to corporate governance, will not be scrutinized by courts. There are certain aspects of company management that are contested by courts and should be looked at when determining liability. Since the company is only a set of rules managers and owners have to follow, it is easier to determine their liability if they do not follow those rules. This quality control that is enshrined in the statutes of companies, forbids "perpetual dictatorships"[54], and enables board members to participate in decision-making. The best theory of the company, therefore, accounts for mandatory norms that cannot be bent, that safeguard the company and its governance, and dispositive norms that enable management to effectively lead the company. Understanding the concept of limited liability is paramount to understanding under what circumstances we should disregard the law (corporate personhood) and pierce the veil to hold shareholders within a company accountable. In other words, if the company is only a façade, what test can we use to determine whether actors within the company have abused its form for illicit purposes? Having established the historical and conceptual roots of corporate personhood, the next step is to examine the doctrinal corollary it enables: limited liability. Understanding this corollary is essential because veil-piercing is ultimately a response to the potential excesses of limited liability

3.2 Limited Liability

As discussed above in Sect. 3.1, limited liability rests on the corporation's status as a legal fiction. Contrary to modern times, partnerships of the 18th century did not have to be incorporated, the partners were unlimitedly liable for debt to creditors. Limited liability was introduced to encourage investment by protecting shareholders from the financial risks of large-scale ventures. This protection has fueled economic growth but has also enabled moral hazard, as highlighted

[53] Grbo (2016), p. 414; Lepetić, 2015, p. 250; Trivun (2011), p. 137.

[54] ibid., p. 1427.

by critics like Ribstein, who argues that it encourages reckless business practices, particularly when corporate assets are misused for personal gain.[55] The first instance of limited liability came with limited partnerships that foresaw limited liability of passive investors[56]. They were seen as money givers and this enabled them to divide risk between different investments, which incentivized risk taking.[57] The positive impact of the limitation of liability was economic prosperity. States finally had the money to finance development projects with financial means of someone else, and investors had access to public goods with guarantees shielding their private assets. In Europe, limited liability was introduced through the French code de commerce from 1807, in Germany in the 19th century through the Prussian corporate law of 1843 and from 1861 through the General German Commercial Code (*Allgemeines Deutsches Handelsgesetzbuch*). There would not have been large investments and in connection with it, large companies, which are seen as a cornerstone of modern society, without limited liability. That this form of incorporation is so popular, proves the fact that limited liability companies account for more than 60% of registered corporate forms in Bosnia and Herzegovina[58] with similar numbers in Croatia[59]. In Germany, the percentages are somewhat lower but remain around 20%. Nevertheless, even though praised for making it possible for companies, to raise capital, limited liability was also criticized for shifting costs to creditors. Criticism of limited liability dates to Adam Smith[60], who questioned its use in the context of joint-stock companies[61]

---

[55] Ribstein (1991), p. 81. For example, mid-18th century Bridgewater Canal, and similar canals were constructed with investment from private enterprises, which used tolls to recoup their investment (however enterprises could only operate with an act of Parliament).

[56] They were called „special partners", 1784 Pennsylvania statute from June 2, 1784, P.L. 271.

[57] Kuntz (2018), p. 442.

[58] In 2024, according to the Agency for Statistics of BiH, from all registered corporate forms in Bosnia and Herzegovina in the FBiH 64% are LLCs, 63% in RS, and 43% in Brčko District. More information here: https://fzs.ba/wp-content/uploads/2024/08/23.1.pdf, accessed March 23, 2025.

[59] In 2022: in Germany there are 3.164.855 registered company forms, 709.564 were limited liability companies. In Croatia from 227.408 registered company forms, 125.760 were limited liability companies. Available information on Business demography by legal form and NACE Rev. 2 activity. Accessed March 24, 2025. https://doi.org/10.2908/BD_L_FORM.

[60] Smith, (1778), vol. II, p. 257.

[61] Fleckner (2016), p. 46.

and continues with more recent scholars like Ribstein, who examined it in relation to reverse limited liability.[62] In the third edition Smiths Wealth of Nations[63] he had a rather pessimistic stance on joint stock companies, primarily because he thought that because managers were not the owners, they had less incentive to manage the business appropriately, and limited liability would diminish accountability making them more prone to recklessness. More precisely he states that: "Negligence and profusion, therefore, must always prevail, more or less, in the management of the affairs of such a company."[64] Similarly Ribstein claimed that limited liability was not always a good idea, especially when it became possible for single-member companies.[65] Debtors would use the business entity to protect their personal debts by placing their money in a corporate form, protecting it from creditors. In literature, authors call this the moral hazard problem associated with limited liability.[66] A particularly interesting research was conducted by Akey & Appel who found that stronger liability protection for parent company in environmental cleanup cases, leads to a 5% to 9% increase in toxic emissions by subsidiaries.[67] Just like Smith has suggested, strengthening limited liability can lead to negligence, which can lead to costs borne by other stakeholders, and not the company or its shareholders.[68] While limited liability has been widely criticized, particularly for enabling companies to externalize social costs, a doctrinal cure has emerged in the form of piercing the corporate veil. Ideally, veil piercing in the context of creditors should involve a careful balance between the economic benefits of limited liability and the social harms caused by negative externalities.[69] However, in practice, it has developed into a highly complex and contested doctrine, characterized by broad and open-ended standards, significant

[62] Ribstein (2005), p. 202.

[63] Smith, (1778), vol. II, p. 124. An Inquiry into the Nature and Causes of the Wealth of Nations is divided into five books.

[64] ibid., p. 124.

[65] Ribstein (1991), p. 102.

[66] Shavell (1986), p. 45; Biais et al (2010), p. 74.

[67] Akey & Appel (2021), p. 7. These environmental cases refer to toxic facilities that are eligible for cleanup based on threats to human health or the environment. Costs associated with the cleanup are large, but most of the time the companies file for bankruptcy before being able to pay for cleanup costs. In the U.S. Congress passed CERCLA in 1980 and established the polluter pays principle, one aspect being that: parents are liable for cleanup costs as owners of subsidiaries, under the standard veil-piercing doctrine in corporate law.

[68] Smith, (1778), vol. II, p. 124.

[69] Lafarre (2023), p. 214.

comparative variation, and case-by-case judicial discretion. While limited liability catalyzed modern economic growth, it also created avenues for opportunistic behavior. The ensuing section therefore analyses the veil-piercing doctrine as the legal system's primary corrective to such abuse.

3.3 Piercing the Corporate Veil

Scholars have been criticizing veil piercing similarly to limited liability, with calls for its abolition.[70] The main reason for the need of its abolishment, according to critics is its unprincipled and unpredictable way courts have deployed this tool.[71] Advocates of neoclassical economic theory view holding shareholders personally liable as a disruptive intervention. While it may appear to promote efficiency on the surface, they argue that it leads to higher costs for investors due to the increased risk of liability, ultimately making it a counterproductive measure.[72] Bainbridge, in his article „Abolishing LLC Veil Piercing“ advocates for the abolishment of veil piercing, proposing that shareholders who abused the corporate form, committed fraud, should be held responsible under principles of direct liability.[73] However, Millon, stressed that veil piercing can perform a useful function by policing limits of limited liability.[74] Even though Easterbrook and Fischel famously described the piercing doctrine as severe as lightning, they also acknowledged that understanding when lightning strikes offers valuable insight, highlighting the importance of not creating conditions that invite corporate bad weather in the first place.[75] They have suggested that the incidence of veil piercing can be explained by reference to efficiency considerations. They write, "the doctrine of piercing the corporate veil, and the distinctions drawn by the courts, makes more economic sense than at first appears. The cases may be understood, at least roughly, as attempts to balance the benefits of limited liability against the costs“.[76] The piercing the corporate veil doctrine blurs the line between corporate

[70] See Stephen M. Bainbridge, Abolishing Veil Piercing, 26 J. Corp. L. 479 (2005); Douglas C. Michael, To Know A Veil, 26 J. Corp. L. 41 (2001). Jonathan Macey & Joshua Mitts, Finding Order in the Morass: The Three Real Justifications for Piercing the Corporate Veil 100(1) Cornell Law Review 99–156 (2014).

[71] Millon (2006), p. 1307.

[72] Merkt & Spindler (2006), p. 227.

[73] Bainbridge (2005), p. 79.

[74] Millon (2006), p. 1339.

[75] Easterbrook & Fischel (1985), p. 89.

[76] Easterbrook & Fischel (1985), p. 93.

entities and the individuals behind them. Because the corporation is, at core, a legal construct (see Sect. 3.1), veil piercing functions as an exceptional corrective mechanism. Companies possess human rights, they own property, enter contracts, establish other companies, sometimes they are criminally liable, they are subject to obligations and rights. Limited liability further confirms and emphasizes that shareholders are not liable for the obligations of the company beyond the capital that they contribute in exchange for their shares.[77] Whether stemming from moral hazard or the misuse of the corporate structure, it has become clear in practice that a corrective mechanism is necessary to prevent owners and shareholders from exploiting the protections of limited liability. One of the most prominent cases that elaborated on this subject was Salomon v. A. Salomon & Co. Ltd.,[78] in which the UK court found that there are limits to corporate separation, and those limits are the protection of public interest. This is when the company becomes legal fiction. It retains its corporate personhood as long as it is not contrary to positive social and economic outcomes. Because that is why this organizational framework, this company, was "born" in the first place: to facilitate business transactions and economic prosperity. The court stated that separate corporate identity cannot override other significant public interests which the state seeks to protect through legislation or regulation.[79] This legislation and/or regulation came in the form of a doctrine. This doctrine allows creditors to satisfy their claim out of the personal assets of shareholders, instead of the company. A more recent study conducted by Gevurtz, examined a set of over 300 court decisions with piercing claims in the last four years in the US and identified that in three quarters of the cases courts got it right when deciding to pierce the corporate veil.[80] The factors were fraud or siphoning performed by shareholders. In response to the ongoing debate over whether the doctrine of piercing the corporate veil should be abolished in favor of alternative legal remedies or retained as a vital tool for protecting creditor claims, this dissertation will examine the legal tests and doctrines applied by courts in deciding whether to disregard the corporate veil. The analysis will focus on the consistency, rationale, and evolution of judicial standards. This literature review will explore the key factors identified by corporate

---

[77] Thompson (1990), p. 1039.

[78] Salomon v. A. Salomon & Co. Ltd., (1897) A.C. 22 (H.L.) 38.

[79] Cheng-Han et al (2019), p. 152.

[80] Gevurtz (2025), p. 3. (self-determined, no page number provided in the article). Article available at SSRN: https://ssrn.com/abstract=5110762 or http://dx.doi.org/10.2139/ssrn.5110762).

law scholars and courts across various legal systems as relevant in determining whether the corporate personality should be set aside.

3.3.1 Factors for Piercing the Corporate Veil

The factors for piercing the corporate veil are crucial as they provide courts with a structured framework for determining when the principle of limited liability should be disregarded in exceptional circumstances. As Millon describes, these factors function as a policing mechanism, helping to ensure that veil piercing is applied consistently and justifiably.[81] By offering clear guidelines, they also serve to reduce judicial unpredictability and enhance the doctrinal coherence of this otherwise flexible and discretionary legal tool. In his article „Piercing the Corporate Veil: An Empirical Study", Thompson stated that piercing the corporate veil is the most litigated and least understood concept in US corporate law.[82] In terms of it being least understood, he points out that courts have a high discretional power to use the doctrine or to ignore it. In his research he argues that the doctrine does not apply to joint stock companies, because "limited liability's positive role in facilitating the public market for shares is strong enough to overcome any justification for piercing."[83] This means that the legal and practical setup in joint stock companies is so solid, due to regulations, governance standards, separation between ownership and management, that it is nearly impossible to pierce the corporate veil and hold shareholders personally liable. Conversely, limited liability companies are in his opinion more private, limited liability is contractual, the parties involved know that the risk of owners and shareholders is limited to

[81] Millon (2006), p. 1329.

[82] Thompson (1990), p. 1036. To support this claim, Thompson conducted research using Westlaw, searching for the terms "piercing the corporate veil" and "disregard! the corporate entity", and identified approximately 2,000 cases. He then compared this to another prominent topic in 1990, "corporate takeover" and "hostile takeover", which appeared in fewer than 300 cases. Using the same methodology, this research replicated his approach in 2025. A search of the same terms, "piercing the corporate veil" and "disregard! the corporate entity", yielded 10,000.00 cases on Westlaw and LexisNexis. In comparison, "corporate takeover" matched 806 cases on Lexis, while "hostile takeover" returned 1,286 cases. Notably, the figure of 10,000 cases likely underrepresents the actual total, as this is the maximum number of results displayed by Westlaw and LexisNexis search engines. These results undoubtedly recognize that Thompsons argument still holds truth. The evidence of this can be found in an empirical study done by Macey, J., & Mitts, J. (2014), who found more than 9,000 cases using the same search keys in 2014.

[83] Thompson (1990), p. 1071; Barber (1980), p. 371; Bainbridge (2005), p. 106.

the amount of their shares. In these instances, courts may more frequently disregard the corporate veil, if the bargain between limited liability and investment is jeopardized by fraud. It must be evident that owners or shareholders abused the privilege of limited liability. There are many factors that scholars have identified over the years that could be relevant for veil piercing. Scholars such as Bainbridge (2005)[84], Thompson and Oh, have tried to group these factors, but they state that the more factors are identified, the more likely it is that it gives courts more discretionary power to decide as they see fit.[85] In his empirical study Oh concluded that courts tend to mostly pierce the veil in fraud cases (61%) and criminal claims cases (67%). The following list of factors was grouped after an extensive literature review on most relevant indicators for abuse of the corporate entity:

1. undercapitalization,[86]
2. fraud,[87]
3. commingling (of assets/lack of separation), failure to follow corporate formalities,[88]
4. violation of criminal law or policy.[89]

Ottolenghi suggested a classification of veil piercing that progresses in intensity, starting with "Peeping behind the Veil"[90], followed by "Penetrating the Veil", then "Extending the Veil", and ultimately "Ignoring the Veil".[91] However, while Ottolenghi's categorization remains conceptually useful, it is somewhat outdated. Information that would traditionally fall under "Peeping behind the Veil", such

---

[84] Bainbridge (2005), p. 88.

[85] Thompson (1990), p. 1044; Oh (2010).

[86] Berle (1947), p. 349; Thompson (1990), p. 1062; Ayres 1992, p. 1398.

[87] Berle (1947), p. 352; Posner (1975), p. 521; Lopez (1982), p. 143; Thompson (1990), p. 1066; Merkt & Spindler (2006), p. 205; Oh (2010), p. 103; Gerner-Beuerle & Schillig (2019), p. 51–52, 825–826, 850, 884; Gevurtz, 2025, p. 23.

[88] Berle (1947), p. 348; Thompson (1990), p. 1042; Merkt & Spindler (2006), p. 203; Oh (2010), p. 121; Gerner-Beuerle & Schillig (2019), p. 62–64; Gevurtz, 2025, p. 25.

[89] Berle (1947), p. 354; Merkt & Spindler (2006), p. 202; Gerner-Beuerle & Schillig (2019), p. 528, 532.

[90] In this instance, the corporate veil is lifted solely to obtain information about those who control the company, for example, identifying the shareholders, determining the proportion of their holdings, and understanding their interrelationships in exercising control over the company.

[91] Ottolenghi (1990), p. 340.

as the identity of shareholders, their shareholdings, and their relationships, has become publicly accessible in many jurisdictions. In the European Union, for example, such data is often available through official company registers, including beneficial ownership registers and commercial registries, which promote transparency and allow access to shareholder information as part of broader corporate disclosure obligations.[92,93,94,95] These registers provide judges and investigators with valuable information that is crucial to making decisions on whether factors for veil piercing occurred. Contrary to authors who grouped factors for piercing the corporate veil, Lopez, states that court should not only consider the factors, but also the policies underlying the separate entity concept as well as other policies underlying the alternative challenges.[96] In this dissertation I have grouped most relevant factors for veil piercing based on an extensive literature review. The following factors were mostly cited and are further elaborated here.

3.3.1.1 Undercapitalization

Ayres stated that there is a default rule that creditors can pierce the corporate veil of a limited liability company if the company is undercapitalized.[97] This is consistent with Berle who linked insufficient capitalization as evidence that the company is used as an instrumentality of its owners.[98] This discourse changed when Thompson published his study in which he found that there are a lot of cases in which undercapitalization is mentioned, but there is a small number of cases in which courts pierce because of undercapitalization.[99] In an empirical study from 2014, conducted by Macey & Mitts, they concluded that courts rarely use undercapitalization as a factor to pierce the corporate veil and if they do,

---

[92] Directive (EU) 2015/849—the 4th Anti-Money Laundering Directive (AMLD4) Introduced the requirement for EU countries to maintain a central register of beneficial owners of companies and legal entities.

[93] Directive (EU) 2017/1132 requires Member States to ensure public access to certain company information via central, commercial, or companies registers. Articles 14–18 (on disclosure and access to company data).

[94] Amended AMLD4, Directive (EU) 2018/843—the 5th Anti-Money Laundering Directive (AMLD5) expanding access to beneficial ownership registers.

[95] Directive (EU) 2019/1151—Digitalization Directive (amending Directive 2017/1132) It supports cross-border access to company and shareholder information via the Business Registers Interconnection System (BRIS).

[96] Lopez (1982), p. 132.

[97] Ayres 1992, p. 1398.

[98] Berle (1947), p. 349.

[99] Thompson (1990), p. 1062.

it is not so successful.[100] Bainbridge confirms this by emphasizing that there is no default undercapitalization rule, and that undercapitalization alone, is an insufficient factor to pierce the corporate veil.[101] Similar findings were presented in Europe. In Germany for example, undercapitalization alone is not a case of veil piercing anymore either, even though authors such as Vasiljević claim otherwise[102]. The Bundesgerichtshof (BGH) in the GAMMA case, emphasized that even if a company is undercapitalized, it does not automatically imply bad faith or moral wrongdoing.[103] Liability requires intent and immoral damage, which undercapitalization alone does not show. Undercapitalization is not immoral under article 826 BGB[104]. Another case concerning undercapitalization was the Trihotel case[105] in which the court stressed that shareholder liability for undercapitalization is not codified in law and is not recognized as a general principle in German corporate law. Only in specific cases may liability arise under Article 826 BGB (intentional immoral damage). Two cases illustrate the (un)importance of undercapitalization as a factor for piercing the corporate veil, the Coral Rose Case[106] and the Films case[107]. Atlas Maritime Co. SA v. Avalon Maritime Ltd. established that even where a company is deliberately structured with inadequate equity by its sole shareholder, this does not automatically result in personal liability. English courts are generally reluctant to interfere with the principle of corporate personality unless there is evidence of fraud, sham, or the misuse of the company structure to evade legal obligations. The case reinforces the principle that the

---

[100] Macey & Mitts (2014), p. 103.

[101] Bainbridge (2005), p. 90.

[102] Vasiljević (2020), p. 155. Vasiljević claims that German courts use undercapitalization as an important factor for unlimited liability of shareholders. This might have been the case prior to the GAMMA case of 2008.

[103] BHG (2008), p. 11 (point 17).

[104] Article 826 BGB: "Anyone who, in a manner that violates good morals, intentionally causes damage to another person is liable to compensate that person for the damage." Only intentional, immoral interference that destroys the company's existence (*existenzvernichtender Eingriff*) can lead to personal shareholder liability under Article 826 BGB (intentional damage contrary to good morals). General economic decisions, such as providing limited initial capital, even if objectively risky, are not enough to justify lifting the corporate veil.

Limited liability remains protected unless there's clear intentional misconduct with morally reprehensible consequences.

[105] BGH. Urteil vom 28. April 2008—II ZR 264/06 (TRIHOTEL-Fall). Retrieved from https://juris.bundesgerichtshof.de.

[106] Atlas Maritime Co. SA v. Avalon Maritime Ltd. (The Coral Rose (No. 3)), (1991) 4 All E.R. 783 (C. A.).

[107] Re F.G. (Films) Ltd., (1953) 1 All E.R. 615 (Ch. D.).

legal autonomy of a company must be respected, and the threshold for piercing the veil remains high, undercapitalization may be a red flag, but it is not decisive without accompanying elements of impropriety. In Re F.G. (Films) Ltd., an English company was set up ostensibly as the producer of a film, but it had minimal capital and no real decision-making power. The entire financing and actual production were managed by an American company. This case demonstrated the court's willingness to pierce the corporate veil where a company is a mere façade or agent for another entity. The decision turned not on undercapitalization per se, but on the lack of genuine corporate independence and substance. Unlike in Atlas Maritime, where the company operated independently (albeit undercapitalized), F.G. Films concerned a shell company with no real function beyond legal formalities. This underscores the principle that undercapitalization alone is not sufficient; what matters is whether the company is being used as a mere device or sham to conceal the true facts or to evade legal responsibilities. Courts will lift the veil only when the company structure is abused, not merely when it is financially weak.

3.3.1.2 Fraud—Misinterpretation

Thompson identified that the percentage in which courts most likely pierce the corporate veil are fraud cases (81,82%), mostly related to tax issues.[108] Oh underlined this in his empirical study, showcasing that the most successful veil piercing cases are supported by specific evidence of fraud or misrepresentation.[109] Most successful in this case refers to the plaintiff being successful with his claim, and the court piercing the corporate veil to hold the shareholder liable. Fraud requires a form of misrepresentation of false facts, and intent to obtain unlawful financial benefit. This was not the case in Castleberry v. Branscum[110] in which for the court to pierce the corporate veil, a plaintiff only needed to proof constructive fraud: "…the breach of a legal or equitable duty which, irrespective of moral guilt, the law declares fraudulent because of its tendency to deceive others, to violate confidence, or to injure public interests."[111] Merkt & Spindler have elaborated on fraudulent intent and a lesser form of culpability, specifically, acting with awareness of potential harm without necessarily intending to deceive or act

---

[108] Thompson (1990), p. 1061. 9 of 2 cases.

[109] Oh (2010), p. 90.

[110] The case stands as a leading authority for allowing veil piercing without proof of intent to defraud, so long as there is abuse of the corporate form that results in unfairness or deception. https://case-law.vlex.com/vid/castleberry-v-branscum-no-892535421, accessed April 2, 2025.

[111] Texas Supreme Court (1986), p. 273.

maliciously.[112] In cases of fraud, courts typically require evidence of intent to deceive and knowledge that the conduct is wrong or dishonest. However, in some legal contexts, it is sufficient if the party causing the damage must foresee the causal chain, though bad intent is not necessary. On the contrary, in the case VTB Capital Plc v. Nutritek International Corp, the Court of Appeal refused to pierce the corporate veil, despite allegations of fraud. VTB had loaned $225 million to RAP, which used the funds to buy overvalued assets from Nutritek, both allegedly controlled by the same individuals. VTB argued that the corporate structure had been misused to commit fraud and sought to hold the individuals contractually liable. However, the court found no evidence that the companies were used as sham or façade specifically to conceal wrongdoing and emphasized that veil piercing requires an independent legal wrong involving the misuse of the corporate form. Since VTB already had legal remedies in tort for fraudulent misrepresentation, veil piercing was deemed unnecessary and unjustified. These cases only illustrate that factors for veil piercing can be viewed differently, and it depends how strictly courts view the separation of legal personality. If the standard of separation is high, courts tend to be stricter in applying the rule. Krendt & Krendl created a list of examples of fraud and misrepresentation, and it included fraudulent transfers of property,[113] agency,[114] and breach of fiduciary duty[115,116] In the US, the plaintiff would only need to proof fraud, in the UK for example, all factors resulting in fraud would needed to be showcased, for the court to pierce the corporate veil, as showcased in VTB Capital Plc vs Nutritek International Corp. Elements of fraud would then include: control of the company by the wrongdoer, improper/fraudulent use of corporate form, use of company to conceal wrongdoing, that there is no other adequate legal remedy.

3.3.1.3 Commingling of Assets

In his recent empirical study, Gevurtz found that piercing the corporate veil often involves acts of deception and the siphoning of corporate assets.[117] His explanation for the frequent success of veil-piercing claims involving siphoning is the

[112] Merkt & Spindler (2006), p. 205.

[113] When money or assets were improperly transferred from the company or the subsidiary to the parent.

[114] When the company (subsidiary) acted at the direction of the owner or shareholder (or parent).

[115] When the directors and officers of the company or subsidiary wasted its assets in order to benefit the parent or themselves.

[116] Krendt & Krendl (1978), p. 31.

[117] Gevurtz, 2025, p. 25.

prevalence of such practices among controlling shareholders of closely held corporations. In many cases, the surrounding facts, such as the failure to comply with corporate formalities in employment contracts, loans, or dividend declarations, are critical to demonstrating that the owner's withdrawals are not legitimate business transactions, but rather improper extractions of value. In assessing the unity of interest and ownership of the piercing test, courts examine indicators such as the absence of separate corporate books and records, the commingling of corporate and personal assets, the absence of separate offices, and the treatment of the corporation as an empty shell with no employees or independent activity. For example, German courts found that personal liability applies only when the shareholder actively caused the commingling, typically by exercising dominant influence as a sole or majority shareholder. This is referred to as "*Verhaltenshaftung*" (behavioral liability), not "*Zustandshaftung*" (state-of-affairs liability). Mere financial or accounting deficiencies are not enough to trigger personal liability.[118] In SHAL and SHAM, the French Commercial Chamber affirmed that confusion of assets between group companies justified the extension of collective insolvency proceedings[119].

Contrary to this, Thompson identifies noncompliance with formalities through omissions such as failure to hold regular board or shareholder meetings, failure to appoint directors, or failure to issue stock certificates.[120] Empirical research supports the relevance of these factors: courts pierce the veil in about two-thirds of cases where noncompliance with formalities is explicitly found, while piercing is denied in over 90% of cases where compliance with corporate formalities is found.[121] Nevertheless, some scholars caution against overstating the role of formalities. As Merkt and Spindler note, failure to comply with procedural

---

[118] BGH (2005). p. 14, point 23. Urt. v. 14.11.2005—II ZR 178/03. Available here: https://www.bundesgerichtshof.de/SharedDocs/Entscheidungen/DE/Zivilsenate/II_ZS/2003/II_ZR_178-03.pdf?__blob=publicationFile&v=1. Accessed January 26, 2026.

[119] Cour de cassation (2000). Available here> https://www.legifrance.gouv.fr/juri/id/JURITEXT000007408068. Accessed January 26, 2026. In this case, the court upheld the extension of SEAM's insolvency proceedings to SHAL and SHAM based on factors including:

(1) excessively long and irrevocable lease agreements between the companies,

(2) abnormal financial flows, such as SEAM financing property acquisitions for SHAL/SHAM through rent and fees, and.

(3) economic dependence and shared interests that rendered their operations indistinguishable. The court found these elements sufficient to establish a confusion des patrimonies, thereby justifying the disregard of corporate separateness. (Cour de cassation, 2000).

[120] Thompson (1990), p. 1064.

[121] Thompson (1990), p. 1064.

requirements alone is generally insufficient to impose shareholder liability.[122] The doctrine of piercing the corporate veil is typically invoked in circumstances where shareholders leverage corporate protections without assuming the corresponding responsibilities, or where they expressly agree to cover corporate liabilities and later seek to evade those obligations. In the EU, Article 11 of the Directive (EU) 2017/1132, stipulates nullity of a company when legal formalities were not complied with.[123] Consequences of nullity are winding up of the company or its dissolution.[124] While judicial entities have exercised caution in implementing the doctrine of veil piercing, due to concerns about creating windfall profits for creditors, the doctrine is ultimately justified by the principle that shareholders should not be allowed to benefit from the privileges of incorporation while ignoring the corresponding obligations.

3.3.1.4 Violation of Criminal Law

Rarely do civil law scholars write about piercing the corporate veil in connection with criminal activity. In his empirical study, Thompson had a rather small sample of criminal cases (15 cases).[125] However, the court decided to pierce the corporate veil in 10 of them. Bainbridge and Henderson argue that "tax cheats should be punished for tax fraud under criminal law; we should not twist and distort corporate law to achieve criminal law ends."[126] That court are not sure about this either proofs the case of R v. Boyle[127], that serves as a critical authority on the intersection of criminal law and corporate veil piercing. The Crown Court (Ireland) had appointed an Enforcement Receiver over company assets by treating them as the realizable property of two convicted individuals, Patrick and Mark Boyle, following their guilty plea to conspiracy involving tachograph fraud. The central issue

[122] Merkt & Spindler (2006), p. 218.

[123] European Parliament and Council (2017), Art. 7. Available here: https://eur-lex.europa.eu/legal-content/EN/TXT/?uri=CELEX%3A02017L1132-20220812. Accessed January 28, 2026.

[124] European Parliament and Council (2017), Art. 12.

[125] Thompson (1990), p. 1058.

[126] Bainbridge and Henderson (2016), p. 115.

[127] Although the Boyles were the "operating minds" of the company, and their conduct led to criminal convictions, the company itself was not a sham, nor was it wholly under their ownership or control. The Court stressed that the company's assets and turnover did not automatically become the personal property of the Boyles simply because of their managerial roles (Royal Courts of Justice, 2016). As such, the attempt to enforce confiscation through veil piercing was not substantiated. Judgment available here: https://crimeline.co.uk/wp-content/uploads/2017/12/boyle2016ewccrim19.pdf, accessed April 14, 2025.

was whether the assets of the family-run company could be attributed personally to the Boyles, thereby justifying veil piercing to satisfy confiscation orders. The Crown Court pierced the corporate veil, but the Court of Appeal overturned the Crown Court's decision, reaffirming the principle that a company is a separate legal person, and this principle cannot be bypassed using a "broad brush" approach. The Court emphasized that the corporate veil may only be pierced in specific, narrowly defined circumstances. These include cases where the offender uses a company to conceal criminal conduct, commits the criminal act in the company's name, or manipulates corporate structures to deceive others.[128] This case, again, emphasizes that courts apply the reasoning for implementing the doctrine, or not, differently, which brings us back to Bainbridge's argument that piercing should be abolished all together[129], or Gevurtz's argument that the doctrine needs to be narrowly defined.[130] However, criminal law uses doctrinal tools to impose liability beyond the entity, for example, in its 1985 decision, the Cour de cassation (France) emphasized that intercompany financial support must serve the interest of the group as a whole, not merely the personal interest of directors. The so called Rozenblum criteria (economic coherence, group strategy, reciprocal benefits) mirrors conditions under which veil piercing would be allowed in other systems like U.S., UK, or Germany. While French civil law rarely pierces the corporate veil explicitly, criminal courts may look beyond the formal legal personality of companies to hold individuals accountable for abuse.[131] This is in line of Merkt & Spindler's argument that the decisive factor can be whether the legal entity was used as a vehicle for fraud.[132] Courts pierce the corporate veil in situations in which the legal entity was used as a vehicle of fraud, something EC warned about in 2021 in their research on letterbox companies. The criminal

---

[128] Rv.Boyle Transport (Northern Ireland) Ltd, Patrick Boyle and Mark Boyle (2016] EWCA Crim 19. Judgment from 25 February 2016.

[129] Bainbridge (2005), p. 106.

[130] Gevurtz, 2025, p. 19.

[131] In this case, the managers used multiple companies they controlled to shift funds in ways harmful to some and beneficial to others. The formal separation of the companies was disregarded, because the real economic control was unified, and it was exercised in the interest of the managers, not the companies themselves. The court refused to let the corporate structure shield individuals from liability when it was used to commit abuse or fraud.

[132] Merkt & Spindler (2006), p. 202.

law context is particularly significant, as violations of tax[133], insolvency[134], or antitrust law[135] may give rise to personal criminal liability. In these areas, the doctrine of piercing the corporate veil is most often invoked in cases where the corporate structure has been misused to circumvent legal obligations. Due to the critical nature of these legal fields, specific statutory provisions and special regulatory frameworks have, in some instances, evolved to address and prevent such abuses. The criminal law context is important because the breach of tax, insolvency or anti-trust law, lead to criminal liability.[136] If there is criminal liability of companies, do we need to pierce the corporate veil at all

3.3.2 The Totality of Circumstances Test

Building on the previously discussed factors, it is evident that fraud remains one of the most consistent grounds for piercing the corporate veil, with courts frequently holding shareholders personally liable. However, as Lopez argues, the mere presence of such factors is not sufficient.[137] Courts require structured and systematic evaluation mechanisms to thoroughly examine the factual matrix of each case and to assess whether disregarding corporate personhood is warranted. This type of analytical framework not only compels courts to clearly articulate the rationale for their decisions but also contributes to the development of a coherent and principled body of case law governing exceptions to the doctrine of separate legal personality.

Consistent with this approach, any decision to pierce the corporate veil must carefully balance two competing legal policy considerations: the promotion of

---

[133] It is essential to examine whether the corporation was founded and operated with a legitimate, independent business purpose, or whether it served primarily as a vehicle for tax avoidance. Additionally, it must be determined whether the shareholders acted in good faith throughout the course of the company's operations.

[134] It is essential to examine whether an insolvency creditor or administrator may pierce the corporate veil of the insolvent company in order to seek recourse against solvent shareholders. For example, German case BGH (2005), Nr. II ZR 178/03, in which the insolvency administrator of a GmbH is authorized to assert a claim of veil piercing (*Durchgriffshaftung*) against shareholders in cases where commingling of assets (*Vermögensvermischung*) has occurred.

[135] It is essential to examine whether affiliated enterprises have been formally separated solely to evade antitrust regulations. Are the companies under unified control and is the competition between them genuine or merely superficial.

[136] Trivun (2023), p. 50.

[137] Lopez (1982), p. 140.

private investment through the principle of limited liability, and the prevention of unjust outcomes, which underpins the very rationale for veil piercing. Where the balance tips in favor of lifting the veil, the court must then assess whether the company was used with the intent to engage in fraudulent or otherwise unlawful conduct vis-à-vis a third party who was not party to the company's internal arrangements.

In conducting this evaluation, a court may consider the following questions, as adapted from Merkt and Spindler[138]:

1. Did commingling of funds and assets occur, i.e., did the shareholders use company funds for private purposes?
2. Did the shareholder misrepresent himself in dealings with third parties, giving the impression of personal responsibility for the company's liabilities?
3. Was the company undercapitalized, and did the director pursue business decisions involving disproportionate risk?
4. Did the company lack its own assets, distinct from those of the shareholders? Were all shares held by a single person or family?
5. Was the company formed with the purpose of assuming the liabilities of another person or legal entity?
6. Was the company operated merely as a shell or conduit for the business of another individual or enterprise?
7. Were false, incomplete, or misleading statements made about the company's financial condition or structure?
8. Were assets distributed by or to shareholders or third parties to the detriment of the company's creditors?
9. Were assets and liabilities artificially split across multiple enterprises so that one held all the assets and another bore the liabilities?

In this context, piercing the corporate veil to reach a shareholder who has actively participated in the management of the company is typically subject to two core preconditions. This situation is most frequently observed in closely held corporations, family-owned businesses, and single-shareholder (one man) companies.[139]

First, the business operations and financial interests of the company and the shareholder must be so closely aligned that the legal separation between the entity

138 Merkt & Spindler (2006), p. 213.

139 Merkt & Spindler (2006), p. 213.

and the individual becomes a mere legal fiction. Second, maintaining that separation would result in an inequitable outcome, particularly where it would allow the shareholder to escape liability for conduct that, in substance, should be attributed to them personally. Despite identifiable factors, courts still apply veil-piercing inconsistently. This inconsistency is particularly acute in Bosnia and Herzegovina, where statutory guidance is scarce. The next section isolates this gap.

3.4 The Gap in Research

In his book Corporate Fraud Handbook: Prevention and Detection, Wells defines fraud as "any crime for gain that uses deception as its principal modus operandi," and identifies four essential elements: (1) a materially false statement; (2) knowledge of its falsity at the time of utterance; (3) reliance by the victim; and (4) resulting damages.[140] Limited liability companies often serve as ideal vehicles for illicit activity due to the protective veil of legal personhood, which shields the identities of owners and shareholders. Empirical evidence presented by Gup & Beekarry indicates a rise in the use of limited liability entities, with increasing concerns over their misuse for unlawful purposes.[141] Furthermore, Uzun et al. established a significant relationship between board composition, the structure of oversight committees, and the incidence of corporate fraud.[142] These findings underscore that fraud is a central element of corporate misconduct and a key factor in establishing corporate responsibility. As such, the presence of fraud is a strong indicator of shareholder liability and remains a cornerstone justification for piercing the corporate veil. The question of shareholder liability in criminal law has been explored through the broader framework of corporate criminal liability. Coffee critiques the systemic underenforcement of corporate crime and highlights how shareholders indirectly bear the cost of corporate sanctions.[143] Laufer argues that corporate criminal liability often fails to attribute blame accurately within complex corporate structures, calling into question its deterrent effect.[144] Arlen & Kraakman analyze liability regimes and argue that different enforcement models impact whether and how individual actors, including shareholders, can be held

---

140 Wells (2017), p. 2.

141 Gup & Beekarry (2009), p. 7.

142 Uzun et al. (2004), p. 37.

143 Coffee (2020), p. 100.

144 Laufer (2006), p. 6.

responsible.[145] Stiglitz & Pieth emphasize shareholder awareness and complicity in corruption-related offenses, proposing that criminal liability should extend to those exercising control[146]. From a European perspective, Tiedemann analyzes economic criminal law and identifies conditions under which shareholder liability may arise, particularly when shareholders act as de facto managers or benefit directly from criminal activity.[147]

While extensive literature exists on the doctrine of piercing the corporate veil and its doctrinal development in civil liability cases, there is limited empirical and doctrinal analysis on how veil piercing interacts with corporate fraud in the context of criminal liability, particularly in transitional legal systems such as BiH. Although the criminal liability of legal persons in Bosnia and Herzegovina is based on the derivative model, where liability is attributed to the company through the culpability of its responsible persons[148] (*rukovodeća ili nadzorna tijela*), the role of shareholders, particularly those exercising de facto control or acting as shadow directors, remains underexplored in both legislative frameworks and scholarly analysis, highlighting a critical gap in addressing the potential criminal liability of shareholders in corporate structures, and with that proof of fraud in civil proceedings related to piercing the corporate veil.[149] This research aims to investigate how fraud and bad faith can serve as legal and evidentiary grounds for piercing the corporate veil in both civil and criminal contexts. Recognizing this doctrinal vacuum in BiH, the dissertation proceeds to draw on EU legislation and case law to propose a model that could fill it.

3.5 Conclusions

Scholars largely agree on the core indicators of abuse of the corporate form, such as fraud, misrepresentation, and commingling of assets, as justifications for piercing the corporate veil. Research has shown that claims for veil piercing are more compelling when supported by evidence that the company is not underperforming due to some kind of asset-related abuse or malfeasance.[150] However, the

[145] Arlen & Kraakman (1997), p. 692.

[146] Stiglitz & Pieth (2016), p. 12.

[147] Tiedemann (2012), p. 145.

[148] Art. 124 Criminal Law of BiH, Art. 128 Criminal Law of FBiH, Art.127 Criminal Law of BiH RS.

[149] Primorac (2011), p. 295.

[150] Oh (2010), p. 139.

issue of undercapitalization remains controversial. Macey and Mitts argue that undercapitalization alone rarely provides sufficient grounds for veil piercing, a view supported by judicial reluctance to rely on this factor in isolation.[151] Furthermore, empirical research by Thompson indicates that courts are more inclined to pierce the corporate veil in closely held corporations with few shareholders, particularly when those behind the company are natural persons rather than legal entities.[152] Notably, no court has yet permitted veil piercing to reach shareholders of publicly traded corporations, underscoring the functional limits of the doctrine in corporate group settings. This research focuses specifically on veil piercing in the context of closely held corporations, where creditors seek to hold the controlling natural person shareholder liable. While alternative contexts for veil piercing exist, such as in tort claims or complex corporate group structures,[153] the empirical data suggest that courts in the United States, are more willing to pierce the veil in contractual claims (42%) than in tort claims (31%), potentially due to the presence of third-party liability insurance in tort contexts, which encourages settlements and reduces the need for judicial intervention.

Beyond civil liability, the issue becomes even more complex in the realm of criminal law. Courts and prosecutors may need to confront the question of whether the misuse of corporate form for criminal purposes, such as tax fraud, insolvency fraud, or antitrust violations, warrants disregarding legal personality. As Berle noted, the corporate form must not become a shield for criminality or policy evasion.[154] If a company does not reflect its corporate documentation or operational independence, courts may justifiably treat it as merely an instrumentality of its controller. This issue is particularly pressing in jurisdictions like Bosnia and Herzegovina, where prosecutorial practice demonstrates a clear focus on individual liability, often neglecting the corporate entity itself, even when the company is clearly used as a vehicle for criminal conduct. This raises critical questions about the separation of legal personhood in criminal law:

- Is there a coherent and consistent prosecutorial approach to corporate crime?
- Should criminal law permit or require veil piercing to hold the company, or alternatively the controlling individuals, accountable in cases of regulatory evasion or corporate misconduct?

---

[151] Macey & Mitts (2014), p. 103.

[152] Thompson (1990), p. 1038.

[153] Bainbridge (2005), p. 91.

[154] Berle (1947), p. 353.

- What role does prosecutorial discretion play in shaping the reality of corporate accountability?

Ultimately, the gap between legal theory and enforcement practice especially in systems where corporate criminal liability exists de jure but is rarely applied de facto, exposes structural deficiencies in institutional capacity, legal culture, and enforcement priorities. This gap underscores the importance of developing a best-practice model for veil piercing that reflects both doctrinal coherence and practical applicability, particularly in transitional legal systems such as Bosnia and Herzegovina. This research project aims to close this gap by analyzing the relationship between civil liability for corporate abuse and criminal liability, and how the court can successfully pierce the corporate veil to combat economic crime.

(Criminal) Shareholder Liability 4

Many authors[1] have written about corporate criminal liability and discussed whether criminal sanctions against corporations generate the necessary behavior modifications compared to civil liability.[2] They argue that the concept is an inequitable practice of collective retribution and therefore unnecessary, since civil sanctions exist for corporations. The social utility of criminal liability is the probability of incarceration and other non-monetary penalties, which are impossible for companies as artificial constructs.[3] However, as Geis & DiMento point out, over time, there was a need to curb the illegalities of the corporate world and their destructive acts, with a legal doctrine that would hold corporations criminally liable.[4] Modern legislative frameworks[5], acknowledge that legal persons (e.g., companies) can be held criminally liable, but always through the conduct of natural persons (directors, shareholders, agents) acting on behalf or for the benefit of the company. The separation of ownership and control and the risk of ownership conflicts between managers and shareholders can lead to decisions that

[1] For example Wells (1993), Wolgast (1992), Becker (1991), Choudhury & Petrin (2019), Bratton (2017).

[2] Wells (2001), p. 11.

[3] Lee (2017), p. 185; Choudhury & Petrin (2019), p. 165.

[4] Geis & DiMento (2002), p. 343.

[5] This dissertation will focus on EU member states Croatia and Germany, and non EU member state: BiH, when refering to comparative legal norms.

L. Hasanovic, *Piercing the Corporate Veil: Shareholder Liability*,
Juridicum – Schriftenreihe zum Wirtschafts-, Unternehmens- und Bankrecht / Series on Business, Corporate and Banking Law,
https://doi.org/10.1007/978-3-658-52987-1_4

are made by the management that are not in alignment with shareholder preferences, or that are even criminal.[6] Across most legal instruments[7], two recurring themes justify holding individuals accountable:

1. Control or decision-making power over the company (typically shareholders or directors).
2. Intentional use of corporate form to perpetrate or conceal criminal acts.

Within these parameters, the doctrine of piercing the corporate veil in company law is generally applied through the shareholder, as the owner of the company's capital, rather than through its legal representative, although, in some cases, the two roles may coincide. This raises a fundamental question of fairness: Is it just to impose liability on an individual who merely holds shares but exercises no control over the company's operations? In this context, the evolving EU legal framework on beneficial ownership plays a crucial role. It provides increasingly refined tools for identifying the natural persons who ultimately exercise control over legal entities, whether directly or indirectly. This development is particularly relevant for judicial analyses of veil piercing, as it enables courts to more accurately distinguish between nominal shareholders and those who exercise real influence over corporate conduct. The implications of this refinement will be further examined in the following section.

4.1 The Internationalization of Corporate Criminal Law

There are several international and EU legal acts that are influential in determining criminal liability of legal entities, and there are more so important since they aim to harmonize rules across the EU related to organized crime, money laundering, and other criminal offences. These laws aim to provide stability and security in Europe and the integrity of financial markets.[8] Two major international events, the second conference of the *Association internationale de droit pénal* held in

[6] Neville (2011), p. 218.

[7] Elaborated further in text.

[8] As emphasized here: https://finance.ec.europa.eu/financial-crime/anti-money-laundering-and-countering-financing-terrorism-overview_en, accessed May 20, 2025.

1921, and the Seventh UN Congress on the Prevention of Crime and the Treatment of Offenders from 1985, stressed the importance of national states to adopt measures against criminal offences of legal persons especially when the criminal offence is committed for their benefit and with the resources of the legal entity.[9] This was accounted to the rise of cross-border corporate crime[10] (especially corruption) and in order to avoid forum-shopping, a minimum harmonization of legal standards was necessary[11]. The adoption of Recommendation No. R (88) 18 on the Liability of Enterprises for Offences by the Council of Europe on 20 October 1988 marked a cornerstone in the development and subsequent harmonization of corporate criminal law across member states.[12] Article I of the Recommendation addresses the liability of enterprises, affirming that both the legal entity and the natural person may be held liable for an offence. Notably, it provides that the entity can be held liable even when the individual perpetrator is identifiable, thereby emphasizing the autonomous responsibility of legal persons.[13]

For instance, both the Republic of Croatia[14] and Bosnia and Herzegovina[15] have adopted a derivative liability model, whereby the criminal liability of a legal

---

[9] Adam et. al (2008), p. 373.

[10] As emphasized in the Council of Europe (CoE) Recommendation R(81)12 on economic crime, 25 June 1981.

[11] UN Convention against corruption (2003), Article 26; OAS Inter-American Convention against Corruption (1996), Article VIII; OECD Convention on Combating Bribery of Foreign Public Officials in International Business Transactions (1997), Article 2, 3(2); CoE Criminal Law Convention on Corruption (1999), Article 18, 19 (2); EU Second Protocol, drawn up on the basis of Article K.3 of the treaty on European Union, to the Convention on the protection of the European Communities' financial interests (1997), OJ C 221/12, 19 July 1997, Article 3, all established liability of legal persons for serious offences.

[12] Available here: https://rm.coe.int/16804c5d71, accessed May 20, 2025.

[13] CoE (1990), P. 10. Available here: https://rm.coe.int/16804c5d71.

[14] The Act on the Liability of Legal Persons for Criminal Offences (Official Gazette Nos. 151/2003, 110/2007, 45/2011, 143/2012, 114/2022, 114/2023); the Criminal Procedure Act (Official Gazette Nos. 152/2008, 76/2009, 80/2011, 91/2012, 143/2012, 56/2013, 145/2013, 152/2014, 70/2017, 126/2019, 126/2019, 80/2022, 36/2024, 72/2025), and the Criminal Code of the Republic of Croatia (Official Gazette Nos. 125/2011, 144/2012, 56/2015, 61/2015, 101/2017, 118/2018, 126/2019, 84/2021, 114/2022, 114/2023, 36/2024).

[15] The Criminal Code of Bosnia and Herzegovina (Official Gazette of BiH Nos. br. 3/2003, 32/2003—corr., 37/2003, 54/2004, 61/2004, 30/2005, 53/2006, 55/2006, 8/2010, 47/2014, 22/2015, 40/2015, 35/2018, 46/2021, 31/2023 and 47/2023); Criminal Code of the Federation of Bosnia and Herzegovina (Official Gazette of the Federation of BiH Nos. 36/2003, 21/2004—corr., 69/2004, 18/2005, 42/2010, 42/2011, 59/2014, 76/2014, 46/2016, and 75/2017); the Criminal Code of the Brčko District (Official Gazette of the Brčko District of BiH Nos. 19/2020—consolidated text, 3/2024, and 14/2024); Criminal Code of the Republic of

person is contingent upon the liability of the responsible natural person within the entity who committed the offence. However, this derivative liability is limited in scope, meaning that a legal person is not automatically liable for every criminal act committed by its responsible representatives; specific legal conditions must be met for corporate liability to arise.[16] In contrast, Article I.5.b of the Recommendation draws upon the German model of *Ordnungswidrigkeiten*, a system of quasi-criminal liability, under which administrative authorities impose sanctions that are subject to judicial review. This model is recommended particularly for addressing illicit conduct that, regardless of its seriousness, does not necessitate criminal sanctions. It offers an alternative approach to enforcement, particularly useful for ensuring accountability in regulatory or economic offences that fall short of criminal gravity, however in the case of Germany where we do not have criminal liability of corporations. Three primary theories of corporate criminal liability emerge across European jurisdictions, reflecting different approaches to attributing culpability to legal persons. Vicarious liability[17] (as seen in Denmark, Article 27.1 of the Danish Criminal Code) is based on the *respondeat superior* model, whereby a legal person is liable for offences committed by any natural person connected to the entity, provided the offence was committed within the scope of their function. This model focuses on the relationship between the natural person and the entity, allowing for broader attribution. In contrast, Croatia and Bosnia and Herzegovina follow an alter ego or identification theory, where liability arises only if the offence stems from the acts or omissions of persons in managerial or supervisory positions, those who are the "directing mind and

---

Srpska (Official Gazette of RS Nos. 67/17, 104/2018—Constitutional Court decision, 15/21, 89/21, and 73/2023).

The Criminal Procedure Code of Bosnia and Herzegovina (Official Gazette of BiH Nos. 3/03, 32/03, 36/03, 26/2004, 63/2004, 13/2005, 48/2005, 46/2006, 29/2007, 53/2007, 58/2008, 12/2009, 16/2009, 53/2009, 93/2009, 72/2013 i 65/2018); Criminal Procedure Code of the Federation of Bosnia and Herzegovina (Official Gazette of the Federation of BiH Nos. 35/03, 37/03, 56/03, 78/2004, 28/2005, 55/2006, 27/2007, 53/2007, 9/2009, 12/2010, 8/2013, 59/2014 i 74/2020); Criminal Procedure Code of the Republic of Srpska (Official Gazette of RS 53/2012, 91/2017, 66/2018 i 15/2021); Criminal Procedure Code of the Brčko Distrikt (Official Gazette of BD 34/2013, 27/2014, 3/2019 i 16/2020).

[16] Primorac (2011), p. 295.

[17] Danish Criminal Code, Order No. 909 of September 27, 2005, as amended by Act Nos. 1389 and 1400 of December 21, 2005. Article 27(1), which extends the attribution of responsibility to the offences committed by each natural person connected to the legal person. "*Criminal liability of a legal person is conditional upon a transgression having been committed within the establishment of this person at the fault of one or more persons connected to this legal person or at the fault of the legal person himself*." https://www.legal-tools.org/doc/606ecd/pdf. Accessed May 20, 2025.

will" of the entity (e.g., Articles 124 CC BiH, 128 CC FBiH, 105 CC RS, and Articles 3 and 4 of Croatia's Act on Corporate Liability)[18]. This model narrows liability to upper management and excludes rank-and-file employees unless they acted under direct influence or oversight failure. Switzerland, by contrast, adopts an aggregate or corporate culture model[19], imposing liability on legal persons regardless of individual culpability, where the company failed to implement adequate organizational measures to prevent crimes such as money laundering, bribery, or terrorism. This reflects a systemic fault model, focusing on internal control and compliance structures rather than individual actions. Thus, Denmark emphasizes delegation and representation, Croatia and Bosnia emphasize control and intent, and Switzerland emphasizes organizational responsibility and prevention. Germany fits most closely with the aggregate/corporate culture model, though it implements this through administrative rather than criminal law, using the Ordnungswidrigkeitengesetz (OWiG), particularly Art. 30 and 130 OWiG[20].

---

[18] Criminal Codes in Bosnia and Herzegovina: only managers or employees endowed with certain responsibilities within the company may cause corporate criminal liability. Article 124 Criminal Code BiH, Article 128 Criminal Code FBiH, Article 105 Criminal Code RS: A legal person shall be liable for a criminal offence committed by a perpetrator in the name of, on behalf of, or for the benefit of the legal person, if: a) the nature of the committed offence stems from a decision, order, or approval of the managing or supervisory bodies of the legal person; b) or if the managing or supervisory bodies of the legal person influenced the perpetrator or enabled them to commit the offence; c) or if the legal person possesses unlawfully acquired property or objects resulting from the criminal offence; d) or if the managing or supervisory bodies failed to exercise proper supervision over the legality of the employees' conduct.

See also Article 3 of the Act on the Liability of Legal Persons for Criminal Offences in Croatia: The responsible person within the legal entity must have committed a criminal offence, and through that offence, a duty of the legal person must have been violated, or the legal person must have obtained or was intended to obtain unlawful material gain for itself or another. Article 4 further defines the "responsible" person within the legal entity as the person who manages the affairs of the legal person or has been entrusted with managing the affairs of the legal person.

[19] Article 102 of the Swiss Criminal Code: "....the undertaking is penalized irrespective of the criminal liability of any natural persons, provided the undertaking has failed to take all the reasonable organizational measures that are required in order to prevent such an offence." (with such offence related to: terrorism, organized crime, money-laundering, bribery. Available: https://legislationline.org/sites/default/files/2023-10/Criminal%20Code%20of%20the%20Swiss%20Confederation.pdf. Accessed May 20, 2025.

[20] Germany: Gesetz über Ordnungswidrigkeiten (OWiG) Article 30 Geldbuße gegen juristische Personen und Personenvereinigungen: If a person:

1. as a representative body of a legal person or as a member of such a body,

The OWiG stipulates that responsible persons in a legal entity are liable when senior officials commit offences (direct liability, Art. 30), or leadership fails to supervise properly, enabling others to offend (organizational fault, Art. 130). The EU legislative framework does not oblige Member States to sanction legal entities through criminal penalties. EU law follows the principle of procedural autonomy allowing Member States to choose administrative, civil, or criminal sanctions, provided the measures are effective, proportionate, dissuasive.[21] However, the EU introduces directives in which criminal liability of legal persons is required.

---

2. as the board of a non-incorporated association or as a member of such a board,
3. as a representative partner of a legal partnership,
4. as a general attorney (Generalbevollmächtigter) or in a senior position as a procurator (Prokurist) or authorized representative (Handlungsbevollmächtigter) of a legal person or an association of persons referred to in numbers 2 or 3, or
5. as any other person responsible for the management of the business or enterprise of a legal person or an association of persons referred to in numbers 2 or 3, including those responsible for supervising management or otherwise exercising control functions in a senior capacity,

commits a criminal offence or regulatory offence that violates obligations imposed on the legal person or the association of persons, or by which the legal person or the association was or was intended to be enriched, a monetary fine may be imposed on the legal person or the association.

(OWiG) Article 130—Violation of Supervisory Duties.

(1) Any person who, as the owner of a business or enterprise, intentionally or negligently fails to implement the supervisory measures required to prevent violations within the business or enterprise of obligations imposed on the owner, the breach of which is punishable by criminal penalty or administrative fine, commits a regulatory offence if such a violation occurs which could have been prevented or significantly hindered by proper supervision. The required supervisory measures include the appointment, careful selection, and monitoring of supervisory personnel.

[21] Art.4(3) TEU. For example, the European Court of Justice (ECJ) cases: 1. Österreichische Unilever GmbH v. Smithkline Beecham Markenartikel GmbH in which the ECJ concluded that a national sanctioning regime disturbs the functioning of the internal market beyond what the effectivity of Community law necessitated (Point 36). Available here: https://eur-lex.europa.eu/legal-content/EN/TXT/?uri=CELEX%3A61997CJ0077, accessed May 20, 2025.; 2. Suzanne Criel, née Donckerwolcke and Henri Schou v. Procureur de la République au tribunal de grande instance de Lille and Director General of Customs in which the ECJ emphasized that penalties for failing to declare the true origin of goods must be proportionate to the administrative nature of the violation. Severe sanctions, such as seizure of goods or fines based on their value, are deemed incompatible with EU law as they impede the free movement of goods. More broadly, any administrative or penal measure exceeding what is strictly necessary to ensure accurate import information constitutes a measure equivalent to a prohibited quantitative restriction under the Treaty. (Point 36). Available here: https://eur-lex.europa.eu/legal-content/EN/TXT/?uri=CELEX%3A61976CJ0041. Accessed May 20, 2025.

It will be elaborated further how and whether these directives establish criminal liability of legal entities, and who, in the name, or along with the legal entity, is to be held liable. In the following paragraph, the dissertation will investigate relevant EU legal framework that puts emphasis on liability of legal entities and that identifies how the responsible person within a legal entity is defined. Who is the natural person "hiding" behind the corporate veil and how do we establish their liability?

4.1.1 Liability of Legal Persons

There is one united opinion in the EU and its Member States, that legal persons, especially companies, are key actors capable of significantly impacting EU revenues, particularly through practices involving tax fraud, money laundering, and corruption. The EU has therefore established a unified legal framework for criminal liability in cases affecting the financial interests of the EU. The European-level enforcement regime addresses cross-border economic crime by including common sanctions for natural and legal persons, enforced by the European Public Prosecutor's Office (EPPO). Directive (EU) 2017/1371 of the European Parliament and of the Council of 5 July 2017 on the fight against fraud to the Union's financial interests by means of criminal law (PIF Directive), for example, provides for liability of legal persons for criminal offences committed for their benefit by other persons in leading positions within the legal entity.[22] These criminal offences are related to fraud affecting EU's financial interests[23], intentional misappropriation and corruption[24] and inciting, and aiding and abetting in those crimes[25]. Article 6 of the PIF Directive stipulates that: „Member States shall take the necessary measures to ensure that legal persons can be held liable for any of the criminal offences referred to in Articles 3, 4 and 5 committed for their benefit by any person, acting either individually or as part of an organ

[22] Article 2, Directive (EU) 2017/1371 of the European Parliament and of the Council of 5 July 2017 on the fight against fraud to the Union's financial interests by means of criminal law. Official Journal of the European Union, L 198, 29.7.2017, 29–41. Available here: https://eur-lex.europa.eu/eli/dir/2017/1371/oj/eng.

[23] Art. 3, PIF Directive.

[24] Art. 4, PIF Directive.

[25] Art. 5, PIF Directive.

of the legal person, and having a leading position within the legal person, based on:

(a) a power of representation of the legal person;
(b) an authority to take decisions on behalf of the legal person; or
(c) an authority to exercise control within the legal person."

The PIF Directive is important for two reasons, firstly, it establishes the obligation for Member States to ensure criminal liability of legal entities, and secondly, it points us to the legal basis for the responsibility of the natural person who is in control of the legal entity. Since this is a directive, Member States such as Germany, can implement the Directive through non-criminal channels (OWiG), for countries such as Croatia that already recognize corporate criminal liability in their national legislation, sanctions like criminal fines, exclusion from public procurement, or dissolution of a company are enforceable as primary criminal penalties. There are Member States that had to amend their national legislation with the requirements of the PIF Directive[26], for example Italy, and there are member states that claimed that the PIF Directive is applicable in their legal framework without the need for additional amendments of domestic legislation.[27] The PIF Directive, however, does not provide for definitions of "leading positions" or "authority", so that it is unclear who and how, within the legal entity would be held liable. The exact same wording can be found in Article 6 of the Directive 008/99/EC on the protection of the environment through criminal law.[28] Due to the rise in environmental offences, the EU has strengthened environmental compliance by criminalizing environmental misconducts. However, it remains unclear who the holders of leading position within a legal entity are, who would be held responsible for the offence. Germany's Action Plan to prevent the misuse

[26] Italy, Legislative Decree no. 231 of June 8th, 2001, which concerns the criminal and administrative liability of legal entities, underwent amendments to align with the requirements of the PIF Directive.

[27] Bartolucci (2024), p. 78.

[28] Article 6, Directive 008/99/EC on the protection of the environment through criminal law. Available here: https://eur-lex.europa.eu/legal-content/EN/TXT/HTML/?uri=CELEX:32008L0099.

of legal persons[29] stipulates that companies should know who owns and controls them and this information should be up to date and available. Shareholders with controlling rights should be required to disclaim whether they hold their respective shares on their own or on someone else's behalf. In the forthcoming paragraph it will be elaborated on how beneficial ownership is relevant in the context of piercing the corporate veil. This issue is of particular importance in the legal and regulatory context of Bosnia and Herzegovina. The current legal framework does not provide adequate mechanisms for identifying beneficial owners across all legal entities, nor does it effectively empower authorities to verify or challenge nominee arrangements that obscure real ownership. Consequently, the lack of transparency facilitates the misuse of corporate entities for illicit purposes. In such an environment, piercing the corporate veil becomes not only a theoretical legal remedy but a realistic enforcement tool.

4.1.2 Beneficial Ownership in EU Legislation

In their guidance manual on legal persons and money laundering, the World Bank established that there are certain reasons for setting up shell companies (or other legal structures) for illicit purposes. Among them were fraud, and tax evasion, hiding true ownership of assets, providing an apparent legitimate commercial justification for large movements of funds, comingling proceeds of crime with legitimate sources of funds. In their study they found that "limited liability partnerships have emerged as a primary mechanism for moving large amounts of illicit funds around the world".[30] The reason legal entities are an attractive vehicle for criminals is their separate legal personality that enables limitation of liability, and privacy. Natural or legal persons can hide their beneficial ownership and access the financial system through the legal entity.[31] The concept of the corporate veil is frequently invoked in criminal law contexts to denote the concealment of a company's true ownership, particularly in cases involving illicit activities. Criminal law often plays a leading role in efforts to identify beneficial owners and shareholders as part of investigations into financial crimes. Examining

---

[29] Available here: https://www.bundesregierung.de/resource/blob/974430/388980/9bc2bd31db6d650254f566e957385037/g8-lough-erne-deutscher-aktionsplan-data.pdf?download=1. Accessed May 27, 2025.

[30] World Bank (2022), p. 9.

[31] FATF (2025), p. 41.

anti-money laundering legislation and legal frameworks addressing financial misconduct involving legal entities offers valuable insight into the conditions under which the corporate veil may be pierced. This, in turn, helps clarify whom the law targets when corporate structures are misused to shield criminal and civil responsibility for fraud.

4.1.3 Anti-Money Laundering

In the context of this dissertation, it is essential to clearly define the concept of beneficial ownership, as it determines the allocation of responsibility within a legal entity. As established, under EU law as well as in the legal frameworks of Croatia and Bosnia and Herzegovina, the attribution of corporate criminal liability ultimately requires the identification of the responsible natural person behind the legal entity. Beneficial ownership encompasses both, significant ownership and effective control over a legal entity, whether exercised formally or informally, to promote transparency and prevent the misuse of corporate structures for illicit purposes. Regulation (EU) 2024/1624[32] (AML Regulation) defines the beneficial owner as "any natural person who ultimately owns or controls a legal entity or an express trust or similar legal arrangement".[33] Directive (EU) 2015/849 (AMLD Consolidated)[34]further defines the case when the beneficial owner is a corporate entity, focusing again on the natural person(s) who ultimately own or control the "legal entity through direct or indirect ownership of a sufficient percentage of the shares or voting rights or ownership interest in that entity, including through bearer shareholdings, or through control via other means." An indication of direct ownership is:

---

[32] Regulation (EU) 2024/1624 of the European Parliament and of the Council of 31 May 2024 on the prevention of the use of the financial system for the purposes of money laundering or terrorist financing (OJ L, 2024/1624, 19.6.2024, ELI: http://data.europa.eu/eli/reg/2024/1624/oj).

[33] Art. 2 (28), AML Regulation.

[34] Directive (EU) 2015/849 on the prevention of the use of the financial system for the purposes of money laundering or terrorist financing, amending Regulation (EU) No 648/2012, and repealing Directive 2005/60/EC and Commission Directive 2006/70/EC. Official Journal of the European Union, L 141, 73–117. The consolidated version includes amendments of Directive (EU) 2018/843, Directive (EU) 2019/2177, Regulation (EU) 2023/1113, and Directive (EU) 2024/1640.

1. a shareholding of 25 % plus one share or an ownership interest of more than 25 % in the customer held by a natural person.
2. a shareholding of 25 % plus one share or an ownership interest of more than 25 % in the customer held by a corporate entity, which is under the control of a natural person(s), or by multiple corporate entities, which are under the control of the same natural person(s).

Since this is a directive, and not a regulation, Member States can decide on a lower percentage which can also be an indication of ownership or control. If no natural person(s) who own or control the legal entity through direct or indirect ownership can be identified, AMLD Consolidated points to the natural person(s) who hold the position of senior managing official(s).

When determining control of an entity, obliged entities[35] must identify and verify the identity of the beneficial owner(s), understand the ownership and control structure, and assess whether any natural or legal person exert significant influence, particularly through ownership, management positions, or financial benefit, as outlined in Article 20 of the AML Regulation. Beneficial ownership information, according to Article 62 of the AML Regulation, includes the following:

"(a) all names and surnames, place and full date of birth, residential address, country of residence and nationality or nationalities of the beneficial owner, number of identity document, such as passport or national identity document, and, where it exists, unique personal identification number assigned to the person by his or her country of usual residence, and general description of the source of such number;

(b) the nature and extent of the beneficial interest held in the legal entity or legal arrangement, whether through ownership interest or control via other means, as well as the date as of which the beneficial interest is held;

(c) information on the legal entity of which the natural person is the beneficial owner in accordance with Article 22(1), point (b)[36], or, in the case of

[35] As defind n Article 3 of AML Regulation, those entities are: credit institutions; financial institutions; auditors, external accountants and tax advisors, lawyers, notaries, trust or company service providers; estate agents and other real estate professionals, traders, etc.

[36] Article 22. 1 (b) of the AML Regulation—Identification and verification of the identity of customers and beneficial owners for a legal entity:

(i) legal form and name of the legal entity;

(ii) address of the registered or official office and, if different, the principal place of business, and the country of creation;

legal arrangements of which the natural person is the beneficial owner, basic information on the legal arrangement;

(d) where the ownership and control structure contains more than one legal entity or legal arrangement, a description of such structure, including names and, where it exists, identification numbers of the individual legal entities or legal arrangements that are part of that structure, and a description of the relationships between them, including the share of the interest held;

(e) where a class of beneficiaries[37] is identified under Article 59, general description of the characteristic of the class of beneficiaries; (f) where objects of a power and default takers are identified under Article 60[38]..."

Information on beneficial ownership can be requested through the Central beneficial ownership registers, as stipulated in Article 10 of the AMLD Consolidated, but this information is not open to the public. Parties requesting beneficial ownership information must demonstrate legitimate interest[39], as outlined in Article 12 (2) of the AMLD Consolidated. Previous versions of the AMLD Consolidated stipulated that beneficial ownership information are open to the public, however, a judgement of the Court of Justice in joined Cases C-37/20 and C-601/20, WM and Sovim SA v. Luxembourg Business Registers[40] annulled the amendment emphasizing that general public access to beneficial ownership information constitutes a serious interference with Articles 7 and 8 of the Charter of Fundamental Rights of the EU, which guarantee respect for private life and

---

(iii) the names of the legal representatives of the legal entity as well as, where available, the registration number, the tax identification number and the Legal Entity Identifier;

(iv) the names of persons holding shares or a directorship position in nominee form, including reference to their status as nominee shareholders or directors.

[37] According to Article 59, this refers to beneficiaries that have yet to be determined, then the class of beneficiaries and its general characteristics shall be identified. Beneficiaries within the class shall be beneficial owners as soon as they are identified or designated.

[38] Related to discretionary trusts.

[39] For example, legitimate interest have: journalists and media, civil society and academia, potential business counterparties, entities in non-EU countries, third-country AML/CFT authorities, EU company registries and supervisory auuthorities, Recovery and Resilience Facility Authorities, public procurement authorities, Developers of AML/CFT tools.

[40] Court of Justice of the European Union. (2022, November 22). Judgment of the Court (Grand Chamber) in WM and Sovim SA v. Luxembourg Business Registers (Joined Cases C-37/20 and C-601/20). ECLI:EU:C:2022:912. Available at:

https://eur-lex.europa.eu/legal-content/EN/TXT/?uri=celex:62020CJ0037. Accessed May 22, 2025.

protection of personal data.[41] However, even though beneficial ownership registries, are not publicly available, the list of persons with legitimate interest is very broadly defined. According to the AML Regulation, beneficial ownership of legal entities refers to natural persons who:

1. Directly or indirectly own 25% or more of the shares, voting rights, or other ownership interests in a company (Art. 52), or

2. Exercise control by other means, such as voting arrangements, veto rights, or the power to appoint or remove board members (Art. 53). Control and ownership must be assessed in parallel, not hierarchically (Art. 51). For entities with high risk of money laundering or terrorist financing, the threshold may be reduced to 15% (Art. 52(2)). Nominee arrangements, family ties, and informal agreements can establish indirect control. In multi-layered structures, beneficial owners include persons who control entities holding shares, or who hold shares in entities that control the company (Art. 54). Where legal arrangements or trusts hold shares, the beneficial owners of those arrangements themselves must be traced (Art. 55). When comparing the AML Regulation with the AMLD Consolidated, we find that the Directive allows Member States some discretion in ownership thresholds and access rules, whereas the AML Regulation provides a more detailed definition of control, including explicit references to nominee arrangements, family relationships, and informal agreements. Findings are summarized in the table below (Fig. 4.1).

[41] Point 36 of Judgment of the Court (Grand Chamber) in WM and Sovim SA v. Luxembourg Business Registers (Joined Cases C-37/20 and C-601/20). ECLI:EU:C:2022:912. Available here: https://eur-lex.europa.eu/legal-content/EN/TXT/?uri=celex:62020CJ0037.

Criteria	AMLD (Directive)	AML Regulation
Ownership Threshold	25% + 1 share or >25% (Art. 3(6))	25% or more (may be reduced to 15% for high-risk entities, Art. 52(2))
Control Criteria	Control via ownership, voting rights, or other means (Art. 3)	Control via Majority of voting rights (even if shared) 1. Right to appoint/remove majority of board 2. Veto or decision rights on profit/assets 3. Control via informal/formal agreements 4. Family relationships 5. Use of nominee arrangements (Art. 53)
Fallback Option	Senior managing officials if no natural person can be identified	Not explicitly stated; more focus on tracing through all layers
Multi-layered Structures	Implied but not detailed; general tracing expected	Detailed treatment in Art. 54 & 55; includes full chain of ownership/control
Nominee Arrangements & Informal Control	Mentioned under indirect control (Art. 3)	Explicitly listed in Art. 53(4) with detailed definitions
Public Access to BO Information	Initially yes, but annulled by ECJ ruling (WM & Sovim, C-37/20 and C-601/20)	Not publicly accessible due to ECJ ruling; reflects Charter rights (Art. 62 ref.)
Registers & Legitimate Interest	Access based on legitimate interest (Art. 12(2))	Broad definition of 'legitimate interest'; structured data required (Art. 10, 12, 62)
Reduction of Threshold for High-Risk Entities	Left to discretion of Member States	Commission may lower threshold to 15% for certain categories (Art. 52(2))

Fig 4.1 Table on Beneficial Ownership in EU Legislation

The EU has established a robust anti-money laundering and countering the financing of terrorism (AML/CFT) framework. Directive (EU) 2024/1640[42] and Regulations (EU) 2023/1113[43], (EU) 2024/1624[44], and (EU) 2024/1620[45] of the European Parliament and of the Council govern the AML/CFT requirements including the establishment of an Authority for anti-money laundering and countering the financing of terrorism (AMLA). The legislative AML package is also related to non-EU countries that have a link with EU, requiring them to disclose beneficial ownership when entering into contracts with EU entities. Besides the definition of beneficial ownership, the AML framework influences changes to the Company Law Directives (Directive (EU) 2017/1132[46] (Company Law Directive) and Directive (EU) 2019/1151[47] (Digitalization Directive), which will be elaborated further as consolidated versions of the EU Company Law framework.

[42] Directive (EU) 2024/1640 of the European Parliament and of the Council of 31 May 2024 on the mechanisms to be put in place by Member States for the prevention of the use of the financial system for the purposes of money laundering or terrorist financing, amending Directive (EU) 2019/1937, and amending and repealing Directive (EU) 2015/849 (Text with EEA relevance). Available here: https://eur-lex.europa.eu/legal-content/EN/TXT/?uri=CELEX:32024L1640#ntr4-L_202401640EN.000101-E0004. Accessed May 21, 2025.

[43] Regulation (EU) 2023/1113 of the European Parliament and of the Council of 31 May 2023 on information accompanying transfers of funds and certain crypto-assets and amending Directive (EU) 2015/849 (OJ L 150, 9.6.2023, p. 1).

[44] Regulation (EU) 2024/1624 of the European Parliament and of the Council of 31 May 2024 on the prevention of the use of the financial system for the purposes of money laundering or terrorist financing (OJ L, 2024/1624, 19.6.2024, ELI: http://data.europa.eu/eli/reg/2024/1624/oj).

[45] Regulation (EU) 2024/1620 of the European Parliament and of the Council of 31 May 2024 establishing the Authority for Anti-Money Laundering and Countering the Financing of Terrorism and amending Regulations (EU) No 1093/2010, (EU) No 1094/2010 and (EU) No 1095/2010 (*OJ L, 2024/1620, 19.6.2024, ELI:* http://data.europa.eu/eli/reg/2024/1620/oj).).

[46] European Parliament and Council. (2017). Directive (EU) 2017/1132 of the European Parliament and of the Council of 14 June 2017 relating to certain aspects of company law. Official Journal of the European Union, L 169, 46–127. Available here: https://eur-lex.europa.eu/legal-content/EN/TXT/?uri=CELEX%3A32017L1132. Accessed May 24, 2025.

[47] European Parliament and Council. (2019). Directive (EU) 2019/1151 of the European Parliament and of the Council of 20 June 2019 amending Directive (EU) 2017/1132 as regards the use of digital tools and processes in company law. Official Journal of the European Union, L 186, 80–104. Available here: https://eur-lex.europa.eu/legal-content/EN/TXT/?uri=celex%3A32019L1151. Accessed May 24, 2025.

4.1.4 The Company Law Connection

The Preamble of the AML Regulation emphasizes that some phases of lifecycles of legal entities are prone to higher risks for criminals to acquire control of the legal entity. Those are: the company formation stage and changes in the company structure.[48] The Company Law Directive and the Digitalization Directive, establish a legal framework for public authorities and interested parties, to acquire information on legal entities and the natural persons controlling them.[49] The Digitalization Directive, introduces reforms to enhance transparency of company data and cross-border use of company data.[50] The EC has identified various cases in which legal entities are used as vehicles for fraudulent activities, which has been further stressed in Reports conducted by the Financial Action Task Force (FATF) for Germany[51], Croatia[52] and Bosnia and Herzegovina[53]. The consolidated EU Company Law Directive also sets out important provisions that define shareholder liability, particularly in instances where there is an abuse of the corporate form. These provisions help to bridge the gap between the formal organs of the company and the individuals who, through control or ownership, exercise real influence, yet may evade liability through misuse of the company's legal personality. In the following paragraphs, relevant articles of the Company Law Directive will be identified and analyzed, in terms of shareholder liability.

---

[48] Point 29 of the Regulation (EU) 2024/1620 of the European Parliament and of the Council of 31 May 2024 establishing the Authority for Anti-Money Laundering and Countering the Financing of Terrorism and amending Regulations (EU) No 1093/2010, (EU) No 1094/2010 and (EU) No 1095/2010 (*OJ L, 2024/1620, 19.6.2024, ELI:* http://data.europa.eu/eli/reg/2024/1620/oj).

[49] Point 22 of Directive (EU) 2019/1151 of the European Parliament and of the Council of 20 June 2019 amending Directive (EU) 2017/1132 as regards the use of digital tools and processes in company law. Available here: https://eur-lex.europa.eu/eli/dir/2019/1151/oj/eng.

[50] Schmidt (2025), p. 578.

[51] Anti-money laundering and counter-terrorist financing measures Germany. Mutual Evaluation Report 2022. Available here: https://www.fatf-gafi.org/content/dam/fatf-gafi/mer/Mutual-Evaluation-Report-Germany-2022.pdf.coredownload.inline.pdf. Accessed May 25, 2025.

[52] Anti-money laundering and counter-terrorist financing measures Croatia. 2nd Enhanced Follow-up Report &Technical Compliance Re-Rating. 2024. Available here https://rm.coe.int/moneyval-2024-18-hr-5thround-2ndenhfur/1680b2bbbc. Accessed May 25, 2025.

[53] Anti-money laundering and counter-terrorist financing measures Bosnia and Herzegovina. Fifth Round Mutual Evaluation Report. 2024. Available here: https://www.fatf-gafi.org/content/dam/fatf-gafi/fsrb-mer/MONEYVAL-MER-Bosnia%20and%20Herzegovina.pdf.coredownload.inline.pdF. Accessed May 24, 2025.

These articles will serve as point of connection for the comparative analysis of Bosnia and Herzegovina, Croatia, and Germany, in Section 5. The identification of these provisions serves as a comparative tool for assessing legal convergence and divergence in the regulation of shareholder responsibilities and misconduct across jurisdictions. It also provides a basis for identifying red flags in company law frameworks. Understanding who had de facto control and decision-making power within a company, and how that power was exercised, is fundamental to evaluating whether and when the corporate veil may be pierced. This is especially relevant in cases involving fraud, money laundering, and misuse of corporate assets. The doctrine of piercing the corporate veil, though not expressly regulated at the EU level, finds indirect application through national transpositions of EU law and is reflected in jurisprudence from the CJEU, the ECtHR, and other international courts across Europe. These cases underscore the principle that the legal personality of a company cannot be used as a shield for personal misconduct or illicit activity by shareholders or company representatives.

4.1.4.1 Representatives vs Owners

4.1.4.1.1 Pre-formation Liability

Several articles in the consolidated Company Law Directive are of essence in determining shareholder liability. Articles that are related to company statutes and pre-authorization liabilities provide that the instrument of incorporation of a company needs to provide information on the members of bodies responsible for representing the company as well as, management, supervision or control of the company and the allocation of powers among those bodies. The identification of the identity of natural and legal persons representing the company is information that constitutes compulsory information[54], it is not only important for a valid formation of a company, but also because the persons who acted in the name of the company that has not been formed yet assume joint and several liability.[55] Article 4 (i) is particularly interesting since the Company Law Directive identifies them as responsible persons within the company. Those persons are "natural or legal persons or companies or firms by which or in whose name the statutes or the instrument of incorporation, or where the company was not formed at the same time, the drafts of those documents, have been signed."[56]

---

[54] Article 3e & 4.

[55] Article 7.2.

[56] Article 4 (i) of the Consolidated text: Directive (EU) 2017/1132 of the European Parliament and of the Council of 14 June 2017 relating to certain aspects of company law (codification). Available here: https://eur-lex.europa.eu/legal-content/EN/TXT/?uri=CELEX%3A02017L1132-20220812.

4.1.4.1.2 Ultra-Vires

If the organs of a company and its representation act outside the stated business purpose (ultra vires), the company is still bound by their actions in relation to third parties (Art. 9). This protects third parties acting in good faith, who should be able to rely on a company representative's apparent authority. The company may avoid being bound if it proves that the third party knew (or could not reasonably have been unaware) that the act was outside its corporate objects. This provision cannot be overruled by the company's internal rules (statutes, board decisions) that limit the powers of a representative.

4.1.4.1.3 Company Formation

The Company Law Directive was amended in 2024 with the Digitalization Directive addressing, among others, transparency of company data.[57] Disclosure requirements for limited liability companies were particularly emphasized.[58] Particularly interesting are Articles 13i (Disqualified directors) and 14 (Documents and particulars to be disclosed by companies). Article 13i refers to the rules on disqualification of directors, and directors include the persons referred to in point (i) of Article 14(d). Article 14(d)(i) defines "directors" as: "the persons who either as a body constituted pursuant to law or as members of any such body authorized to represent the company in dealings with third parties and in legal proceedings; it shall be apparent from the disclosure whether the persons authorized to represent the company may do so alone or are required to act jointly."[59] Besides authorized representatives, Article 14(d)(ii) further defines that compulsory disclosure by companies includes persons that "take part in the administration, supervision or control of the company." All of this information is available in commercial, or companies registers, that are part of a European central platform of company registers in the EU.

4.1.4.1.4 Control Through Shareholding

The Company Law Directive does not define the controlling shareholder or owner of a legal entity, but there are relevant articles that require disclosure or examination of ownership and control structures. For example, articles on cross-border

---

[57] Hasanović (2024), p. 211.

[58] Schmidt (2025), p. 569.

[59] Article 14(d)(i) Company Law Directive (consolidated).

mergers of limited liability companies, require disclosure of ownership and control structures for merger approval[60] in terms of shareholders holding special rights (Art. 86d(c)), Any special advantages for board members (Art. 86d(g)), and disclosure of cash compensation to members (Art. 86d(i)). This helps identify persons exercising control, including through voting rights or indirect shareholding. In the Case C-81/09, Idryma Typou A.E. v. Ypourgos Typou kai Meson Mazikis Enimerosis[61] the CJEU affirmed that EU law does not prevent Member States from deviating from the principle of limited liability in specific, regulated contexts, however that imposing joint and several liability on shareholders of public limited companies, holding more than 2,5% of a company's capital, solely based on their shares, is not justifiable. The Court found that the national measure constituted a restriction on both the freedom of establishment and the free movement of capital, as it deterred investment, especially from foreign investors, applied indiscriminately to all shareholders over the 2,5% threshold regardless of their actual ability to influence the company.[62] The ruling not only supports the broader EU regulatory trend that seeks to enhance transparency and accountability by looking beyond the formal ownership structure to the actual influence exercised within corporate entities, but also the fact that veil-piercing generally does not occur in public limited companies. In a separate Opinion to this case issued by the Advocate General Trstenjak[63], he noted that EU law permits veil-piercing in exceptional circumstances, as acknowledged in Directive 2009/102/EC on single-member companies[64]. This also confirms that veil-piercing in EU

[60] Article 86d: The draft terms of a cross-border conversion shall include at least the following particulars: (e) the rights conferred by the converted company on members enjoying special rights or on holders of securities other than shares representing the company capital, or the measures proposed concerning them; (g) any special advantages granted to members of the administrative, management, supervisory or controlling bodies of the company; (i) details of the offer of cash compensation for members.

[61] On 11 May 2001, the defendant (Greek Government) adopted a decision imposing a fine of GRD 10 000 000 jointly and severally on the public limited company Nea Tileorasi, owner of the television station Star Channel, and on its shareholders and the members of its board of directors. Case: Tipou A.E. v. Ipourgos Tipou Kai Meson Mazikis Enimerosis (C-81/09). Available at: https://eur-lex.europa.eu/legal-content/en/TXT/?uri=CELEX:62009CC0081. Accessed May 29, 2025.

[62] Point 69 and 70. Tipou A.E. v. Ipourgos Tipou Kai Meson Mazikis Enimerosis (C-81/09). Available at: https://eur-lex.europa.eu/legal-content/en/TXT/?uri=CELEX:62009CC0081.

[63] Available here: https://curia.europa.eu/juris/document/document.jsf?text=&docid=81189&pageIndex=0&doclang=EN&mode=lst&dir=&occ=first&part=1&cid=2391857. Accessed June 5, 2025.

[64] Advocate General's Opinion, Case C-81/09. In its Preamble (point 4), the Directive stipulates that: "A legal instrument is required allowing the limitation of liability of the individual

law is permitted when there is no ownership and control issue, that and that limited liability is not an absolute principle under EU law. However, it is not enough to own shares, for veil-piercing, but to proof control over activities that cause veil-piercing in the first place.

4.1.4.2 Nominal Owners vs Beneficial Owners

In the Company Law Directive, shareholders or legal owners are identified as natural or legal persons who hold shares in the company and are named in the register of members. They may be nominal owners, but not necessarily the beneficial owners of the company. Company organs and legal representatives are identified as directors, managing board, or supervisory board members, they legally represent the company. They are not the owners of the company (even though it is possible that those two overlap). These natural or legal persons sign documents, conclude contracts, represent the company externally. They do not necessarily own any part of the company. The Company Law Directive, however, does not define the ultimate owners of the company. It only records legal shareholders, not those behind the scenes who may control the company indirectly. If a person owns or controls shares through another company, trustee, nominee, or through informal agreements, this information will not be captured under the Company Law Directive. From a company law perspective, beneficial ownership bridges the gap between formal legal structures (as regulated by the Company Law Directive) and the actual exercise of influence or control (as captured by the AML framework). The disclosure and transparency obligations under the Company Law Directive support the identification of beneficial owners under AML rules, enabling regulators, courts, and counterparties to assess risk, detect abuse, and assign responsibility. This connection is particularly relevant when courts consider piercing the corporate veil, as both frameworks assist in establishing which natural persons effectively dominate or benefit from the company's activities, thus potentially justifying the lifting of limited liability protections in cases of fraud, abuse, or criminal misconduct. This is why beneficial ownership should be defined in company law legislation. If provisions on piercing the corporate veil exist, especially if they are targeted at shareholders (owners) of the legal entity, the legislative framework should provide for the definition of those natural or legal persons. In the following subchapter, relevant case law on piercing

entrepreneur throughout the Community, without prejudice to the laws of the Member States, which, in exceptional circumstances, require that entrepreneur to be liable for the obligations of his undertaking." (European Parliament and Council of the European Union, 2009).

the corporate veil will identify how courts justified piercing and who the natural persons behind the veil were.

4.2 Discussion of Relevant Case Law

The misuse of companies as conduit entities, created solely to enable their owners to exploit one legal system or circumvent another, has been widely recognized by both scholars and the international community.[65] This problem was enshrined into the G20 Declaration and G8 Action Plan that stated that: "We encourage all countries to tackle the risks raised by opacity of legal persons and legal arrangements."[66] As seen above, the EU has enacted Directives aimed at ensuring insight into beneficial ownership and restricting the use of bearer shares.[67] However, do courts see through the abuse of companies, and do they detect fraud? The Panama Papers have shown that criminal organizations were formed and legal entities abused for tax evasion purposes, and even though in 2020, German authorities issued international arrest warrants[68] for some of the natural persons entangled in the scandal, in June 2024, a judge in Panama acquitted all former Mossack Fonseca employees, including the two founders, due to insufficient evidence and problems with the chain of custody of evidence.[69] The following cases presented before international and EU courts, will demonstrate how the courts identify abuse of companies, fraud, illicit conduct, and why transparency of beneficial ownership is crucial in the identification of liability.

4.2.1 Court of Justice of the European Union

The CJEU is using a two-element test to identify abuse of EU law, and in this context abuse of EU law by companies. When referring to abuse of EU law, it is

[65] Birkmose et al (2019), p. 3.

[66] Point 77, G20 Declaration available on http://www.g20.utoronto.ca/2013/2013-0906-declaration.html and the G8 Action Plan available at https://www.gov.uk/government/uploads/system/uploads/attachment_data/file/207532/G8-Action-Plan-principles-to-prevent-the-misuse-of-companies-and-legal-arrangements.pdf (both accessed 29 May 2019).

[67] Munkholm (2019), p. 343.

[68] https://www.icij.org/investigations/panama-papers/germany-seeks-arrest-of-senior-panama-papers-lawyer/. Accessed June 5, 2025.

[69] Obermaier & Obermayer (2024), p. 11.

meant that the CJEU has jurisdiction to prevent circumvention of national legislation to fraudulently take advantage of provisions of Community law. The test CJEU applied in the Case C-110/99, Emsland-Stärke[70] required a combination of objective circumstances indicating that, despite the formal fulfilment of the conditions set out in Union law, the purpose of those rules has not been achieved, and, a subjective element, namely the intention to obtain an advantage under Union law by artificially creating the conditions required for its application.[71] This test has been used in various cases since then[72] and has been codified in secondary EU law.[73] Interestingly, the CJEU found that no abuse of EU law exists if companies are forum shopping.[74] This was confirmed in the Case C-212/97, Centros where the CJEU found that formation of a company in another Member State

[70] Emsland-Stärke GmbH v. Hauptzollamt Hamburg-Jonas, Case C-110/99, ECLI:EU:C:2000:695. Available here: https://eur-lex.europa.eu/legal-content/EN/TXT/?uri=celex:61999CJ0110. Accessed June 3, 2025.

[71] Case C-110/99, Emsland-Stärke (2000), point 39. Emsland-Stärke, a German company, exported processed potato starch to Switzerland to obtain an export refund under EU agricultural law. Shortly after, the goods were re-imported into the EU through France by the same company's trading partner. Although the formal requirements for the export refund were met, because the goods had technically left the customs territory, the economic purpose of the export rule was not fulfilled. The refund was intended to support genuine exports outside the EU market, not artificial transactions aimed at circular trading or exporting on paper only.

[72] See Case Halifax plc and Others v. Commissioners of Customs & Excise, Case C-255/02, ECLI:EU:C:2006:121. Available: https://curia.europa.eu/juris/liste.jsf?num=C-255/02. Accessed June 3, 2025. Halifax, a UK bank, set up a complex corporate structure involving the creation of subsidiaries and service contracts to recover VAT on construction services for call centers. Although the formal structure followed UK tax rules, the setup was aimed primarily at obtaining VAT advantages. Additional relevant case law: see, in particular, regarding freedom to supply services, Case 33/74 Van Binsbergen v. Bedrijfsvereniging Metaalnijverheid (1974) ECR 1299, paragraph 13, Case C-148/91 Veronica Omroep Organisatie v. Commissariaat voor de Media (1993) ECR I-487, paragraph 12, and Case C-23/93 TV 10 v. Commissariaat voor de Media (1994) ECR I-4795, paragraph 21; regarding freedom of establishment, Case 115/78 Knoors (1979) ECR 399, paragraph 25, and Case C-61/89 Bouchoucha (1990) ECR I-3551, paragraph 14; regarding the free movement of goods, Case 229/83 Leclerc and Others v. "Au Blé Vert" and Others (1985) ECR 1, paragraph 27; regarding social security, Case C-206/94 Brennet v. Paletta (1996) ECR I-2357, "Paletta II", paragraph 24; regarding freedom of movement for workers, Case 39/86 Lair v. Universität Hannover (1988) ECR 3161, paragraph 43; regarding the common agricultural policy, Case C-8/92 General Milk Products v. Hauptzollamt Hamburg-Jonas (1993) ECR I-779, paragraph 21, and regarding company law, Case C-367/96 Kefalas and Others v. Greece (1988) ECR I-2843, paragraph 20).

[73] Sørensen (2019), p. 263.

[74] Gelter & Vicente (2019), p. 5.

which has less restrictive rules, and in which the company will perform proper business operations, cannot be regarded as abuse of EU law, in this case right of establishment.[75] However, this does not apply to situations in which Member States can proof "fraudulent evasion of statutory law", "false representation", or "abuse of rights", as seen in Case C-367/96, Kefalas and Others v. Greek State.[76] The objective element of the test focuses on the effect of the legal arrangement or transaction and poses questions to whether the result contradicts the spirit or objective of the EU legal provision, and whether the legal or natural entity is taking advantage of EU law in a way that defeats its purpose. The subjective element must show intention to obtain an advantage from EU law by artificially creating the conditions required for obtaining it. CJEU assesses this intent by identifying whether the arrangement was set up solely or primarily to gain a benefit under EU law, and whether there is a lack of genuine economic activity, substance, or commercial rationale. The test the CJEU uses to identify abuse of EU law is relevant for the rationale on fraud and artificiality. How does the Court conclude that in some instances the law was abused, and in others not. How does it justify intent for abuse? Similar reasoning could be applied by courts when deciding on whether to pierce the corporate veil. Could the objective and subjective elements be applied by courts to identify fraud and abuse of companies? The test will be reviewed in two cases in which fraud and abuse of legal entities occurred.

---

[75] CJEU (1999), point 27. In Centros Ltd v. Erhvervsog Selskabsstyrelsen, Centros Ltd was a UK-registered private company formed by two Danish nationals. The company conducted no business in the UK but wanted to open a branch in Denmark. Danish authorities refused registration, claiming that the real purpose was to avoid Danish minimum capital rules by incorporating in the UK, where capital requirements were lower. The Court stated that a Member State cannot refuse the registration of a branch of a company validly incorporated in another Member State even if the purpose is to benefit from more favorable laws in that state (e.g., lower capital requirements). Available here: https://eur-lex.europa.eu/legal-content/EN/TXT/?uri=celex:61997CJ0212. Accessed June 3, 2025.

[76] CJEU (1998), point 27. Kefalas and Others v. Greek State, concerned the misuse of the EU's freedom of establishment provisions by Greek nationals who sought to exploit EU law for financial gain by invoking Treaty rights in a situation that lacked genuine cross-border economic activity. The Greek government argued that the claimants were abusing EU law. The CJEU confirmed that Community law cannot be relied on for abusive or fraudulent ends. The prevention of such abuse or fraud is a legitimate objective. Available here: https://eur-lex.europa.eu/legal-content/EN/TXT/?uri=CELEX:61996CC0367. Accessed June 3, 2025.

4.2.1.1 Joined Cases C-116/16 & C-117/16 (T Danmark and Y Danmark ApS)

The issue in T Danmark and Y Danmark ApS[77] was whether a Member State can refuse to grant an exemption from withholding tax under the EU Parent-Subsidiary Directive (2011/96/EU)[78] when dividends are paid to an EU-based intermediary holding company, which is ultimately owned by a non-EU parent and appears to lack real substance. Under Article 5 of the Parent-Subsidiary Directive, dividends distributed between companies in different Member States are generally exempt from withholding tax to avoid double taxation. The Danish tax authority denied the exemptions, arguing that the intermediary companies were conduit vehicles with no real substance. The Court tested the case for abusive practices applying the objective elements (the arrangement defeats the purpose of the Directive which is to eliminate double taxation) and subjective elements (the structures were set up with intent to unlawfully gain the withholding tax exemption), emphasizing that there are indicators for abuse of rights, and they must be objective and consistent. Such indications are:

1. existence of conduit companies which are without economic justification,[79]
2. the purely formal nature of the structure of the group of companies,[80]
3. the financial arrangements and the loans.[81]

---

[77] Judgment of the Court (Grand Chamber) of 26 February 2019 (requests for a preliminary ruling from the Østre Landsret Denmark) Skatteministeriet v. T Danmark (C-116/16), Y Denmark Aps (C-117/16). Available here: https://eur-lex.europa.eu/legal-content/EN/TXT/?uri=oj:JOC_2019_139_R_0004#ntr1-C_2019139EN.01000701-E0001. Full judgement available here: https://curia.europa.eu/juris/document/document.jsf?text=&docid=211047&pageIndex=0&doclang=EN&mode=lst&dir=&occ=first&part=1&cid=5854259. Accessed June 5, 2025.

[78] Directive available here: https://eur-lex.europa.eu/legal-content/EN/TXT/?uri=CELEX%3A02011L0096-20150217. Accessed June 5, 2025.

[79] The absence of actual economic activity must, in the light of the specific features of the economic activity in question, be inferred from an analysis of all the relevant factors relating, in particular, to the management of the company, to its balance sheet, to the structure of its costs and to expenditure actually incurred, to the staff that it employs and to the premises and equipment that it has. (Point 104 of the Judgement)

[80] A group of companies may be regarded as being an artificial arrangement where it is not set up for reasons that reflect economic reality, its structure is purely one of form and its principal objective or one of its principal objectives is to obtain a tax advantage running counter to the aim or purpose of the applicable tax law. (Point 108 of the Judgement).

[81] CJEU (2019), point 3. Existence of an arrangement intended to obtain improper entitlement to the exemption, and that all dividends are, very soon after their receipt, passed on

The Court found that the beneficial owner of the dividends must have substantive control and not merely act as a conduit. These indications are seen in the factors for piercing the corporate veil in regard to fraud, however, the fraud and abuse in this case only lead to exemption of certain Community law benefits, but they could have been grounds for creditors' claims under the piercing the corporate veil doctrine.

4.2.1.2 Joined Cases C-115/16, C-118/16, C-119/16 & C-299/16, N Luxembourg 1 and Others

In the Joined cases C-115/16, C-118/16, C-119/16 & C-299/16, N Luxembourg 1 and Others[82] Danish companies made interest payments to companies in Luxembourg, which then forwarded them to ultimate parent companies in third countries. These payments were claimed to be exempt from withholding tax under the Interest and Royalties Directive (2003/49/EC)[83]. The Luxembourg companies had no substance and acted solely as intermediaries. In terms of the objective element, the legal structure respected the form of the Directive but subverted its purpose, which is to avoid double taxation within the EU, not to channel payments. In terms of the subjective element, the intermediary companies were set up with the intent to obtain a tax advantage, they were conduit companies.[84] They had no economic function, no employees, no management, and no risk exposure. The Court denied the benefits of the Directive, affirming that EU law cannot be invoked abusively even in the absence of domestic anti-abuse rules.

---

by the company that has received them to entities which do not fulfil the conditions for the application of exemption. (Point 101 of the Judgement).

[82] Judgment of the Court (Grand Chamber) of 26 February 2019 N Luxembourg 1 and Others v. Skatteministeriet. Available here: https://curia.europa.eu/juris/document/document.jsf?text=&docid=211053&pageIndex=0&doclang=en&mode=lst&dir=&occ=first&part=1&cid=5882533. Accessed June 5, 2025.

[83] Available here: https://eur-lex.europa.eu/legal-content/EN/TXT/?uri=CELEX%3A02003L0049-20130701. Accessed June 5, 2025.

[84] With (Z Luxembourg's) acquisition of the private equity fund's debt claim against (Z Denmark), and the company's simultaneous acquisition of the shares in (Z Denmark) through a loan from the private equity fund of almost the same amount and on almost the same terms as the debt claim against the company, (Z Luxembourg's) tax on interest payments from the Danish company would be offset by the company's interest payments to the private equity fund, which is why there would not be taxable net income on the overall transactions falling to be taxed in the hands of the company. The Luxembourg company is therefore regarded as a conduit company without any real powers or opportunities to take decisions on disposals of the transferred amounts received. (Judgement, point 74).

4.2.2 European Court of Human Rights Cases

The European Court of Human Rights (ECtHR) case law regarding piercing the corporate veil is important for the purpose of this dissertation for two reasons. Firstly, to assess the tests the ECtHR uses to determine whether the veil piercing was in breach of Article 1 of Protocol No. 1[85] of the European Convention of Human Rights (ECHR). Secondly, to identify who the shareholders of legal entities are and their level of control of the pierced legal entity. The ECtHR emphasizes that all interference by a national public authority with the peaceful enjoyment of possessions of natural and legal persons, should be lawful. Lawfulness presupposes that the law that is provided by public authorities, needs to be accessible, precise and foreseeable[86]. The law or measure imposed should also be proportionate in the sense that there should be a balance between public and private interest.[87] In terms of piercing the corporate veil, the ECtHR identified two situations in which the veil of the legal entity can be pierced:

1. Lifting the corporate veil of limited liability companies in the interest of its shareholders' to be identified with companies for the purposes of "victim" status that is, "from within".
2. Lifting of the corporate veil of a limited liability company in the interest of its creditors—or "from without".[88]

For the purposes of this Dissertation, two cases will be presented as examples of piercing from within and from without.

---

[85] Article 1 Protocol 1 of the ECHR: "(1) Every natural or legal person is entitled to the peaceful enjoyment of his possessions. No one shall be deprived of his possessions except in the public interest and subject to the conditions provided for by law and by the general principles of international law.

(2) The preceding provisions shall not, however, in any way impair the right of a state to enforce such laws as it deems necessary to control the use of property in accordance with the general interest or to secure the payment of taxes or other contributions or penalties."

[86] Council of Europe/European Court of Human Rights (2020), pt. 111 and 114. There should be a level of protection against arbitrary interferences by public authorities.

[87] There should be a relationship od proportionality between means employed and the aim sought to be realized by measures applied by the State.

[88] Council of Europe/European Court of Human Rights, 2020, pt. 33 and 39.

4.2.2.1 Lekić v. Slovenia

In the case Lekic vs Slovenia the ECtHR decided that there had been no violation of Article 1 of Protocol No. 1 to the ECHR, and that the interference with the peaceful enjoyment of possessions Mr. Lekić, were both lawful and proportional.[89] In its judgement, the court had several observations that are relevant to the piercing the corporate veil doctrine. Mr. Lekić was a minority shareholder (11,11% shares) in the limited liability company (transformed from public limited liability company), that was a dormant company with additional shareholder who, over the course of several years, died. The Slovenian Government, in order to protect creditors from companies that had frozen accounts, debts and or no employees (dormant companies[90]), brought the Financial Operations of Companies Act 1999 (FOCA), that allowed registry courts to strike off dormant companies and hold the companies "active members" personally liable for the companies' debts. Active members were members holding more than 10% of shares. The ECtHR found that FOCA was lawful since the Companies Act of Slovenia (similarly to all former Yugoslav republics) provided for piercing of the corporate veil when: "members have abused the corporate form in order to attain an objective that was forbidden to them as individuals; members have abused the corporate form such as to cause damage to creditors; members have used the assets of a company, in breach of the law, as their own personal assets; or members have reduced a company's assets, for their own benefit or for the benefit of another person, where they knew or should have known that the company would not be capable of meeting its liabilities to third persons."[91] (ibid.) The ECtHR found that the piercing was justified because:

1. The FOCA was lawful within the meaning of Art 1 of Protocol 1 of ECHR;
2. Mr. Lekić was an active member of the company, holding more than 10% of its shares.

The active member status and the percentage of 10% was considered just and not arbitrary by the ECtHR, because members of limited liability companies with at

---

[89] Lekić v. Slovenia, 2018, point 130. Application No. 36480/07, Judgment of 11 December 2018. Available here: https://hudoc.echr.coe.int/eng#{%22appno%22:[%2236480/07%22],%22itemid%22:[%22001-188268%22]}. Accessed June 7, 2025.

[90] In 1999 Slovenia had 6,587 such companies that accumulated debt over EUR 352,412,000. (Judgment, point 41).

[91] Lekić v. Slovenia (2018), point 56.

least 10% shares enjoyed certain rights.[92] The ECtHR also pointed to relevant tests used by other international organizations such as the Organization for Economic Co-operation and Development (OECD) and the International Monetary Fund (IMF), in terms of distinguishing between investors who do not control a company (portfolio investors) and those who do (direct investors).[93] A definition of "significant influence" by the OECD is as follows: "Power to participate in the financial and operating policy decisions of a unit but not control those policies. Significant influence may be gained by an ownership interest, statute or agreement. In the case of foreign direct investment, a direct investor is considered to have a significant degree of influence if it owns between 10% and 50% of the voting power in a direct investment enterprise."[94] (ibid.) Even though Mr. Lekić did not abuse the right of the company, he and other shareholders, neglected to uphold the corporate form, the company had no director, it was undercapitalized, it did not hold general meetings, nor did they initiate insolvency proceedings. The general conclusion of the case was that only those who are in the position to actively influence the operation of a company should be held liable for the debts of the company.

4.2.2.2 Radelić v. Croatia

In the case Radelić v. Croatia[95] Radelić was found guilty of business fraud and sentenced to one year's imprisonment, including confiscation of 854,743.39 HRK

---

[92] Lekić v. Slovenia (2018), point 100. For example: the right to be informed of the company's affairs; the right to access the company's records and files; the right to request the convening of a general meeting; the right to request that a specific issue be included on the agenda of a general meeting; the right to lodge an action with the competent court requesting that the company be wound up.

[93] OECD (2025), p. 85. While the core principle of the 10% ownership threshold as an indicator of a direct investment relationship remains unchanged, the new OECD framework provides a more detailed criteria for assessing control and influence. It also introduces new classifications and emphasizes the importance of tracing the ultimate sources and destinations of investments, thereby offering a more comprehensive and accurate representation of global foreign direct investment (FDI) flows. Ownership percentages should be considered alongside other factors, such as voting rights and the ability to influence management decisions, to determine the nature of the investment relationship.

[94] OECD (2025), p. 295.

[95] Radelić v. Croatia (Application No. 12432/22, Judgment of 13 May 2025). Strasbourg: Council of Europe. Available here: https://hudoc.echr.coe.int/eng#{%22itemid%22:[%22001-243081%22]}. Accessed June 7, 2025.

(approximately EUR 113,440), offences for which one of the constitutive elements is the acquisition of an unlawful pecuniary gain for the company that the perpetrator was representing. However, the company ceased to exist the day proceedings were initiated against Radelić[96]. Radelić was also the sole shareholder and director of the company. During domestic proceedings, besides criminal law provisions on business fraud and forgery, courts relied on Article 252 of Croatia's Company Law (Duty of care and liability of management board members) and confirmed the rightness of prior rulings that Radelić needs to pay back the money. However, the ECtHR (with a vote 4:3), found that there had been a violation of Article 1 od Protocol No. 1, because the confiscation measure was not foreseeable under domestic law and inconsistent with the nature of the offence he was convicted of. The reason the ECtHR found that the measure was unforeseeable for Radelić, is because the Government applied Article 252(5) of the Company Law, which provides for tort liability of management board members of a commercial company to creditors, in conjunction with Article 77 of the Penal Code, which provides for the confiscation of proceeds of crime, which, the Court found, is inconsistent with the nature of that measure and thus impossible to foresee. Even though the Government in this case did cite Article 10 of Croatia's Company Law[97] in proceedings before the ECtHR, the ECtHR found that: "The Government, in addition to those provisions, referred to Article 10(3) of the Commercial Companies Act, a provision on piercing the corporate veil, which they also considered to be of relevance (see paragraphs 24 and 45 above). However, the Court cannot take that provision into account because the domestic courts did not refer to it."[98] It is worth considering whether the outcome might have differed had

---

[96] Radelić initiated bankruptcy proceedings a year prior to his conviction for business fraud.

[97] Liability of company members Article 10(1).

(2) Members of a limited liability company ... are not liable for the company's obligations unless otherwise provided by this Act.

(3) Whoever abuses the fact that, as a member of a company, he or she is not liable for the company's obligations, may not rely on not being liable for those obligations under the law.

(4) The requirement for the liability of members of the company referred to in paragraph 3 is considered to have been met, particularly if:

1. they use the company to achieve a goal that is otherwise prohibited to them;
2. they use the company to damage creditors;
3. contrary to the law, they manage the assets of the company as if they were their own;
4. they reduce the company's assets for their own benefit or for the benefit of another person, even though they knew or must have known that the company would not be able to meet its obligations."

[98] Radelic v. Croatia (2024), pt. 52.

domestic courts invoked the explicit veil-piercing provision. The implication is that doing so could have provided a clearer legal basis and potentially satisfied the foreseeability requirement. In the case Khodorkovskiy and Lebedev v. Russia[99], the court even stated: "Where a limited liability company was used merely as a façade for fraudulent actions by its owners or managers, piercing of the corporate veil may be an appropriate solution for defending the rights of its creditors, including the State. That being said, there should be clear rules allowing the State to do so, otherwise an interference would be arbitrary."[100] In a dissenting opinion judge Pisani stated that: "national authorities applied the law in a perfectly foreseeable way, or at least, to paraphrase this Court's frequent qualification, with the clear-sighted advice of a sensible professional."[101] The reason for judge Pisani's statement was based on the fact that Croatia has adopted and ratified the United Nations Convention against Transnational Organized Crime, the Convention on Laundering, Search, Seizure and Confiscation of the Proceeds from Crime and the Convention on Laundering, Search, Seizure and Confiscation of the Proceeds from Crime and on the Financing of Terrorism and they provide for the confiscation of direct or indirect proceeds of crime without consideration as to where they may be found. Nevertheless, the failure of domestic council to refer to provisions of piercing the corporate veil, may have been detrimental to the decision in this case before the ECtHR.

4.2.3 Veil-Piercing Beyond National Courts: Insights from Arbitration

There are two doctrines dominantly written about by prominent scholars in the field of arbitration when it comes to the extension of the arbitration agreement to non-signatories: the group of companies' doctrine and the piercing the corporate veil doctrine. The reason why those two doctrines are sometimes not distinguished is because the third parties that are included in the arbitration, even though they did not sign the contract, belong to a group of companies. In the case of piercing, the shareholder abused the corporate form to limit their liability.[102]

---

[99] Khodorkovskiy and Lebedev v. Russia (Applications Nos. 11082/06 and 13772/05, Judgment of 25 July 2013). Strasbourg: Council of Europe. Retrieved from https://hudoc.echr.coe.int/eng#{%22itemid%22:[%22001-122697%22]}. Accessed June 7, 2025.

[100] Khodorkovskiy and Lebedev v. Russia (2013), pt. 877.

[101] Radelic v. Croatia (2025), Dissenting opinion Pisani, pt. 6.

[102] Besson (2010), p. 147.

Gary Born highlighted the difference of those theories emphasizing that the piercing the corporate veil doctrine "….is invoked to disregard or nullify the otherwise applicable effects of incorporation of separate legal personality. The outcome of this analysis is that one entity is deemed either non-existent or merely an unincorporated part of another entity. (…) In contrast, the group of companies doctrine is ordinarily a means of identifying the parties' intentions, which does not disturb or affect the legal personality of the entities in question."[103] It is therefore of essence to acknowledge the difference between the group of companies doctrine in terms of the extension of the arbitration agreement[104], and the piercing the corporate veil doctrine and extension of the arbitration agreement, because the corporate veil can be pierced only if there is behavior contrary to good faith and fair dealing, and the prohibition of abuse of rights.[105] As Berger emphasizes, control must have been used to commit an abuse of right or fraud.[106] In the case ICC award 5721 the court emphasizes that: "The theory of "Durchgriff" (piercing the corporate veil) is grounded on the prohibition of the abuse of rights. From that perspective one always has to examine in a given case whether the institution of the juridic person (and the juridic independence that is attached to it) has been deprived of its very purpose by the persons who are behind that juridic person … therefore, the exceptional principle of piercing the corporate veil may only be applied with great caution. The independence (of the juridic person from the physical persons behind it) may only be ignored in exceptional cases when this independence is invoked with an intention to cause damages, i.e. in a way that is contrary to the principle of good faith."[107]

Extending the arbitration agreement to third parties based on the group of companies' doctrine, is not considered piercing of the corporate veil, it is just another means of determining the real intentions of the parties. Third parties are included in the arbitration agreement not because they have abused the corporate form, but because they relate to the parties to the arbitration agreement through other circumstances. One of the most well-known cases concerning the extension of an

---

[103] Born (2009), p. 1154.

[104] They relate to relationships of representation in all its forms (agency), implied consent, contracts for the benefit of third parties, assignment, transfer of contracts, subrogation, and guarantees.

[105] Ceronja (2022), p. 728.

[106] Berger (2022), p. 200.

[107] ICC award 5721 (1990) p. 1025). Clunet 1990, at 1019 et seq., Available here: https://www.trans-lex.org/205721/mark_962000/#3b. Accessed June 14, 2025.

arbitration agreement to third parties is Dow Chemical v. Isover Saint Gobain[108]. However, this case is not classified as a piercing the corporate veil case, rather, it falls under the group of companies' doctrine, which permits the extension of arbitration agreements within affiliated corporate entities. This distinction is crucial because the question of whether a third party may be bound by an arbitration agreement is generally considered a procedural issue. The applicable law is that of the jurisdiction in which the company whose legal personality is being disregarded has its seat, *lex societatis.* This means that the determination of whether the legal personality of a company should be disregarded is primarily governed by the company law of the relevant jurisdiction[109]. Even if a tribunal decides to pierce the corporate veil, the award may be set aside in national courts[110] that have jurisdiction over the arbitration venue.[111] Shareholders that want to avoid piercing the corporate veil doctrinal implications, will choose incorporation of companies in jurisdictions that do not foresee veil piercing in their domestic law. A distinction between the group of company's doctrine and piercing the corporate veil doctrine could be made in regard to shareholders participation in

[108] ICC Award No. 4131, YCA 1984, at 131 et seq. (also published in: Clunet 1983, at 899 et seq.) Available here: https://www.trans-lex.org/204131/_/icc-award-no-4131-yca-1984-at-131-et-seq-/. Accessed June 14, 2025. The tribunal relied on the common intent of the parties, such as it appears from the circumstances that surround the conclusion and characterize the performance and later the termination of contracts. The tribunal also followed usages conforming to the needs of international commerce, in particular in the presence of group of companies. According to the single entity theory applied by the tribunal, "(a) group of companies, despite the legal status of each of the companies, represents a single economic reality which the arbitral tribunal must take into account when ruling on its jurisdiction."

[109] The doctrine of piercing the corporate veil, is based on (i) a conflict of law analysis; and (ii) the application of a specific domestic law as shown in these specific cases: Ad hoc arbitration 1989, ASA Bul. (1990) p. 270 (applying Swiss and Italian laws); Ad hoc arbitration 1991, ASA Bul. (1992) p. 202 (applying Swiss law); ICC case No. 7626, YCA (1997) p. 132 (applying English law); ICC case No. 8163, ICC Ct. Bull. 16(2) (2005) p. 81 (applying German law); ICC case No. 11160, ICC Ct. Bull. 16(2) (2005) p. 103 (applying Venezuelan law); but see ICC case No. 8385, JDI (1997) p. 1061 (preference for international standards but noting that New York and Belgian law would lead to the same result).

[110] Under the New York Convention for example, in Peterson Farms Inc. v. C&M Farming Ltd., the arbitration award was successfully challenged in England on the basis that the tribunal had no jurisdiction to entertain claims by entities that were not specifically named as parties to the arbitration agreement. Not under the International Centre for Settlement of Investment Disputes (ICSID) Convention. ICSID awards do not need to be recognized in national courts or defended at the arbitration venue. They are recognized and enforced by States as a public international law obligation.

[111] Kryvoi (2010), p. 170.

arbitration proceedings raised by scholars who raise the question whether arbitration could be a better option for the annulment of shareholders decision in a company.[112] Even though the procedure would be initiated by the shareholder who voted against the General Assemblies decision, against the company, shareholders would need to be informed and would be able to join the proceedings as joining parties on the side of the defendant or the respondent. This situation would not be considered as piercing the corporate veil, because the shareholders belong to a company and have therefore interest in the outcome of the case. As Grbo confirms, arbitration can only be agreed upon in dispositive legal relations, which the parties are free to regulate by agreement.[113] It is therefore an interesting observation whether annulment of shareholders decisions or piercing of the corporate veil, as stipulated by domestic law, could be regarded as dispositive, or rather *ius strictum.* Only if the shareholders abuse the corporate form for personal gain, does the court consider lifting the corporate veil, looking behind the juridic person of the company. The tribunal determines lifting the corporate veil, regardless of the consent of the company or its shareholders and decides to pierce predominantly when there is an abuse of the good faith principle and if the domestic law foresees it. However, problems arise in regard to the enforcement of those arbitral awards in domestic courts. These problems are less predominant in proceedings before the ICSID[114], therefore relevant caselaw will be analyzed to understand when the tribunal accept or refused to exercise personal jurisdiction over non-signatories to ICSID arbitration clauses.

ICSID Cases

In Tshinvali v. Georgia[115] the ICSID tribunal was unwilling to extend its jurisdiction over non-signatories. The investor submitted claims on behalf of itself as well as its

---

[112] Grbo (2024), p. 71; Gagula (2020), p. 53; Jevremović (2018), p. 223. Article 338 of the Law on Companies of FBiH, which states that "A shareholder has the right to challenge a decision of the general assembly against which they voted by filing a lawsuit with the competent court within 30 days from the date the decision was adopted."

[113] Grbo (2024), p. 76.

[114] Grbo (2017a), p. 181.

[115] Zhinvali Development Ltd. v. Republic of Georgia, ICSID Case No. ARB/84/3, f 392–405 (Jan. 24, 2003).

three shareholders who had not been registered as claimants in those ICSID proceedings. Rule 2 and 59[116] of the ICSID Arbitration Rules provide that the request for arbitration needs to designate parties to the dispute and that the award must contain a designation of each party. These rules are sometimes so well implemented by the UCSID tribunals that arbitrators do not even go beyond them. In Rumeli Telecom v. Kazahstan[117], the Respondent (Kazakhstan) challenged ICSID jurisdiction by alleging that the claimants, although incorporated in Turkey (a contracting state), were effectively controlled by nationals of Kazakhstan, and thus lacked foreign nationality for the purposes of the ICSID Convention (Art. 25(2)(b)). Kazakhstan invoked the idea of "piercing the corporate veil" to identify the real controllers of the investment and deny the protection of ICSID arbitration. The arbitral tribunal rejected the application of the effective nationality test[118] to pierce the corporate veil and reach the real controllers of the corporate group, arguing that the ICSID Convention does not foresee piercing the corporate veil. There are other cases in which the tribunal disregarded the foreign control test. In AMCO and others v. Republic of Indonesia, Autopista Concesionada de Venezuela, C.A. v. Bolivarian Republic of Venezuela[119] and Aguas del Tunari v. Republic of Bolivia[120], the tribunals refused to lift the veil beyond the formal legal criterion, that of nationality.

Contrary to those cases there are several in which the tribunals did pierce the corporate veil to establish foreign control as stipulated by Article 25(2)(b) of the ICSID

[116] Available here: https://icsid.worldbank.org/sites/default/files/documents/ICSID_Convention.pdf. Accessed June 22, 2025.

[117] Rumeli Telecom A.S. and Telsim Mobil Telekomikasyon Hizmetleri A.S. v. Kazakhstan.

[118] The issue of determination of foreign control was raised in Tokios Tokelds v. Ukraine, ICSID Case No. ARB/02/18, Dissenting Opinion, (Apr. 29, 2004). Chairman Prosper Weil strongly objected to the majority's approach in recognizing jurisdiction. He argued that the formal incorporation test alone was insufficient, and that the tribunal must consider effective foreign control to prevent abuse of the ICSID system. In the aforementioned case, the tribunal recognized jurisdiction even though claimant Tokios Tokelės, was a company incorporated in Lithuania but largely owned and controlled by Ukrainian nationals. Ukraine challenged jurisdiction on the grounds that there was no genuine foreign control, and thus the claimant did not qualify as a "foreign investor" under Article 25(2)(b) of the ICSID Convention. The tribunal rejected Ukraine's argument that Tokios Tokelės was a shell used to abuse ICSID jurisdiction.

[119] Autopista Concesionada de Venezuela, C.A. v. Bolivarian Republic of Venezuela, ICSID Case No. ARB/00/5, available here: https://www.italaw.com/cases/3458. Accessed June 22, 2025.

[120] Aguas del Tunari, S.A. v. Republic of Bolivia, ICSID Case No. ARB/02/3. Available here: https://www.italaw.com/cases/57. Accessed June 22, 2025.

Convention[121]. In the case TSA Spectrum de Argentina S.A. v. Argentine Republic[122] TSA argued that it was controlled by a Dutch company, thereby invoking protection under the Argentina–Netherlands BIT. The tribunal, however, conducted a detailed analysis of the ownership structure and found that the supposed foreign parent was merely an intermediary and that ultimate control remained with Argentine nationals. The tribunal emphasized that ICSID jurisdiction cannot be based on formalistic corporate layering and held that to establish jurisdiction, it must identify the real source of control, tracing ownership through all corporate layers. Since TSA was not ultimately foreign controlled, the tribunal concluded that it lacked jurisdiction to hear the dispute and dismissed the claim. In its Opinion the tribunal stated:

"Significant difference between the two clauses of Article 25(2)(b) is that the first uses a formal legal criterion, that of nationality, whilst the second uses a material or objective criterion, that of "foreign control" in order to pierce the corporate veil and reach for the reality behind the cover of nationality."[123] The tribunal further stated that Article 25(2)(b) allows the parties to agree to lift the corporate veil, because the existence and materiality of foreign control must be objectively proven to establish jurisdiction. There are various other cases in which the tribunal decided to establish foreign control (and lift the corporate veil)[124], and deny jurisdiction of the ICSID, but it is clear that ICSID tribunals have not been consistent in dealing with this issue.

[121] Article 25(2)(b) of the ICSID Convention reads as follows: (A)ny juridical person which had the nationality of a Contracting State other than the State party to the dispute on the date on which the parties consented to submit such dispute to conciliation or arbitration and any juridical person which had the nationality of the Contracting State party to the dispute on that date and which, because of foreign control, the parties have agreed should be treated as a national of another Contracting State for the purposes of this Convention.

[122] TSA Spectrum de Argentina S.A. v. Argentine Republic, ICSID Case No. ARB/05/5, 147 (Dec. 19, 2008) (Award). Available: https://www.italaw.com/sites/default/files/case-documents/ita0874.pdf. Accessed June 22, 2025.

[123] TSA Spectrum de Argentina S.A. v. Argentine Republic (2008), pt. 140.

[124] For example Société Ouest Africaine des Bétons Industriels (SOABI) v. Senegal, Case No. ARB/82/1, Decision on Jurisdiction, 19 July 1984. and African Holding Company of America and Société Africaine de Construction au Congo S.A.R.L. v. Republic of Congo, Case No. ARB/05/21, Award, 29 July 2008. tribunals did not hesitate to pierce the corporate layers in identifying foreign control and the nationality of those holding it.

4.3 Conclusion

Criminal liability of legal entities was seen as a mechanism to prevent impunity for anonymous fault and avoid situations in which shareholders do not have to bear the consequences of a corporate policy they would otherwise have profited from.[125] By exploring how criminal or quasi-criminal measures (like anti-fraud and anti-money laundering laws) demand transparency and accountability, this Chapter supports the hypothesis that clearer standards for veil-piercing are needed to hold shareholders liable in cases of abuse. The corporate form should not shield individuals from liability when used illicitly. To address economic crime effectively, the EU has established (or is trying to), a unified approach to criminal liability including common sanctions for natural and legal persons. The evolving EU framework on beneficial ownership, provides increasingly precise tools for identifying the natural persons who ultimately control legal entities. This refinement is particularly relevant for judicial considerations of piercing the corporate veil.[126]

While traditional company law doctrines focus primarily on formal ownership and statutory obligations, the AML Regulation introduces a layered and substantive approach to determining control. It extends beyond formal ownership thresholds to encompass indirect control through voting arrangements, nominee structures, familial ties, and informal influence mechanisms. This broader evidentiary framework, especially the obligation to trace beneficial ownership in multilayered structures (Art. 53–55), can significantly support judicial reasoning when assessing whether a company has been used as a mere façade. In cases where natural persons intentionally obscure their involvement through shell or conduit companies, the data made available under AML rules, particularly through central beneficial ownership registers (even if subject to legitimate interest access), provides courts with a concrete basis to establish control and personal accountability. Consequently, the AML Regulation enriches the doctrinal basis of corporate veil-piercing by enabling courts to shift from purely formalistic criteria to a more substance-oriented analysis rooted in EU harmonized transparency standards. Without knowing who the beneficial owners are, any legal provision allowing veil-piercing would be ineffectual. Conversely, robust transparency regimes (as now mandated by EU law) enable courts and regulators to

[125] Radelic v. Croatia (2025), Dissenting opinion Pisani, pt. 6.

[126] Kuntz (2017), p. 178.

actually pierce the veil and hold the correct persons liable. The research found that EU directives require Member States to ensure that legal entities and the individuals behind them can be sanctioned for financial crimes. This reflects a consensus that corporate liability must go together with personal liability. A shell company may face penalties or dissolution, but without pinning liability on the natural persons orchestrating the scheme, justice is incomplete.

The case law and rules set out by international courts is important in order to address the principles under which courts implement international standards with national laws. Abuse of rights, fraud, and evasion of legal obligations are universally condemned bases for looking past the corporate form. The CJEU's jurisprudence on abuse of EU law provides a useful analytical template: it asks whether a given arrangement, despite formal compliance, defeats the purpose of the law (objective element) and whether there was intent to obtain an illegitimate advantage (subjective element). These criteria resonate with domestic veil-piercing cases, which frequently turn on whether the company was a mere façade concealing true facts or responsibilities. The ECtHR's decision in Lekić v. Slovenia underscored that an "active" shareholder (holding a sizeable stake and rights in the company) could be held personally liable for corporate debts when the company was essentially abandoned with outstanding obligations.[127] This finding aligns with a broader principle seen throughout the study: those who actively direct or benefit from a company's wrongful acts cannot hide behind its separate personality. The ECtHR case also highlights the delicate balance between preventing abuse and maintaining the rule of law: arbitrary or ad hoc piercing of the veil is unacceptable, but carefully crafted legal provisions can strike that balance. This section also provided insights from arbitration cases and how the tribunals sometimes seek the real controlling party (as seen when ICSID tribunals determine "foreign control" by looking past formal ownership), underscoring again that substance prevails over form. Where authorities can readily discover who the beneficial owners or controlling shareholders are, they are able to impose liability (or jurisdiction) appropriately. Conversely, opacity in corporate ownership greatly hinders accountability. Thus, the findings from the criminal-law perspective reinforce the hypothesis by demonstrating that legal reforms fostering transparency and clear liability channels significantly bolster the ability to pierce the veil in practice.

[127] Lekić v. Slovenia, 2018, point 130.

In the upcoming Chapter the comparative analysis of shareholder liability across Germany, Croatia, and Bosnia and Herzegovina, will be focused on aspects such as the definition and elements of piercing the corporate veil, the responsibilities of individuals within legal entities, shareholder rights, beneficial ownership, criminal liability, and transparency in relation to foreign legal structures and nominee regulations. This framework sets the stage for a deeper examination of how these jurisdictions approach shareholder accountability and corporate abuse.

Comparative Analysis—Shareholder Liability in Germany and Croatia

5

This research adopts a comparative approach to piercing the corporate veil by examining Croatia and Germany as contrasting case studies. Croatia, sharing Bosnia and Herzegovina's legal heritage, language, and institutional traditions, provides a relevant post socialist comparator, having completed EU accession a decade ago[1] and fully transposed the company law acquis. Its experience offers lessons on integrating transitional legal systems with EU corporate governance standards in contexts with similar legal cultures and administrative capacities. Germany, by contrast, represents a stable, jurisprudentially rich jurisdiction and a key architect of EU legal norms, offering functional and doctrinal benchmarks in corporate accountability, legal certainty, and judicial methodology. Comparing these two jurisdictions enables the study to assess both post socialist legal adaptation and established EU best practices, yielding doctrinal, institutional, and policy insights relevant to Bosnia and Herzegovina's ongoing EU integration. There is no common pattern for piercing the corporate veil on the EU level, the doctrinal anchor is stipulated within national law. In Germany the courts recognize the doctrine and pierce the corporate veil but try to solve liability issues through application of existing legal norms within civil, criminal or administrative law. In Croatia, the doctrine is enshrined in company law. This section will compare the doctrinal focus of piercing the corporate veil in German and Croatian law, and explore situations in which shareholders are jointly and severally liable in limited liability companies. What are the responsibilities of shareholders and under

---

[1] Croatia became the 28th EU member country on 1 July 2013. Treaty available here: https://eur-lex.europa.eu/eli/treaty/acc_2012/sign/eng. Accessed August 17, 2025.

L. Hasanovic, *Piercing the Corporate Veil: Shareholder Liability*,
Juridicum – Schriftenreihe zum Wirtschafts-, Unternehmens- und Bankrecht / Series on Business, Corporate and Banking Law,
https://doi.org/10.1007/978-3-658-52987-1_5

which circumstances could they have foreseen and acted upon fraudulent behaviors of management of the company? What is the level of control and influence and how does it correspond to their responsibilities towards creditors or interested parties of the company? Can the company be held criminally liable, and if yes, do the shareholders bare responsibility? Is beneficial ownership important in the determination of control and responsibility?

5.1 Piercing the Corporate Veil in Germany

5.1.1 Scope and Definition of the Doctrine in Germany

German company law is fundamentally structured around the principle of legal separation (*Trennungsprinzip*), which strictly distinguishes the legal entity from its shareholders.[2] This means that the company, whether a Limited Liability Company (GmbH), Entrepreneurial Company (Limited Liability) (UG)[3], or Stock Corporation (AG), is the sole holder of its assets and is solely liable to third parties with those assets[4]. This foundational rule is codified in Art. 13(2) GmbHG[5] and Art. 1(1) sentence 2 AktG[6], establishing that creditors generally have no recourse to the private assets of shareholders. The piercing the corporate veil doctrine in Germany (*Durchgriffshaftung)* has been established through case law and

[2] Krawczyk-Giehsmann (2020), p. 500; Matschernus (2007), p. 65; Neher (2011), p. 240.

[3] Article 5a of GmbHG. The business name of a company formed with a share capital which falls short of the minimum share capital must bear the designation „*Unternehmergesellschaft (haftungsbeschränkt*)“ (Entrepreneurial Company (Limited Liability)), or „UG (*haftungsbeschränkt*)“ for short.

[4] GmbH are formed by one or more founding shareholder(s) adopting the articles of association and appointing one or more managing directors in a notarial deed. GmbH acquire legal personality upon registration on the Commercial Register. UGs are a special form of limited liability company which is not required to meet the legally mandated EUR 25,000.00 share capital required of a GmbH. It is primarily used for small businesses. They are otherwise the same as GmbH. Together, GmbH and UG are the most common type of legal person in Germany.

[5] Limited Liability Companies Act, as consolidated and published in the Federal Law Gazette III, Index No. 4123–1, as last amended by Article 9 of the Act of 22 February 2023 (Federal Law Gazette 2023 I No. 51). Available here: https://www.gesetze-im-internet.de/englisch_gmbhg/englisch_gmbhg.html. Accessed July 13, 2025.

[6] Stock Corporation Act of 6 September 1965 (Federal Law Gazette I, p. 1089), as last amended by Article 13 of the Act of 11 December 2023 (Federal Law Gazette 2023 I, no. 354). Available here: https://www.gesetze-im-internet.de/aktg/BJNR010890965.html#BJNR010890965BJNG000300308. Accessed July 13, 2025.

related to situations in which shareholders exercise existence destroying interventions (*existenzvernichtende Eingriffe*) towards the assets of a GmbH.[7] The existence destroying interventions refer to the elimination of the economic viability of the company by shareholders, that severely disadvantage the company, mainly motivated by personal interests (using corporate assets to repay private debts or finance personal expenses). Article 30 of the GmbHG is relevant in that regard as it states that: "Those assets which the company requires to maintain its share capital may not be paid out to the shareholders." It prohibits payments to shareholders (e.g., dividends or other distributions) if they lead to undercapitalization (*Unterbilanz*), i.e. when the company's net assets fall below the registered capital.[8] However, it excludes other companies' assets which are vital, but do not fall under Article 30, such as patents, or machinery, or even business opportunities, as long as the total value remained above the minimum capital. That is why in Germany, when it comes to piercing the corporate veil, *lex generalis* is the BGB[9], since it applies to situations in which neither fiduciary duties (*Treuepflicht*) nor statutory capital maintenance rules provide sufficient safeguard towards company's assets. Article 826 BGB states that:"A person who, in a manner offending common decency (*gute Sitten*), intentionally inflicts damage on another person is liable to the other person to provide compensation for the damage."[10] The articles scope is very broad, and protects economic interests of the violated party, addressed in cases of so-called pure financial losses (*reine Vermögensschäden*) that have occurred without the violation of a protective statute (*Schutzgesetz*).[11] For the claim to be successful under the Article 826 of the BGB, courts consider intentional immoral infliction of damage (*vorsätzliche sittenwidrige Schadenszufügung*), which consist of the infliction of damage (5.1.1.1), immorality (5.1.1.2), and intent to cause harm (*Schädigungsvorsatz*) (5.1.1.3).

---

[7] Henzler (2009), p. 68.

[8] Schmidt (1994), p. 837.

[9] As stated in 3.3.1.1. the Trihotel decision limited the scope of piercing the corporate veil to Art. 826 BGB (intentional immoral harm). The BGH abandoned veil piercing as an autonomous doctrine and reclassified existence-destroying liability as a subcategory of tort law under Article 826 BGB. The Court acknowledged gaps in creditor protection but concluded that these could be addressed within the framework of general delict liability, without creating a separate legal doctrine.

[10] Article in German language available here: https://www.gesetze-im-internet.de/bgb/__826.html. Accessed July 24, 2025.

[11] Röthel (2021), p. 259.

5.1.1.1 Infliction Of Damage

According to the Federal Court of Justice[12], damage includes more than just financial loss but relates to any impairment of a legally recognized interest and any imposition of an obligation. However, since Article 826 BGB is seen as a supplement to Article 823 BGB its application arises for financial losses that are not caused by the violation of a legal interest or right protected under Article 823(1) BGB[13]. Article 823 BGB provides for liability in cases of negligent or intentional infringement of specific legally protected interests or the breach of protective statutes, Article 826 BGB enables compensation for pure economic loss only under the stricter condition of intentional and immoral conduct, thereby marking a conceptual boundary and limiting the expansion of Article 823 BGB to unenumerated interests.[14] There must be a causation between the damage inflicted on the claimant by the defendant.

5.1.1.2 Immorality (*Sittenwidrige Handlung*)

The second element of the definition that is commonly used to pierce the corporate veil in Germany, is immorality. According to official legislative materials (*Motivenberichte*) that accompanied the drafting of the BGB, immorality was explained as "... an abuse when someone's conduct contradicts the views expressed in good morals and offends the sense of decency shared by all fair and just individuals. Accordingly, an action is considered wrongful (a tort) even if it is, in principle, permitted under general freedom, but is disloyal and violates public morals, if it causes harm to others. The application of this principle requires prudence and caution, yet there is confidence that the courts will be able to fulfill this task."[15] The courts have discretionally power to evaluate the existence of immorality on a case-by-case basis, looking at the motive and conduct

[12] Judgment of 19 July 2004—II ZR 217/03. Neue Juristische Wochenschrift (NJW), 2004, 2667–2669. Available here: https://www.bundesgerichtshof.de/SharedDocs/Entscheidungen/DE/Zivilsenate/II_ZS/2003/II_ZR_217-03.pdf?__blob=publicationFile&v=1.

[13] Article 823 Liability in Damages: (1) Anyone who, intentionally or negligently, unlawfully injures the life, body, health, freedom, property, or any other right of another person is obliged to compensate the other for the damage arising therefrom. (2) The same obligation applies to anyone who violates a law intended to protect another person. If, according to the content of the law, a violation is possible even without fault, liability to pay compensation arises only in the case of fault. Available here: https://www.gesetze-im-internet.de/bgb/__823.html. Accessed July 24, 2025.

[14] Pure economic interests (e.g., loss of profits, investment losses); mere expectations or hopes (e.g., future contracts); market reputation or competitive position (unless part of a right like business operations).

[15] Motivenbericht (1888), p. 727.

against the standard of fair-minded individuals (*Anstandsgefühl aller billig und gerecht Denkenden*). It requires a particularly blameworthy character (*besondere Verwerflichkeit*). Historic and current interpretation of "*gute Sitten*" under Article 138 BGB[16] stipulates that the standard of morality is not subjective, but is grounded in societal norms, the so-called "sense of decency" (*Anstandsgefühl*), as evaluated by the courts[17]. BGH emphasizes that conduct is not immoral just because it violates a legal provision or because financial damage has occurred.[18] For example the BGH initially affirmed a finding of immoral harm in the VW emissions case[19], but later denied such liability following VW's efforts to disclose and investigate the misconduct,[20] confirming that what is required is a reprehensibility of the conduct, which must result from the purpose pursued, the means employed, the attitude displayed, or the consequences that have ensued. The key legal issue with Article 826 BGB and the liability of companies, is that a company itself cannot act immorally. That is why the court pierced the corporate veil and under Article 31 BGB[21], held board members and development heads liable, attributing liability to the person who had knowledge of the cheating device. VW was found liable for damages due to intentional, immoral harm caused to purchasers of affected vehicles.

In another case, the BGH additionally explained the immorality element:

---

[16] Article 138 reads as follows: Legal transaction offending common decency; usury. (1) A legal transaction that offends common decency is void. (2) In particular, a legal transaction is void by which a person, by exploiting the predicament, inexperience, lack of sound judgment or considerable weakness of will of another, causes a promise to be made to them or to a third party, in exchange for an act of performance, for pecuniary advantages that are clearly disproportionate to the performance, or causes such pecuniary advantages to be granted.

[17] The concept, first articulated in Reichsgericht (RGZ 48, 114), remains central in recent case law like BGH NJW 2020, 2798.

[18] BGH (2004), p. 2670; BGH (2014), p. 1380.

[19] BGH (2020a), p. 7 point 12. Judgment No. VI ZR 252/19. of 25 May 2020, available here: https://www.bundesgerichtshof.de/SharedDocs/Entscheidungen/DE/Zivilsenate/VI_ZS/2019/VI_ZR_252-19.pdf?__blob=publicationFile&v=1;

Röthel (2020), p. 261.

[20] BGH (2020b), p. 2802; see also BGH (2004), p. 2670; BGH (2014), p. 1380.

[21] Article 31 BGB, Liability of an association for organs. "The association is liable for the damage to a third party that the board, a member of the board or another constitutionally appointed representative causes through an act committed by them in carrying out the business with which they have been entrusted, where the act gives rise to a liability in damages."

> "The failure to disclose material irregularities in a capital investment does not automatically constitute a violation of public morals within the meaning of Article 826 BGB, even if there is a contractual duty to provide such disclosure. The serious allegation of immoral conduct (*sittenwidriges Verhalten*) is only justified if the silence of the person obligated to provide information also offends the sense of decency shared by all fair and just individuals. Immoral conduct could only be attributed to the defendant if he remained silent despite having positive knowledge that the investment was hopeless, i.e., with knowledge that a prohibition of the business activity was imminent".[22]

In its decision of June 17, 2016, the Oberlandesgericht Oldenburg applied Article 826 BGB to hold a former shareholder-managing director personally liable for damages resulting from a deliberate "company burial" (*Firmenbestattung*). The defendant had orchestrated the merger and rapid dissolution of the GmbH and its successor entities, thereby eliminating the plaintiff's ability to enforce existing claims. Unlike the BGH's Trihotel doctrine, which limits existence-destroying intervention to an internal liability of shareholders toward the company, the court found that no company remained to assert such claims. This exceptional situation justified granting the creditor a direct claim under Article 826 BGB, since the defendant's actions constituted a deliberate and immoral obstruction of creditor rights[23].

5.1.1.3 Intent to Cause Harm

To establish liability under Article 826 BGB, two key components of intent must be satisfied, the intent to cause harm (*Schädigungsvorsatz*)[24], and knowledge of the factual circumstances that render the conduct immoral, even if the actor is not aware of the immorality. According to the BGH[25], intent under Article 826 BGB requires both knowledge and acceptance of harm (*Wissens- und Wollenselement*), as stated in the VW judgment in which the BGH emphasized that the intent (*Vorsatz*) required under Article 826 BGB includes both a cognitive (*Wissenselement*) and a volitional element (*Wollenselement*). The actor must have known or foreseen the harm to the claimant and incorporated it into their will, or at

[22] BGH (2010), pt. 15.

[23] Oberlandesgericht Oldenburg (2016), Urt. v. 17.06.2016, Az. 6 U 22/16. Judgment available at: https://voris.wolterskluwer-online.de/browse/document/8c4dc2e7-ec65-3fe6-9c9f-ceb417e86d36. Accessed August 30, 2025.

[24] Reichsgericht (1904); BGH (1987).

[25] BGH (2014), p. 1381; BGH (2020), p. 1969.

the very least considered it possible and consciously accepted it.[26] Even though courts apply this element flexibly[27] the BGH reaffirmed in the VW judgments from 2023 that mere negligence or regulatory violations without immoral intent do not suffice for buyers to claim full rescission-like damages. The manufacturers needed to have acted with intentional and immoral deception, notably by issuing false conformity certificates. The damage needs to be part of the legal consequence.[28] For Article 826 of the BGB to be applicable, the parties need to prove particularly reprehensible conduct, which requires a higher threshold of culpability than ordinary negligence. In the 2023 VW cases no concrete evidence existed that the vehicle manufacturers or their senior management consciously and deliberately intended to deceive buyers. Unlike in an earlier VW scandal from 2020[29] in which the BHG found that the core immorality lies in the systematic deception of the Federal Motor Transport Authority and consumers over years, pursued in

---

[26] BGH (2023a), p. 4 point 7. Judgment No. VIa ZR 335/21 of 26 June 2023 available here: https://www.bundesgerichtshof.de/SharedDocs/Entscheidungen/DE/Zivilsenate/VIa_ZS/2021/VIa_ZR_335-21.pdf?__blob=publicationFile&v=1.

BGH (2023b), p. 8 point 14. Judgment No. VIa ZR 533/21 of 26 June 2023 available here: https://www.bundesgerichtshof.de/SharedDocs/Entscheidungen/DE/Zivilsenate/VIa_ZS/2021/VIa_ZR_533-21.pdf?__blob=publicationFile&v=1.

BGH (2023c), p. 7. point 14. Judgment No. VIa ZR 1031/22 of 26 June 2023 available here: https://www.bundesgerichtshof.de/SharedDocs/Entscheidungen/DE/Zivilsenate/VIa_ZS/2022/VIa_ZR_1031-22.pdf?__blob=publicationFile&v=1.

[27] It is sufficient that the actor foresees the general nature and direction of the harm.

[28] Wagner & Kötz (2021), p. 237.

[29] In the landmark case VI ZR 252/19, the BGH ruled on a claim brought by a consumer who purchased a used VW Sharan 2.0 TDI vehicle equipped with the EA189 diesel engine, which included an illegal defeat device. This device enabled the car to produce artificially low nitrogen oxide (NOx) emissions during regulatory testing, while operating with higher emissions during regular driving. This constituted intentional and strategic deception, violating European emissions regulations (Regulation (EC) No. 715/2007). After Volkswagen publicly admitted the manipulation in 2015 and the German Federal Motor Transport Authority (KBA) ordered corrective action, the plaintiff had a software update installed in 2017. Nevertheless, he filed suit under Article 826 BGB (intentional immoral injury), seeking full repayment of the purchase price in exchange for returning the vehicle. The Regional Court (Landgericht) initially dismissed the case, but the Higher Regional Court (Oberlandesgericht) reversed this, awarding partial compensation of EUR 25,616.10 based on the principle of "*Vorteilsausgleich*" (benefits received from using the vehicle). Both parties appealed. The BGH confirmed that Volkswagen's conduct in the EA189 scandal met the strict requirements of Article 826 BGB due to: 1. Deliberate strategic deception; 2. Mass distribution of affected vehicles; 3. Violation of consumer trust and environmental standards. This decision became the defining precedent for successful Article 826 BGB claims related to diesel emissions fraud.

the company's own profit interest.[30] German case law has further clarified the scope of Article 826 BGB in situations where liability extends to the heirs of a managing director. During his tenure, the managing director engaged in insolvency concealment and involvement in a fraudulent investment scheme, thereby triggering potential liability under Article 826 BGB. The BGH acknowledged that claims based on intentional immoral conduct, such as the deliberate concealment of insolvency or the operation of a Ponzi scheme, may pass to heirs, provided the harmful acts were committed during the deceased's tenure as managing director.[31]

5.1.2 Joint and Several Liability of Shareholders in the GmbHG

Even though Article 826 of the BGB has its established elements which the court considers, it is important to establish in which cases joint and several liability of shareholders exist, regardless of fraud and abuse. To establish shareholder liability, we need to understand how the GmbHG defines their obligations. The organ-bound fiduciary duty applies to corporate directors (e.g., managing directors of a GmbH). It obliges them to perform their functions diligently and in strict alignment with the interests of the company, excluding personal or external interests. The membership-based fiduciary duty (*mitgliedschaftliche Treuepflicht*), by contrast, governs the conduct of shareholders in their internal dealings. It requires shareholders to exercise their rights with appropriate regard for the interests of fellow shareholders and the integrity of the company structure. It applies regardless of whether it is explicitly agreed upon in the articles of association, reflecting its quasi-mandatory character within German legal doctrine. While Article 45 GmbHG allows shareholder rights to be shaped by the articles of association, this flexibility does not extend to blanket waivers of the membership-based fiduciary duty.[32] According to Article 46 of the GmbHG, duties of shareholders are:

---

[30] BGH (2020a), p. 5 point 8. Judgment No. VI ZR 252/19. of 25 May 2020, available here: https://www.bundesgerichtshof.de/SharedDocs/Entscheidungen/DE/Zivilsenate/VI_ZS/2019/VI_ZR_252-19.pdf?__blob=publicationFile&v=1.

[31] See https://www.rechtsprechung-im-internet.de/jportal/portal/t/aj8/page/bsjrsprod.psml?doc.hl=1&doc.id=jb-KORE718272025&documentnumber=1&numberofresults=317&doctyp=juris-r&showdoccase=1&doc.part=L&paramfromHL=true#focuspoint. Accessed August 30, 2025.

[32] Fleischer & Harzmeier (2015), p. 1297.

1. the approval of the annual financial statements and the appropriation of earnings;
2. decisions concerning the disclosure of separate financial statements and the approval of consolidated financial statements prepared by the directors;
3. the calling in of capital contributions and the repayment of additional contributions;
4. the division of, grouping and collection of shares;
5. the appointment and dismissal of the directors, as well as their discharge;
6. the regulation of audits and oversight of the management;
7. the appointment of those vested with the general commercial power of representation and those vested with the commercial power of attorney for the entire business establishment;
8. the assertion of claims for compensation to which the company is entitled as a result of formation or management vis-à-vis directors or shareholders, as well as the representation of the company in proceedings being conducted against the directors. The authority to pursue legal action against managing directors lies squarely with the shareholders. This principle is reflected in Article 46 Point 6 and 8 GmbHG, which entrust shareholders with the power to decide whether to pursue liability claims against managing directors, or waive such claims entirely. This discretionary power gives the general meeting substantial influence over the legal accountability of the company's executives. It also opens the door to potential tensions between internal corporate governance and creditor protection, particularly in closely held GmbHs where managing directors often control or influence the shareholder majority. A core instrument of shareholder control is the discharge resolution (*Entlastungsbeschluss*), governed by Article 46 point 5 GmbHG. By granting discharge, the shareholders declare their approval of the managing director's past conduct during the preceding fiscal year.[33] This resolution carries significant legal consequences. It precludes any damage claims already in existence at the time of discharge, provided that these claims were discoverable with reasonable diligence by the shareholders. However, certain statutory violations are so serious that they may override or limit the effect of discharge, they include:

1. Article 30 GmbHG that stipulates that managing directors may not authorize distributions to shareholders (such as dividends or loan repayments) that cause the company's net assets to fall below the registered share capital. Payments made

---

[33] Schmidt (1994), p. 837.

in violation of Art. 30 GmbHG are strictly prohibited, and any managing director who facilitates such a payment is personally liable.

2.Article 33 GmbHG that stipulates that the company may not purchase or take in pledge own shares for which capital contributions have not yet been paid in full.

These provisions related to the director are important especially if he acted in bad faith.[34] Pursuant to Article 6 Point 5 GmbHG, shareholders who intentionally or gross negligently leave a person who may not act as director to manage the company's business are held jointly and severally liable to the company for that damage which arises on account of the fact that this person violates the obligations which he or she is under vis-à-vis the company. This is also the only reference to joint and several liability the GmbHG makes in terms of shareholders, but an important one. This provision holds shareholders of limited liability company's liable if they knowingly keep a disqualified director to manage the company, and that director commits fraud or abuse to creditors. There is an internal division of authority that corporate managers need to respect and they cannot make decisions unilaterally especially where the law or in other instances, internal governance rules reserve decision making power shareholders or the supervisory board. That is why the GmbHG shares these liabilities with shareholders pursuant to article 6 Point 5 GmbHG. There are also harmful shareholder influences towards the company, especially when they have various business interests and the shareholders loses interest in the company's long-term success. Shareholders may attempt to extract remaining assets, thereby accelerating the company's collapse and harming its creditors. In cases in which the above-mentioned articles do not apply, an exceptional remedy may lay in Article 826 BGB.

5.1.3 Criminal Shareholder Liability in Germany

In Germany criminal liability of legal entities does not exist as previously explained but is focused on individuals within the company who direct or oversee the wrongful actions. For companies without a specific legal framework for liability, the liability of shareholders may come into play, particularly if they are actively involved in the decisions leading to criminal actions. Kuntz stated that effective and substantial control mechanisms are crucial and necessary for assigning responsibility, rather than mere ownership, which is akin to the concept of

[34] Henzler (2009), p. 104.

individual criminal liability.[35] There are two important articles in the German Criminal Code (StGB) relevant for the identification and definition of control and ownership of a legal entity. Article 14 of the StGB[36] stipulates that a person acting in the following capacities is subject to criminal liability under laws that assign liability based on special personal attributes, relationships, or circumstances, even if those characteristics do not apply to the person acting but to the entity, partnership, or individual they represent:

1. As a representative authorized to act for a legal entity or as a member of such a governing body;
2. As a partner authorized to represent a partnership with legal capacity;
3. As a statutory representative of another individual.

If a person is authorized by the owner of a business or by someone delegated by the owner to:

1. Manage the entire business or part of it; or
2. Perform specific duties that belong to the business owner,

then any law that assigns criminal liability based on special personal characteristics also applies to the person commissioned to act, even if those characteristics apply to the business owner and not to the commissioned person. This applies to businesses as well as enterprises. If a similar commission is made for an agency performing public administrative services, the same rule applies. This stance is confirmed by the BGH relating to using a trustee for the establishment of a GmbH. The trustee (*Strohmann*) is treated as a shareholder for the purposes of provisions relevant to them.[37] This trustee is seen as the beneficial owner of the company and has therefore to bear the obligations arising from this status. Using a trustee in German law is not illegal and does not itself meet grounds for piercing, employing trustees is not immoral, but it is an important element

[35] Kuntz (2017), p. 271.

[36] Criminal Code in the version published on 13 November 1998 (Federal Law Gazette I, p. 3322), as last amended by Article 2 of the Act of 22 November 2021 (Federal Law Gazette I, p. 4906). Available here: https://www.gesetze-im-internet.de/englisch_stgb/englisch_stgb.html#p266. Accessed July 14, 2025.

[37] Neher (2011), p. 240.

because beneficial control through a trustee can invoke shareholder responsibilities and liabilities.[38] It also is an indication that not every owner of a company is the one in control of it. Article 74e of the StGB concerns individuals acting in official representative roles such as board members, directors, or managers. It stipulates that they can be held accountable for actions that harm the interests of the legal entity, association, or business they represent. If such acts lead to the confiscation of illegal profits, the responsibility for those acts can extend to the entity or person represented, not just the individual who committed the wrongful act. Shareholders are not typically considered legal organs of the company unless they directly control or influence company operations. In cases where they exercise significant influence or make decisions that impact the company's assets or operations, they can be held liable for criminal offenses, particularly under laws related to fraud, mismanagement, or breaches of trust. Although shareholders do not typically engage in actions on behalf of the company, they can be criminally liable for complicity in crimes like tax evasion, fraud, or insolvency offenses, particularly if they participate in or enable illegal activities such as financial manipulation. Shareholders may also be liable for failure to file for insolvency if the company is leaderless (i.e., without a formally appointed director), with liability applying even in cases of negligence.[39] Since legal entities cannot be held criminally liable in Germany, the OWiG offers important insights into the liability of business owners. Under Article 130 OWiG, which addresses organizational and supervisory failures, the owner of a business or operation, including public enterprises, commits a regulatory offence if they intentionally or negligently fail to take the necessary supervisory measures to prevent violations of legal duties within the enterprise, where such duties carry a criminal penalty or regulatory fine. Liability arises when a violation occurs that proper supervision could have prevented or significantly hindered. This provision explicitly includes the obligation to appoint, carefully select, and oversee supervisory personnel. Reasons for veil piercing related to the failure to follow corporate formalities (as discussed in Sect. 3.3.1 of this dissertation) fall within the scope of this legal norm. The German legislator recognizes such failures as violations, holding owners accountable through substantial penalties. Fines may reach up to one million euros, depending on the severity of the violation, and are calculated based on the maximum penalty for the underlying offence. In this way, the provision ensures that companies face

[38] Habenicht (2011), p. 19. Habenicht's reference to replacing shareholders and directors with "*bezahlte Strohmänner*" (paid straw men) on p. 19 describes a classic nominee structure, formal shareholders appear in the register, but they do not exercise real control, they merely conceal the true controlling person.

[39] Bittmann (2011), p. 944.

sanctions even when the individual offenders are not directly prosecuted.[40] In its remand decision overturning the Higher Regional Court of Stuttgart, the BGH sharpened the contours of delictual liability in Ponzi-scheme contexts for actors performing ostensibly neutral professional services and reaffirmed the evidentiary approach relevant to Article 826 BGB.[41] The Court held that the appellate court had applied an unduly narrow *mens rea* test by demanding proof of actual knowledge of the fraud while neglecting the alternative route to intent, conditional intent, where the assistant regards the fraud as very or overwhelmingly likely and nevertheless furthers it.[42] (BGH, 2025a) In the criminal trial, the managing directors and their close associates were charged with large-scale fraud (Art. 263 StGB) for operating a Ponzi scheme under the guise of a storage-rental business. The criminal court's findings, notably the managing director's conviction, the co-defendant's confession, and extensive evidentiary material (cash flows, falsified invoices, fictitious customers, absence of real assets), provided a factual matrix that civil courts could not ignore. While civil courts are not formally bound by criminal judgments, the confessions and documentary record assembled in the criminal process served as powerful indicia in the civil burden of proof. Thus, in this case, the criminal proceedings functioned as an evidentiary shortcut in civil proceedings: it clarified factual issues of intent, knowledge, and scheme structure that are otherwise opaque, thereby strengthening creditors' ability to invoke piercing of the corporate veil and Article 826 BGB. In this way, criminal law not only sanctions fraudulent actors but also indirectly facilitates the civil law's corrective mechanisms by making veil-piercing claims more viable in Germany.

---

[40] Achenbach (2023), p. 10.

[41] Higher Regional Court of Stuttgart (2024), point 18. Judgment No. 12 U 285/21 from 30 January 2024 available here: https://www.landesrecht-bw.de/bsbw/document/NJRE001613254.

[42] BGH (2025a), point 11. Aider-and-abettor liability in German civil law is also determined according to criminal law principles Pursuant to Article 27(1) StGB, anyone who intentionally assists another in the commission of that person's intentional unlawful act is punishable as an accessory. Aiding and abetting therefore constitutes the intentional provision of assistance to another's intentional offense. Objectively, the act of assistance need not have been causal for the result of the principal offense; it suffices that it promoted or facilitated the commission of the offense or strengthened the perpetrator in his decision to commit it. Accessory intent exists where the aider does not know all the details but is nevertheless aware of the central features of the principal act and of how his conduct furthers it or at least considers this possible in the sense of conditional intent and accepts it. See https://www.rechtsprechung-im-internet.de/jportal/portal/t/aj8/page/bsjrsprod.psml?doc.hl=1&doc.id=jb-KORE714562025&documentnumber=2&numberofresults=317&doctyp=juris-r&showdoccase=1&doc.part=L&paramfromHL=true#focuspoint. Accessed August 30, 2025.

5.1.4 The Controlling Shareholder

In terms of the piercing of the corporate veil provision related to Article 826 BGB, the fact that a shareholder had control or not is relevant in terms of a party proving intent of the harmful act, and that the shareholder knew or must have known that the conduct is immoral. Article 50 GmbHG grants shareholders with at least 10% of the registered share capital the right to request the convening of a shareholders' meeting. Each shareholder, according to Article 51a of the GmbHG has the right to request information on the company's affairs and inspect the books and company documents. It is therefore possible for any shareholder holding at least 10% of shares (or less) to familiarize with internal affairs of the company and be aware of possible fraudulent activities. Article 826 BGB as a special case of intentional immoral damage, confines liability to the internal sphere of the company, making shareholders liable to the company, not directly to creditors.[43] The Act on the Tracing of Profits from Serious Crimes (GwG) in its Article 3, defines the controlling party in a company as the beneficial owner ("*wirtschaftlich Berechtigter*"), as the natural person who ultimately owns or controls the legal entity.

A person is considered the controlling party if they:

1. Directly or indirectly hold more than 25% of the capital shares;
2. Control more than 25% of the voting rights; or
3. Exercise control in a comparable manner (e.g., through agreements, voting arrangements, or indirect ownership chains).

Indirect control is deemed to exist when ownership interests are held by another entity controlled by a natural person, with "dominant influence" defined in accordance with Article 290(2) to (4) of the German Commercial Code (HGB)[44].

[43] Petričević (2023), p. 258.

[44] A parent undertaking will be considered to have dominant influence in all cases in which: 1. it is entitled to the majority of the shareholder voting rights in another undertaking; 2. The right to appoint/dismiss the majority of the governing body while being a shareholder; 3. The right to determine financial and business policy via a domination agreement (*Beherrschungsvertrag)* or corporate charter, or 4. The majority of risks and opportunities in a purpose company (*Zweckgesellschaft*). (Art. 290, HGB).

5.1.5 Discussion

In Germany, the development of the piercing the corporate veil doctrine has been extensive and shaped primarily by judicial interpretation. The most recent doctrinal shift sought to reconcile shareholder liability with the fundamental principle of limited liability. Under current jurisprudence, this principle will be disregarded through the application of Article 826 BGB only when no other remedy is available under company, criminal, or administrative law. By relocating veil piercing into the realm of civil law, Article 826 BGB is considered sufficiently broad to protect not only the company's interests but also those of its creditors. The "Dieselgate" scandal demonstrates how Article 826 BGB has become a primary legal avenue for compensating injured parties, despite the parallel availability of criminal sanctions under provisions such as Article 263 StGB (fraud). The doctrinal narrowing in Trihotel and Gamma marked a decisive retreat from broad shareholder external liability. The Bundesgerichtshof (BGH) now requires proof of *dolus* (including *dolus eventualis*) and immoral conduct, thereby excluding mere negligence or breaches of regulatory duties[45]. As a result, creditor protection under veil piercing depends on demonstrating a targeted, morally reprehensible act directly aimed at causing harm. This same reasoning has been applied in corporate tort contexts. In the EA189 Dieselgate case, the BGH held Article 826 BGB applicable because VW's leadership had made a strategic decision to install defeat devices and deceive the German Federal Motor Transport Authority (KBA), conduct qualifying as deliberate immoral harm. By contrast, in the 2023 VW Audi Mercedes EA288 and related cases the court declined to apply Article 826 BGB, finding no evidence of such strategic, deceptive intent by decision-makers, since KBA had tested EA 288 engines extensively and issued no recalls[46]. Even if unlawful defeat devices were present, without proof of intentional immoral conduct, only Article 823(2) BGB applied, limiting compensation

[45] BGH (2025c). The party asserting a claim under Article 826 BGB bears the full burden of pleading and proof for the facts giving rise to the claim—that is, both for the circumstances establishing the injury and its immorality in objective terms, as well as for the at least conditional intent of the tortfeasor with respect to the existence of those circumstances (Senate, judgment of 27 October 2022—III ZR 211/20, WM 2023, 134 para. 15; BGH, judgment of 25 May 2020—VI ZR 252/19, BGHZ 225, 316 para. 35; each with further references).

[46] BGH (2025b). See here: https://www.rechtsprechung-im-internet.de/jportal/portal/t/b74/page/bsjrsprod.psml?pid=Dokumentanzeige&showdoccase=1&js_peid=Trefferliste&documentnumber=3&numberofresults=317&fromdoctodoc=yes&doc.id=jb-KORE708562025&doc.part=L&doc.price=0.0&doc.hl=1#focuspoint. Accessed August 20, 2025.

to a "difference in damages" (5% to 15% of the purchase price) rather than full rescission and repayment.

Germany's restrictive approach favors established remedies to protect creditors before disregarding corporate separateness. These include strict capital maintenance rules (requiring repayment of unlawful asset withdrawals), personal liability for directors who trade while insolvent or fail to file for bankruptcy, liability for shareholders who retain a disqualified director, and avoidance actions against fraudulent transfers. Since Trihotel, most veil-piercing scenarios have been redirected into the Article 826 BGB tort framework, enforceable by insolvency administrators or, in rare cases, directly by creditors. The piercing the corporate veil doctrine is now subsidiary, used only when orthodox remedies prove inadequate.

The central issue is that, under current law, even proven fraud, such as in the 2023 emissions cases, does not necessarily meet the Article 826 BGB threshold if courts find no intent to cause immoral harm. This raises the question: can a shareholder or manager be shielded from veil-piercing liability merely because such intent was not demonstrably present, even though intentional fraud was committed? The requirement of proving immoral harm, as a subjective element assessed case by case, reveals the high value German law places on the principle of limited liability and the reluctance to erode it without unequivocal evidence of deliberate, morally reprehensible conduct. The framework preserves avenues to hold truly blameworthy shareholders accountable. Those who willfully exploit the corporate form to the detriment of creditors cannot hide behind the veil. The high subjective bar thus targets only abusive behavior, serving as a deterrent against using a GmbH as a vehicle for fraud or deliberate unlawful behavior. In less serious cases, such as mere negligent mismanagement, creditors must rely on other remedies (such as claims against directors or contractual guarantees), since shareholders' personal assets remain protected.[47]

An additional consideration in the German context is the role of controlling shareholders in the application of article 826 BGB. Although German courts apply veil-piercing restrictively, the statutory framework provides objective indicators of control that could support the evidentiary burden for proving intent and knowledge. Shareholders who meet the thresholds for "beneficial owner" under Article 3 GwG, holding more than 25% of capital or voting rights, or exercising comparable influence, or who meet the "dominant influence" criteria under Article 290 HGB, occupy positions where they can access critical company information and influence strategic decisions. These capacities, combined with rights

[47] Steffek (2009), p. 83.

under Articles 50 and 51a GmbHG to convene meetings and inspect company records, make it difficult for such shareholders to claim ignorance of conduct amounting to intentional immoral harm. Consequently, in cases where control can be established through these statutory definitions, the courts may find it easier to satisfy the subjective elements of Article 826 BGB, potentially lowering the practical barriers to shareholder liability in cases of fraudulent or abusive conduct.

5.2 Piercing the Corporate Veil in Croatia

The piercing of the corporate veil doctrine in Croatia is codified in the Law on Companies (ZTD)[48]. The ZTD was enacted in 1993 and modelled after the German and Austrian company law.[49] Members of the limited liability company are not personally liable for its debt, there is a strict division between the members personal assets and the company's assets. However, if a shareholder abuses this limited liability in the limited liability company, provisions on limited liability do not apply and the shareholder shall be personally liable for the companies' obligations. Article 4 and 5 of the ZTD stipulate that the company is granted legal personhood upon registration in the court register, with all the rights and obligations of a legal entity, enabling it to act independently in legal and economic transactions until its deregistration. (Art. 4 & 5 ZTD) Therefore, the liability of the shareholder that arises under specific circumstances, stems from the companies' debts towards creditors, rather than from debts of the shareholder. There is no direct contractual relationship, it is the liability for another's debt, in this case, the debt of the company of the member, a case of suretyship (*solidarno jamstvo*) as defined by the Croatian Law on Obligations (ZOO CRO)[50], however not agreed by the member and creditors, but imposed by law, in this case ZTD as *lex specialis*. The liability of the shareholder is accessory in nature; it exists only as long as the company's obligation towards the creditor exists. In case of veil piercing however, creditors are not required to pursue enforcement against the company's assets before holding members accountable.

[48] Companies Act (*Zakon o trgovačkim društvima*), Official Gazette of the Republic of Croatia Nos. 111/1993, 34/1999, 121/1999, 52/2000, 118/2003, 107/2007, 146/2008, 137/2009, 111/2012, 125/2011, 68/2013, 110/2015, 40/2019, 34/2022, 114/2022, 18/2023, 130/2023, 136/2024. Available here: https://informator.hr/zakoni/10841-zakon-o-trgovackim-drustvima. Accessed August 17, 2025.

[49] Jurić & Braut Filipović, (2020), p. 70.

[50] Article 104 ZOO CRO.

5.2.1 Scope and Definition of the Doctrine in Croatia

Abuse of limited liability is the overarching reason for piercing the corporate veil in Croatia. The abuse of limited liability is defined in Article 10 (3) and (4) ZTD. Article 10 (3) stipulates that the shareholder cannot rely on the exemption from personal liability for the companies' obligations if the shareholder abuses their limited liability. Article 10(4) lists reasons for abuse by members of a limited liability company, shareholders of a joint-stock company, and limited partners in a limited partnership if the:

1. company is used to achieve a purpose that is otherwise prohibited to that member;
2. company is used to harm creditors;
3. company's assets are managed contrary to the law as if they were the member's personal assets;
4. member, in their own interest or in the interest of another person, reduces the company's assets, although they knew or should have known that the company would not be able to meet its obligations.[51]

Based on these circumstances that would assume joint and several liability of shareholders, Croatian courts have created case law with more than 100 final judgements in which the veil of the limited liability company or joint stock company, has been pierced[52] due to:

1. shareholder abuse of influence,[53]
2. abuse of company's corporate form,[54]
3. comingling o assets,[55]

[51] Art. 10, ZTD.

[52] Jurić & Braut Filipović (2020), p. 82.

[53] High Commercial Court of the Republic of Croatia (2003). Decision Pž-1760/02. Retrieved from: https://www.iusinfo.hr/sudska-praksa/SE500B1760S02D20030415?HighlightQuery=proboj+pravne+osobnosti. Accessed August 18, 2025.

[54] High Commercial Court of Croatia, 2003, Pi-1760/02 and High Commercial Court of Croatia, 2003a, Pž-636/03.

[55] High Commercial Court of the Republic of Croatia, 2004. Decision in case Pž-636/03. Retrieved from https://www.iusinfo.hr/sudska-praksa/SE500B6369S03D20040217?HighlightQuery=proboj+pravne+osobnosti. Accessed August 18, 2025. The case concerns the liability of a parent company (founder) for the debts of its subsidiary (daughter company) in

4. undercapitalization,[56,57]
5. tax abuse.[58]

Before turning to the doctrinal details, it is useful to clarify the analytical framework applied in the following subsections. The Croatian case law and doctrine on veil-piercing can be systematized around three interrelated elements:

(i) the claim element—the existence of a creditor's demand against the company which triggers the potential extension of liability to shareholders;

insolvency proceedings. The court found that such liability arises when there is a commingling of assets between the two companies, to the extent that it is impossible to distinguish which assets belong to the parent and which to the subsidiary. The first-instance court, based on the insolvency administrator's report and evidence (such as contracts, treatment of employees, shared premises, identical equipment, blocked bank accounts, and unclear bookkeeping), concluded that the parent company acted as a controlling company and used the subsidiary's operations for purposes it could not otherwise achieve. Where there is mixing of assets and functions between a shareholder (as the parent company) and its subsidiary, the shareholder may be held liable for the subsidiary's debts, as creditors must be allowed to pursue the shareholder's assets for repayment.

[56] High Commercial Court of the Republic of Croatia, 2021. Decision Pž 1820/2020–3 of the High Commercial Court of the Republic of Croatia. Available here: https://odluke.sudovi.hr/decisionView?id=090216ba80c82c12&q=67+Pž-1820%2F2020-3. Accessed August 18, 2025. The Court confirmed shareholder liability under Article 10(3) of the ZTD in a case where the shareholder deliberately diminished the company's assets to the detriment of creditors. The defendant transferred business shares with a nominal value of HRK 15,4 million for only HRK 3,9 million, effectively stripping assets from the company without equivalent consideration. At the same time, he established a new company with an almost identical name and business activity, transferring all operations to it while the original company faced financial distress. The courts concluded that these actions constituted an abuse of the privilege of limited liability, as the shareholder knew or should have known that such conduct would prevent the company from satisfying its obligations.

[57] High Commercial Court of the Republic of Croatia, 2003a. Decision No. Pž-636/03. Available: https://www.iusinfo.hr/sudska-praksa/SE500B636S03D20031118. Accessed November 18, 2025. The shareholder abused the protection of limited liability by creating sixteen subsidiary companies to which he transferred employees (including the claimant) without the transfer of significant assets. The parent company retained the majority of its assets, leaving the subsidiaries with minimal capital (e.g., only 387,800.00 HRK compared to the parent's 17 million HRK). The court found that the shareholder, as the sole shareholder and controlling entity of the subsidiary, abused the corporate form to avoid obligations to employees.

[58] Administrative court in Zagreb, 2021. Decision Nr. Us I-1877/2020–8, from 27 May 2021. Available here: https://odluke.sudovi.hr/Document/View?id=2cfd5ad7-1433-4ba0-9128-19829e6c19da&q=proboj+pravne+osobnosti. Accessed August 20, 2025.

(ii) the substantive grounds—specific forms of abuse of limited liability that justify disregarding the corporate form; and
(iii) the evidentiary standard—the level and type of proof creditors must meet to succeed in establishing shareholder liability.

The subsequent subsections (5.2.1.1 through 5.2.1.3) track these elements in turn, highlighting how Croatian courts have developed them in practice.

5.2.1.1 Infliction of Damage—Abuse of Limited Liability

For piercing to take place the creditor must show a due claim against the company and abusive conduct under Art. 10(4) that occurred to the creditor of the company. Therefore, The burden of proof of abuse of limited liability of the shareholder, lies with the damaged party, the creditor of the company as stipulated in a case before the Supreme Court in Croatia[59]. The court stated that the plaintiff's revision was dismissed as unfounded because he failed to provide clear reasons demonstrating how the defendant had abused the privilege of limited liability. In cases of piercing the corporate veil, it is the plaintiff's burden to present facts indicating such abuse, and the mere non-payment of debts by the company is not sufficient to establish it. Members of limited liability companies are generally not liable for company debts, but liability arises when a creditor's claim is due and the member has abused the privilege of limited liability. Abuse is presumed in cases such as using the company for prohibited purposes, harming creditors, treating company assets as personal property, or depleting company assets while aware of insolvency risk. The liability of the shareholder for debts of the company exists only if the subjective element of abuse is proven. Abuse under Article 10(3) of the ZTD arises when a shareholder uses its influence to achieve objectives that are otherwise prohibited to the company. Examples of actions include:

1. deliberately blocking the companies' accounts to prevent creditor satisfaction,
2. shifting obligations to one company while directing revenues to another,
3. favoring certain creditors over others, thereby undermining equal treatment.

Such conduct constitutes misuse of corporate form, as it results in disposing of assets contrary to law or business practice, or putting creditors in a disadvantaged

[59] Supreme Court in Croatia (2013). Decision Nr. Rev-666/2010–2 from January 16, 2013. Available at: https://odluke.sudovi.hr/Document/View?id=90df48b0-4450-4848-9a99-255cec40ea6f&q=proboj+pravne+osobnosti. Accessed August 20, 2025.

position.[60] The liability for piercing the corporate veil rests with those who abuse the privilege of limited liability. This includes not only formal members but also those in a *de facto* membership position, as their silence may imply consent to the abuse. Parent companies can also be liable for the obligations of subsidiaries if they misuse their non-liability status. Importantly, liability applies to anyone who was a member at the relevant time, even if they no longer hold membership when the lawsuit is filed. Members are responsible for all company obligations, regardless of whether they stem from contracts, statutes, public law (including taxes), or private law.[61] This highlights why, in the Croatian context, the determination of who qualifies as a controlling shareholder assumes particular importance for the development of a more equitable doctrine of piercing the corporate veil. At present, the doctrine primarily focuses on the factual relationship between the shareholder and the company, rather than on the shareholder's abusive conduct vis-à-vis the creditor, however, without the existence of a due claim there is no piercing. To succeed with the claim the creditor will have to prove abuse as stipulated in Article 10(4) of the ZTD. The courts in Croatia have been favorable in identifying such abuse for the following reasons.

5.2.1.1.1 Comingling of Assets

In Croatian company law, the mixing of assets between a limited liability company and its members is recognized as a key indicator for piercing the corporate veil. This occurs when the separation between company and private assets is blurred, most often through inadequate bookkeeping or the diversion of company funds for personal use. Scholarly literature[62], distinguishes between direct abuses, such as the transfer of profitable opportunities, client base, or loss-making obligations, and indirect abuses, including balance sheet neutral measures like loans to insolvent members, security interests in favor of members, or the free private use of company property. These practices undermine the principle of asset separation and are treated as forms of abuse justifying the extension of shareholder liability. In a judgment of the Commercial Court in Varaždin[63], the court held that the plaintiff did not provide sufficiently concrete facts to establish piercing

---

[60] High Commercial Court of Croatia (2003), Pi-1760/02.

[61] Petričević (2023), p. 264.

[62] Barbić (2020), p. 500; Brnabić & Ivancev (2017), p. 260; Barbić (2009), p. 36.

[63] Commercial Court in Varaždin (2025). Decision P-23/2025–45, from February 28, 2025. Available here: https://odluke.sudovi.hr/Document/View?id=8fc289a7-505a-44ac-8a6f-125ca00b8f37&q=P-23%2f2025-45. Accessed August 20, 2025. The plaintiff claimed that the defendant had managed the company's assets as if they were his own personal property. However, the plaintiff failed to present concrete facts or evidence to prove such misuse. The

of the corporate veil. Allegations that the defendant used company assets (workers, machinery, goods) for private projects or transferred assets below value were considered too vague and general to prove that the shareholder treated company property as his own. For the doctrine of piercing to apply, the plaintiff must clearly state specific acts or omissions by the shareholder that demonstrate abuse of limited liability. Mere inability of the company to pay its debts does not constitute abuse, as this can result from normal business risks and changing market conditions. In order to be successful in his claim, the plaintiff needs to prove that the shareholder for example used company assets to finance personal projects (houses etc.), and that the company was left without sufficient funds to pay put outstanding debt to creditors.

5.2.1.1.2 Harm to Creditors

In a case before the County Court in Split[64] the creditor had purchased an apartment (312 A) from the company A. n. LLC LLC, represented by the defendant as director and shareholder, and paid the full amount. However, the apartment had already been sold to a third party. An amendment to the pre-contract was later signed, shifting the contract to a different apartment (412), but this apartment too had already been sold to another third party by the time of contract conclusion. At the time, the company's account was blocked and in severe financial difficulty. The court found that the defendant, acting as shareholder and director, knowingly sold property that was not owned by the company, thereby deceiving the plaintiff and deliberately preventing fulfillment of contractual obligations. This conduct constituted an abuse of limited liability and justified piercing the corporate veil, making the shareholder personally liable for the company's obligations.

In another case before the High Commercial Court in Croatia[65], the shareholder abused the protection of limited liability by creating sixteen subsidiary companies to which he transferred employees (including the plaintiff) without the transfer of significant assets. The parent company retained the majority of its assets, leaving the subsidiaries with minimal capital (e.g., only 387,800.00 HRK

---

mere fact that the company could not meet its obligations was deemed insufficient to justify piercing the corporate veil, as business risk and changing circumstances are inherent to commercial activity. Piercing is possible only when specific, proven circumstances of abuse exist.

[64] County Court in Split (2014). Decision number: Gž x-533/2013–2 from December 18, 2014. Available at: https://odluke.sudovi.hr/Document/View?id=ec854df4-4e51-4b34-b6d5-8d8abbc53084&q=proboj+pravne+osobnosti. Accessed August 20, 2025.

[65] High Commercial Court in Croatia (2003). Decision No. Pž-636/03. Available: https://www.iusinfo.hr/sudska-praksa/SE500B636S03D20031118. Accessed November 18, 2025.

compared to the parent's 17 million HRK). The court found that the shareholder, as the sole shareholder and controlling entity of the subsidiary, abused the corporate form to avoid obligations to employees. This judgment is of particular importance because employees form part of a circle of creditors who are in an especially disadvantaged position, as they typically lack the bargaining power that other legal entities doing business with these companies have. The Croatian judiciary, by recognizing this imbalance, proves its commitment to strengthening the protection of weaker parties and thereby contributes to the development of a fairer justice system.

5.2.1.1.3 Undercapitalization

As in other jurisdictions, undercapitalization in Croatia cannot, by itself, serve as a sufficient ground for piercing the corporate veil; it must be coupled with evidence of abusive or dishonest conduct.[66] In a judgment by the High Commercial Court of the Republic of Croatia[67] piercing the corporate veil exists in cases where one company is the alter ego of another, acting as its shareholder and managing the affairs of the company from the shadows in an unlawful manner, such as creating benefits for itself while generating debts for the established company, siphoning funds from the other company, or when the other company is a fictitious entity set up solely for the founder's purposes. Undercapitalization is considered to be any conduct of a member by which the company's assets are extracted without consideration or with inadequate consideration. The reduction of the company's assets is generally not permitted when it results in a negative report on the company's financial position, and therefore financial reports on the company's status are of great importance when proving abuse.

5.2.1.1.4 Tax abuse

Croatia has created a very restrictive tax system with their General Tax Act[68] (GTA CRO) replicating the piercing the corporate veil doctrine from the ZTD. Article 30 of the GTA CRO is identical to Article 10(3) and 10(4) of the ZTD, mirroring provisions on abuse of limited liability to shareholders. Practically, this means that shareholders who conduct activities that would result in the inability

---

[66] Jelinić & Akšamović, (2009), p. 544.

[67] High Commercial Court of the Republic of Croatia (2007). Decision Nr. Pž-1250/2004–5 from December 13, 2007. Available here: https://odluke.sudovi.hr/Document/View?id=67fd80ac-e15e-428d-830d-bbbcd06f1fd3&q=proboj+pravne+osobnosti. Accessed August 20, 2025.

[68] General Tax Act (Official Gazette Nos. br. 115/16., 106/18., 121/19., 32/20., 42/20., 114/22, 114/24 and 151/25).

of the company to fulfill its tax obligations, will be held personally liable for tax obligations of the company. This was confirmed in a decision by the Administrative Court in Zagreb[69]. The court looked at a Decision by the tax authority brought against the director and sole shareholder of a company, in which the tax authority confirmed that the shareholder made cash payments from the company's cash register, although daily revenues from business operations should have been deposited into the company's account. This resulted in the inability of the company to fulfill its tax obligations, which meets the requirements for holding the shareholder liable for abuse of rights under the GAT CRO.

5.2.1.2 Immorality—Prohibition of Abuse of Rights

A very important element of the definition on piercing the corporate veil in Croatian law is the abuse of rights. A fundamental principle stipulated in the ZOO CRO, is the prohibition of abuse of rights, which states that "exercising rights arising from an obligation is prohibited if it is contrary to the purpose for which that right was established or recognized by law."[70] This means that liability arises from an objective violation of another's interests. Another relevant article relates to the principle of good faith, and it stipulates that: "In establishing contractual relations and in exercising the rights and obligations arising from such relations, the parties are obliged to adhere to the principle of good faith and fair dealing."[71] When defining the principle of good faith and fair dealing, the German term *Treu und Glauben* was used as a model.[72] In Croatian company law, one of the fundamental duties of members is the duty of loyal conduct. This obligation represents a concretization of the principle of trust, which derives from the broader principle of good faith and fair dealing. The principle of trust is not merely theoretical; its application may lead to the annulment of shareholders' assembly decisions, lawsuits against members, liability of shareholders.[73] Both principles, the principle of prohibition of abuse of law, and the principle of good faith, are similar to the element of immorality as defined in Article 826 BGB, since it relates to good morals and decency shared by all fair and just individuals. The difference is the implementation of those principles in Croatia and Germany. In Germany

[69] Administrative Court in Zagreb (2021). Decision available here: https://odluke.sudovi.hr/Document/View?id=2cfd5ad7-1433-4ba0-9128-19829e6c19da&q=proboj+pravne+osobnosti. Accessed August 20, 2025.

[70] Art. 6, ZOO CRO.

[71] Art. 4, ZOO CRO.

[72] Osrečak, (2014), p. 53.

[73] Barbić (2009), p. 40.

courts see this as a defining element of the piercing the corporate veil doctrine. Without it, there is no piercing. In Croatia, on the other hand, courts mention that principle only to identify whether abuse of limited liability occurred, without going into the specifics of the principles themselves. Another relevant principle enshrined in the ZOO CRO in Article 12, stipulates that in contractual relationships between parties, customary rules and business practices shall apply. In a ruling by the Supreme Court of the Republic of Croatia[74], the court stated that the essence of abuse as stipulated in Article 10(3) ZTD lies in the shareholder using their influence in the company, particularly through its management, to pursue certain goals. Such abuse occurs when the shareholder's influence leads to the company's assets being managed contrary to law or business customs[75], thereby placing some or all creditors in a disadvantaged position.

5.2.1.3 Intent to Cause Harm

The definition for piercing the corporate veil in Croatia regulates the liability of company members for the company's obligations, not liability for damages. Therefore, liability for damages and the fault of a company member are not relevant. The plaintiff (creditor) must prove that the shareholder abused his limited liability, by proving abuse. In cases listed in paragraph 4 of Article 10 the shareholder's fault is presumed and the burden of proof that no fault exists rests with the shareholder.[76] In a case on veil piercing[77], the courts emphasized that shareholder liability for abuse of limited liability is not based on fault (*krivnja*) or damage liability but on the principle of abuse of rights based on Article 6, of the Law on Obligations (ZOO CRO). Because liability arises from an objective violation of another's interests, intent or negligence is not relevant. In such cases, the creditor does not claim damages but can demand performance of the company's obligation directly from the shareholder who abused limited liability. Importantly, it is not necessary to prove that the company itself is unable to fulfil its obligation; the creditor may seek fulfilment simultaneously from both the company and

[74] Supreme Court of the Republic of Croatia (2012). Decision Nr. Revt-159/2011–2, from January 25, 2012. Available here: https://odluke.sudovi.hr/Document/View?id=2d0eb1e3-efbe-4172-b7e3-d00249a9862b&q=proboj+pravne+osobnosti. Accessed August 20, 2025.

[75] Art. 12 ZOO CRO.

[76] As stipulated in a decision by the High Commercial Court of the Republic of Croatia (2003b): Pž-1522/03, available https://www.iusinfo.hr/sudska-praksa/SE500B1522S03D20030923?HighlightQuery=proboj+pravne+osobnosti. Accessed August 18, 2025.

[77] High Commercial Court of the Republic of Croatia (2021). Decision Pž 1820/2020–3. Available here: https://odluke.sudovi.hr/decisionView?id=090216ba80c82c12&q=67+Pž-1820%2F2020-3. Accessed August 18, 2025.

the shareholder. As a result, the statute of limitations that applies to the company also applies to the shareholder. In this case, the relevant limitation period is 10 years under Article 233(1) ZOO CRO, making the creditor's claim against both the company and the shareholder valid.

5.2.2 Joint and Several Liability of Shareholders in the LLC

Besides Article 10 of the ZTD that provides for circumstances in which shareholders are personally liable for the company's obligations, the law provides for situations in which the shareholders have exclusive jurisdiction. This is particularly important for Croatia because the reasons for piercing the corporate veil are less restrictive than in Germany, creating more opportunity for shareholder liability. Since intent is irrelevant, it may happen that a shareholder accidentally bears the burden of personal liability due to unfortunate circumstances. Article 441 ZTD sets out the powers of the shareholders' meeting in a limited liability company. While the articles of association can expand or restrict the shareholders' meeting's jurisdiction, certain powers are mandatory and cannot be excluded:

1. Approval of financial statements and discharge of management (Art. 441(1.1)),
2. Return of additional capital contributions (Art. 441(2.a)),
3. Election/dismissal of supervisory board members (Art. 441(4)),
4. Assertion of company damage claims against management/supervisory board members and appointment of litigation representatives (Art. 441(9)),
5. Approval of high-value contracts exceeding one-fifth of share capital (Art. 441(10)), when concluded within two years of registration.

Similarly to Germany, on shareholders request, managers must provide financial information of the company and access to company records (Art. 447 ZTD)

According to Article 442, shareholders holding together at least 10% of the share capital may request the convening of the shareholders' meeting. This threshold can be lowered through the Articles of Association granting the right to members with less than 10%.[78]

In 2019, the ZTD was amended, with Article 290(2) creating additional obligations towards shareholders. Shareholders who have not paid the full amount of

[78] Art. 442 point 3 ZTD.

cash contributions were obliged to fulfill this obligation one year from the registration of the limited liability company. Shareholders who have not paid the full amount of cash contributions were jointly and severally liable for all company obligations up to the amount of all unpaid cash contributions. This provision was deleted in new changes of the ZTD in 2022.

Similarly to the German Article 6 point 5 GmbHG, the ZTD through Article 423 foresees joint and several liability of shareholders who deliberately or through gross negligence appoint a person who is not eligible to hold a position of a member of the management board. Those shareholders are jointly and severally liable to the company for all damage caused by that person's breach of obligations towards the company. The general assembly can directly influence the management board's business decisions, and the management board is obliged to act in accordance with the instructions of the assembly. This is an important article since it legally connects responsibilities of the management to the shareholders. Article 62a ZTD prohibits persons with outstanding debts from public levies or obligations toward employees from founding companies or from being appointed as management board members or executive directors. The aim of this provision is to prevent repeated company formation by individuals who already have unsettled debts to the state or workers, thereby strengthening corporate accountability and creditor protection. Article 62a ZTD is also an additional explanation of what is considered an ineligible manager as stipulated in Article 423 ZTD.

There are provisions related to bankruptcy proceedings[79] and company incorporation[80] that foresee joint and several liability of shareholders, which are not relevant for this dissertation.

Creditor protection in Croatian company law is primarily framed through a series of statutory remedies, which often remain limited in scope when compared to the doctrine of piercing the corporate veil. Article 273 ZTD provides creditor protection through liability for damages based on abuse of influence within the company, particularly in cases of unlawful interference with company assets. However, this protection is conditional, creditors may only bring claims if they cannot recover from the company itself, making this a derivative claim rooted

---

[79] Article 404 ZTD, if the company enters bankruptcy proceedings, shareholders are jointly and severally liable for payment of unpaid capital contributions, should such payments be necessary to settle the company's creditors.

[80] Article 6, ZTD, obligations and rights arising before a company's registration in the court register fall directly on the founders. Any rights are considered their joint undivided property, while obligations create joint and unlimited liability. If multiple founders or representatives assume obligations, they bear joint and several liability with all their personal assets.

in the company's right to damages rather than a direct action, as is the case in veil-piercing.

Additional safeguards include capital maintenance provisions, such as Article 217 and 408 ZTD (prohibiting repayment of contributions and disguised capital replacement loans) and Article 407 ZTD (prohibiting unlawful distributions to shareholders). These measures are designed to protect only part of the company's assets (i.e., to ensure that equity is preserved), but they do not protect against secondary harms, such as insolvency losses. Similarly, Article 224(2) ZTD allows creditors indirectly to enforce claims against shareholders by targeting unlawful distributions received by them.

Finally, creditor protection is reinforced through insolvency law, particularly the duty of management to file for insolvency within 21 days of over-indebtedness or insolvency. This mechanism primarily protects new creditors, who would otherwise be misled into contracting with a company that can no longer meet its obligations.

5.2.3 Criminal Shareholder Liability in Croatia

Besides chapters within the Criminal Code[81], Croatia regulates criminal liability of legal persons by a *lex specialis*, the Act on the Liability of Legal Persons for Criminal Offences[82] (ALLPC).[83] The liability of the legal entity is derived from the liability of the responsible person within the company. The "responsible person" is defined as a natural person who manages the affairs of the legal entity or is entrusted, at any level, with tasks within its scope of activity.[84] For the criminal offence to take place, the responsible person must have violated its duty of care, and the legal person must have obtained or was intended to obtain unlawful material gain for itself or another. An interesting case was brought before the High

[81] Article 246—265 of the Criminal Code of the Republic of Croatia (Official Gazette Nos. 125/2011, 144/2012, 56/2015, 61/2015, 101/2017, 118/2018, 126/2019, 84/2021, 114/2022, 114/2023, 36/2024), available here: https://www.zakon.hr/z/98/kazneni-zakon. Accessed August 30, 2025.

[82] The Act on the Liability of Legal Persons for Criminal Offences (Official Gazette Nos. 151/2003, 110/2007, 45/2011, 143/2012, 114/2022, 114/2023). Available here: https://www.zakon.hr/z/110/zakon-o-odgovornosti-pravnih-osoba-za-kaznena-djela. Accessed August 30, 2025.

[83] Gotovuša (2020), p. 172.

[84] Art. 4, ALLPC.

Commercial Court of the Republic of Croatia[85] in which the shareholder was convicted for bankruptcy abuse[86] and abuse of authority[87], with the conviction confirmed by the Supreme Court of Croatia. Following the criminal proceedings, the plaintiff (creditor) initiated a civil lawsuit, arguing that the shareholder had abused the corporate form by deliberately diminishing the company's assets, failing to collect receivables, selling assets at below market value, and appropriating company property for personal gain. The plaintiff sought damages amounting to EUR 38,807, representing unpaid invoices owed by the shareholder's company. The civil court held that piercing the corporate veil was justified, as the underlying abuse of limited liability had already been established in the criminal proceedings. Similarly, the County Court in Pula-Pola[88] stressed that the conviction for a criminal offence committed by the responsible person of the company in connection with the damage caused to that company, for instance through the payment of an obligation under the civil claim, may indicate a breach of the duty of a diligent and conscientious businessman. Criminal convictions often establish factual predicates (e.g., asset stripping) that civil courts may rely on, but civil courts still must fit the facts into Art. 10(3) to (4) ZTD.

These cases illustrate a relatively straightforward pathway to veil piercing in Croatia, where a shareholder has been criminally convicted of a commercial offense linked to corporate abuse, and civil courts are inclined to recognize the abuse without requiring creditors to reestablish the factual basis. In such circumstances, creditors gain direct access to the shareholder's personal assets to satisfy claims against the bankrupt or deregistered company.

---

[85] High Commercial Court of the Republic of Croatia (2013). Decision No. Pž-4386/2012–3, from January 23, 2013. Available here: https://odluke.sudovi.hr/Document/View?id=bbb87da7-ea3b-4b06-b2ce-19018b4ca78d&q=proboj+pravne+osobnosti. Accessed August 30, 2025.

[86] Art. 282 Criminal Code.

[87] Art. 337 Criminal Code.

[88] County Court in Pula-Pola (2025), point 9. Decision Kž-400/2024–7. Available here: https://odluke.sudovi.hr/Document/View?id=c979f8dd-9f74-4d65-bdfc-f3cd965fa566&q=Kž-400%2f2024-7. Accessed August 31, 2025.

5.2.4 The Controlling Shareholder

In a ruling by the Supreme Court of the Republic of Croatia[89], the court stated that the essence of abuse as stipulated in Article 10(3) ZTD lies in the shareholder using their influence in the company, particularly through its management, to pursue certain goals. Such abuse occurs when the shareholder's influence leads to the company's assets being managed contrary to law or business customs[90], thereby placing some or all creditors in a disadvantaged position. The Act on the Prevention of Money Laundering and Terrorist Financing[91] (CRO AML Law) defines the beneficial owner as "the ultimate owner of the legal entity, or controls the legal entity, or otherwise manages it, and/or any natural person(s) on whose behalf a transaction is carried out, including those natural person(s) who ultimately exercise effective control over a legal person or legal arrangement".[92] Croatia directly transposed the EU definition of the beneficial owner. Article 28 of the CRO AML Law further defines the beneficial owner as any natural person who ultimately owns, controls, or manages a legal entity, or on whose behalf a transaction is conducted. The law applies a 25% plus one share threshold for both direct and indirect ownership, while also recognizing control through other means, such as shareholder agreements or dominant influence. If, after due diligence, no such person can be identified, the law presumes that a member of the management board or equivalent body is the beneficial owner. This approach is significant as it provides a statutory threshold for determining control within a legal entity. By contrast, under the ZTD, shareholders collectively holding at least 10% of the share capital acquire specific procedural rights, such as convening the shareholders' meeting, but also bear certain responsibilities. This was underscored in Lekić v. Slovenia, where the ECtHR confirmed that a 10% threshold was sufficient to establish shareholder influence and corresponding responsibility.[93] Taken together, these divergences raise the broader normative question of

---

[89] Supreme Court of the Republic of Croatia (2012). Decision Nr. Revt-159/2011–2, from January 25, 2012. Available here: https://odluke.sudovi.hr/Document/View?id=2d0eb1e3-efbe-4172-b7e3-d00249a9862b&q=proboj+pravne+osobnosti. Accessed August 20, 2025.

[90] Art. 12 ZOO CRO.

[91] Act on the Prevention of Money Laundering and Terrorist Financing. Official Gazette Nos. 108/2017, 39/2019, 151/2022.

[92] Art. 4 CRO AML Law.

[93] Lekić v. Slovenia (Application No. 36480/07, Judgment of 11 December 2018). Available here: https://hudoc.echr.coe.int/eng#{%22appno%22:[%2236480/07%22],%22itemid%22:[%22001-188268%22]}.

whether the AML framework and company law provisions should be harmonized. If the underlying objective across AML, criminal law, and company law as *lex specialis* is to identify the true beneficial owner in order to allocate both rights and obligations, then the thresholds and criteria applied by these regimes should be aligned to ensure consistency, predictability, and fairness in attributing responsibility within legal entities.

5.2.5 Discussion

In Croatian limited liability companies, the management board formally runs the company, but the shareholders retain strong influence through instructions, approval rights, and general assembly decisions. The system emphasizes flexibility and shareholder control, with management remaining bound by loyalty, statutory duties, and accountability to the company. The Croatian approach to piercing the corporate veil reflects a codified, shareholder-focused doctrine, situated primarily within Article 10(3) and (4) of the ZTD. Unlike the German model, which grounds liability in general tort law[94] and requires proof of intent and immorality, Croatian law opts for a more objective regime of responsibility. The essence of Croatian doctrine is the abuse of limited liability, which is defined in statutory form and elaborated through extensive case law. Courts have recognized abuse in scenarios including the comingling of assets, deliberate harm to creditors, systematic undercapitalization, and tax abuses. Importantly, Croatian courts have consistently emphasized that mere insolvency or inability to pay debts does not justify piercing; the plaintiff must prove specific acts that constitute abuse as enumerated in Article 10(4) ZTD.

The Croatian judiciary has also relied heavily on the principle of abuse of rights[95] and the principle of good faith and fair dealing[96] as normative backstops, underscoring the civil law orientation of the doctrine. In practice, this means that liability is not fault-based but arises from an objective violation of creditor interests, which reduces the evidentiary burden compared to Germany. At the same time, however, the burden of proof still lies with the creditor, and vague allegations are insufficient, as courts require concrete evidence of abuse.

---

[94] Art. 826 BGB.

[95] Art. 6 ZOO CRO.

[96] Art. 4 ZOO CRO.

Another distinct feature of the Croatian framework is its interlinkage with other legal regimes. The General Tax Act[97] replicates the veil-piercing provisions of the ZTD, empowering tax authorities to pierce directly and impose liability on shareholders in cases of tax abuse. Similarly, criminal convictions for economic offences often function as gateways to civil piercing, with courts more readily attributing liability once corporate abuse has been judicially established in criminal proceedings. The parallel definitions of "beneficial ownership" in the AML legislation (25% threshold) and procedural rights in company law (10% threshold) further illustrate that Croatian law seeks to identify responsible persons across multiple legal contexts, although the lack of harmonization in thresholds raises normative questions.

Taken together, the Croatian regime offers a comparatively broader and more flexible pathway to piercing than the German model, but its focus remains confined to shareholders, excluding other actors such as managers or third parties. For dissertation purposes, this reveals both the strengths and limitations of the Croatian approach: it provides predictability by codifying grounds for piercing, but risks rigidity by not allowing courts to develop broader categories of abuse. The Croatian model thus highlights the tension between creditor protection and legal certainty, which is relevant for the potential reform of the veil-piercing doctrine in Bosnia and Herzegovina.

5.3 Lessons Learned from Germany and Croatia

The private limited company is envisaged as a member-dominated form in both Croatia and Germany, but power allocation varies in ways that influence shareholder liability. Croatian law allows for extensive contractual flexibility; the articles of association can divide administrative powers between directors and the shareholders' assembly, allowing members to participate directly in strategic decisions. In contrast, German law incorporates shareholder primacy into the statutory structure of the GmbHG, allowing shareholders to not only appoint and dismiss directors but also issue binding instructions to management[98] and enjoy comprehensive information rights[99].

[97] Art. 30 GTA CRO.

[98] Art. 37 GmbHG.

[99] Art. 51a GmbHG.

This legally established control system has significant consequences for veil-piercing arguments. If shareholders have the authority to direct and oversee management at their own discretion, their claim to limited liability protection is weakened when such influence is used abusively. In Germany, shareholders cannot claim to be passive investors because they have structural control. Nonetheless, German courts have preferred to confront shareholder wrongdoing through established remedies like capital maintenance or director accountability, rather than systematic veil-piercing. Croatia, on the other hand, has a more flexible contractual structure that blurs the line between ownership and management, potentially making it harder to trace wrongdoing to shareholders who actively interfere. Thus, while both systems maintain the principle of limited liability, the statutory subordination of directors in Germany provides a stronger doctrinal link between shareholder control and potential liability, even though courts remain reluctant to pierce the veil.

When comparing liability standards, Croatian law, through Article 10 ZTD combined with Article 6 ZOO CRO, adopts an objective abuse of rights model. Once abuse is shown, the shareholder is personally liable for company obligations irrespective of fault or intent. Creditors can demand performance directly from both the company and the shareholder, without proving insolvency. Since Trihotel, in Germany, creditors must prove intentional, immoral harm. Negligence or regulatory breaches are insufficient. The result is that Croatia tilts strongly toward creditor protection, while in Germany separate legal personality is prioritized by setting a high evidentiary threshold.

Both the Croatian ZTD and the German GmbHG place the shareholders' meeting at the core of decision-making in limited liability companies, while granting wide freedom of contractual structuring through the articles of association. Yet, each system also prescribes non-transferable competences. Both regimes underline that shareholders retain non-transferable powers such as approval of accounts, appointment/removal of managers, enforcement of company claims, which courts can use as anchors to assess responsibility. Croatia adds capital-protective competences for example, approval of high-value contracts, return of contributions, while Germany emphasizes structural matters such as dissolution. These competences matter for veil piercing as they confirm that shareholders are not mere capital providers but remain the ultimate center of control.

In both Croatia and Germany, members of a limited liability company enjoy statutory rights to request the convening of a shareholders' meeting once they hold at least 10% of the share capital. While this establishes an important minority protection mechanism in both systems, a key distinction lies in the degree of flexibility. Under the Croatian Companies Act[100], the articles of association may lower this threshold, thereby extending the right to even smaller shareholders, whereas in Germany the GmbHG (Art. 50) fixes the 10% requirement as mandatory. This difference reflects Croatia's more flexible approach to minority protection within the LLC, in contrast to Germany's stricter emphasis on legal certainty and uniformity in the GmbH framework.

A key difference between Croatia and Germany in the application of piercing the corporate veil lies in the scope of potential liable parties. In Croatia, the doctrine is narrowly tied to the position of shareholders as members of the company: only those who misuse the privilege of limited liability under Article 10(3) of the ZTD can be held personally liable. The Croatian approach therefore conceptualizes piercing as an exception to the shareholder's statutory shield, grounded in abuse of rights and limited to the shareholder-company relationship. By contrast, in Germany, veil-piercing under Article 826 BGB (intentional immoral harm) is not limited to formal shareholders. Liability can extend to any individual who participates in conduct that deliberately destroys the company's existence or defrauds creditors. This was illustrated, for example, in case law where even a financial advisor was held personally liable for knowingly supporting a Ponzi scheme, despite not being a shareholder.[101] The German doctrine thus focuses less on formal membership status and more on the substantive role and culpability of the actor in causing the harm. The consequence of this divergence is that Croatia adopts a formalistic, membership-based veil-piercing model, while Germany adopts a functional, conduct-based model that allows creditors a broader reach against wrongdoers, even beyond the shareholder circle.

In both cases, however, the 25% share threshold as emphasized in the AML Directive (similarly defined in Croatia as well as Germany) would be relevant to both jurisdictions. The beneficial owner of the legal entity is ultimately the natural person who owns or controls it and whose transaction is ultimately carried out, or a business relationship is ultimately established. This includes any person who holds more than 25% of the voting rights or exercises control in a comparable manner."[102]

[100] ZTD, Art. 442(3).

[101] BGH (2025a), point 11.

[102] Art. 10(1)2, 3(1), 1(3), GwG.

This creates misalignment because the same legal systems treat a 10% shareholder as influential enough to trigger procedural rights (and, in Lekić v. Slovenia, ECtHR-recognized responsibilities), but a 25% threshold to identify "control" for AML. Piercing the veil, by contrast, is threshold-free. A harmonized approach could introduce rebuttable presumptions, e.g., influence above 25% or 10%, to improve predictability while preserving judicial discretion to sanction abuse below these markers.

Shareholder Liability in Bosnia and Herzegovina 6

The General Framework Agreement for Peace in Bosnia and Herzegovina ended the war between Bosnia and Herzegovina (BiH), the Republic of Croatia and the Federal Republic of Yugoslavia.[1] Annex 4 of this Agreement represents the Constitution for BiH which states that BiH shall consist of the two Entities, the Federation of Bosnia and Herzegovina (FBiH) and the Republika Srpska (RS) (the Entities). BiH's constitutional system is classified as a "mild" asymmetric federal-type system.[2] The Constitution of BiH[3] stipulates that the Entities have the right to establish special parallel relationships with neighboring states consistent with the sovereignty and territorial integrity of BiH.[4] They are units within BiH in which RS has a centralized government system, and FBiH a federal system consisting of 10 Cantons. With BD as separate unit, BiH accounts to 14 governments and parliaments.[5] The company law framework is governed by entity and BD legislation and enshrined in Article 5 (Liability for Obligations),

---

[1] General Framework Agreement for Peace in Bosnia and Herzegovina, 14 December 1995, 35 I.L.M. 75 (1996). Available here: https://www.ohr.int/dayton-peace-agreement/. Accessed November 26, 2025.

[2] Sahadžić & Woelk (2023), p. 131.

[3] Annex IV to the Dayton Peace Agreement.

[4] Constitution of Bosnia and Herzegovina (Annex 4 to the General Framework Agreement for Peace in Bosnia and Herzegovina). Office of the High Representative (OHR). Retrieved from https://www.ohr.int/dayton-peace-agreement/annex-4/. Accessed November 26, 2025.

[5] Banović, Gavrić & Mariño (2021), p. Preface (v).

L. Hasanovic, *Piercing the Corporate Veil: Shareholder Liability*,
Juridicum – Schriftenreihe zum Wirtschafts-, Unternehmens- und Bankrecht / Series on Business, Corporate and Banking Law,
https://doi.org/10.1007/978-3-658-52987-1_6

of Company Law of FBiH[6] (ZPDBiH), Article of 15 (Abuse of Business Entity) Company Law RS[7] (ZPDRS), and Article 7 of the Law on Companies of Brčko District BiH[8] (ZPDBD). Even though similarities among the laws are evident, all three laws differ in their definition of piercing the corporate veil. The doctrine of piercing the corporate veil was first introduced in the Law on Companies of the SFRY, where it applied exclusively to sole shareholders.[9] In the subsequent adoption of entity-level legislation in BiH, the scope of the doctrine was expanded. In RS, for example, Article 54 of the Law on Enterprises extended the application of veil piercing to company managers in addition to shareholders.[10] This legislative development is of particular significance, as it has contributed to one of the most persistent confusions in contemporary judicial practice in BiH: courts frequently conflate shareholder liability under veil piercing with director liability. Directors are not encompassed within the statutory definition of veil piercing; their liability arises under a distinct framework, namely the duty of care and related fiduciary duties. In the FBiH, the Law on Companies[11] was enacted in 1999, its Article 6 (now Article 5) stayed unchanged. Therefore, the FBiH still has the same definition of piercing the corporate veil as in 1999, focusing on shareholder abuse within the company, as elaborated under 6.1.1.

[6] Company Law of the Federation of Bosnia and Herzegovina (Official Gazette FBiH, No. 81/15 and 75/2021).

[7] Company Law of Republika Srpska (Official Gazette of RS, nos. 127/2008, 58/2009, 100/2011, 67/2013, 100/2017, 82/2019, 17/2023 and 45/2025).

[8] Law on Companies of the Brčko District of Bosnia and Herzegovina—Consolidated Text (Official Gazette of the Brčko District of Bosnia and Herzegovina, No. 49/11 and 01–02-815/20). Article 140a states that: If the sole shareholder of a joint-stock company, the sole member of a limited liability company, or the sole owner of a private enterprise, through his actions or by mixing his own assets with those of the enterprise, creates for others the appearance of an economic identity with the enterprise, he shall be liable to the creditors for the obligations of the enterprise with unlimited joint and several liability.

[9] Law on Enterprises (SFRY, "Official Gazette of the SFRY" Nos. 77/88, 40/89, 46/90, 61/90; "Official Gazette of the FRY" No. 24/94).

[10] Law on Enterprises, Official Gazette of the Republic of Srpska, Nos. 24/1998, 62/2002, 66/2002, 38/2003, 97/2004, 34/2006. Available here: https://www.vladars.net/sr-SP-Cyrl/Vlada/Ministarstva/mf/Documents/Zakon%20o%20preduzecima.pdf. Accessed September 19, 2025.

[11] Law on Companies (Official Gazette of the Federation of BiH, Nos. 23/99, 45/00, 2/02, 6/02, 29/03, 68/05, 91/07, 88/08 and 63/10). Available here: https://www.pufbih.ba/v1/public/upload/zakoni/88372-zakon-23_99.pdf. Accessed September 19, 2025.

6.1 Scope and Definition of the Doctrine

6.1.1 Piercing of the Corporate Veil in FBiH

Article 5 of ZPDFBiH focuses on limited liability and emphasizes that a limited partner in a limited partnership, a shareholder in a joint-stock company, and a member of a limited liability company is not liable for the company's obligations, except in certain cases stipulated by law. The ZPDFBiH provides for specific statutory grounds for shareholder liability beyond limited liability when:

a) the shareholder uses the company to pursue a personal goal that is not consistent with the goals of the other members and the company as a whole;
b) the shareholder manages the company's assets as if they were his/her own assets;
c) the shareholder uses the company to commit fraud or to harm his/her creditors;
d) the shareholder influences the reduction of the company's assets for his/her own benefit or for the benefit of third parties or causes the company to assume obligations although he/she knew or ought to have known that the company would not be able to fulfil them.[12]

The ZPDFBiH codifies veil piercing through enumerated abuse scenarios, providing specific reasons for veil piercing and several liability of shareholders, such as fraud, misuse of assets, harm to creditors and undercapitalization. This is emphasized in a decision brought by the Supreme Court of the Federation of BiH[13] in which the Court underlined that piercing the corporate veil is possible only if the following cumulative requirements of Article 5(2) were: (i) abuse of the company for unlawful or fraudulent purposes, (ii) disposal of company assets as if they were personal assets, (iii) financial gain of the responsible person (shareholder), (iv) detrimental consequences for the creditor, and (v) a causal link between the abusive conduct and the impossibility of satisfying the creditor's claim. The Court emphasized that veil-piercing functions as a sanction against shareholders who abuse the legal personality of the company by using it for unlawful or fraudulent purposes, disposing of company assets as if they were their own, or reducing corporate assets to the detriment of creditors. Compared to the Croatian

[12] Art. 5(2), ZPDFBiH.

[13] Supreme Court of the Federation of BIH (2019), p. 4. Judgment No. 51 0 Ps 108754 18 Rev, of March 7, 2019. This judgment is not available online. It was made available in hard copy by a Supreme court judge for the purposes of writing this dissertation.

ZTD that has a general piercing clause (*zloupotreba prava*), the ZPDFBiH lists the situations the courts need to assess when piercing the corporate veil. BiH and Croatia both use an objective standard, contrary to Germany where the subjective element (intent to cause harm), needs to be proven by the creditor. In FBiH, liability arises once abuse of limited liability is shown. One of the central difficulties in the jurisprudence of BiH is the lack of conceptual clarity between shareholder liability, through piercing the corporate veil, and director liability, based on the duty of care.

This confusion is well illustrated in a decision of the Supreme Court of the Federation of Bosnia and Herzegovina[14]. The case concerned a short-term credit agreement concluded in 2000 by a limited liability company through its director. The plaintiff, acting as guarantor, later sought repayment both from the company and from its director. The Municipal Court in Sarajevo and Cantonal court in Sarajevo[15] upheld the claim not only against the company but also against the director, invoking the piercing the corporate veil article in the ZPDFBiH, which allows veil piercing when a shareholder uses the company to defraud or harm creditors. The Supreme Court emphasized that this reasoning was flawed. The fact that the defendant acted as director of the LLC did not automatically establish that he was also a shareholder. That there is confusion about Article 5 of the ZODFBIH in terms of who is personally liable within a company, proves the request of the Cantonal Court in Tuzla (Judge Predrag Krsmanović) for a review of the constitutionality of the Law on the Tax Administration of the Federation of BiH (LTAFBiH)[16]. The Cantonal Court in Tuzla requested constitutional review of Articles 29 and 30 of the Law on the Tax Administration of FBiH. These articles make directors or other responsible persons jointly and severally liable for unpaid tax debts of companies, under certain conditions. In its decision, the Constitutional Court of BiH[17] emphasized that there should be a clear doctrinal distinction between the institute of veil piercing under Article 5 ZPDFBiH which is confined *ratione personae* to company owners and founders in cases

[14] Supreme Court of the Federation of Bosnia and Herzegovina (2012). Decision no. 65 0 P 195188 11 Rev from 12 July 2012, retrieved from https://sudskapraksa.pravosudje.ba/case-law-documents/1807/details. Accessed September 15, 2025.

[15] Both decisions have the same case number as the Supreme Court of the Federation of Bosnia and Herzegovina (2012). Decision no. 65 0 P 195188 11.

[16] Law on the Tax Administration of the Federation of Bosnia and Herzegovina ('Official Gazette of the Federation of Bosnia and Herzegovina' nos. 33/02, 28/04, 57/09, 40/10, 29/11—Constitutional Court decision, 27/12, 7/13, 71/14, 91/15 and 44/22).

[17] Constitutional Court of Bosnia and Herzegovina. (2023). Decision on admissibility and merits in case no. U-2/23. Sarajevo: Constitutional Court of BiH.

of abuse of corporate personality, whereas the regime of solidarity under the Tax Law operates within a different normative framework, extending liability to directors and other persons authorized to manage the company's finances for the purpose of securing tax collection. The foregoing analysis reveals a persistent conceptual ambiguity in the jurisprudence of BiH concerning the differentiation between shareholder liability and director liability. Veil piercing under Article 5 ZPDFBiH is a shareholder-focused instrument, intended to sanction the abuse of corporate personality by those who benefit from limited liability. By contrast, the liability of directors arises from a distinct normative regime rooted in their managerial duties and fiduciary obligations. Only in situations where a director simultaneously holds the position of shareholder can the two spheres intersect.

6.1.2 Piercing the Corporate Veil in RS

Article 15 of ZPDRS, stipulates that limited partners in a limited partnership, members of a limited liability company, and shareholders in a joint-stock company may be personally liable towards third parties for obligations of the company if they abuse the company for unlawful or fraudulent purposes, or if they dispose of the company's assets as if they were their own, as if the company as a legal person did not exist. The ZPDRS further stipulates that it is upon the court to consider all circumstances related to the abuse of the company, particularly the fact that limited liability will not be taken into consideration.

Therefore, two overarching reasons for piercing prevail in the ZPDRS:

1. abuse of company for unlawful and fraudulent purposes
2. commingling of assets.

The ZPDRS uses a more general clause with the wording "unlawful or fraudulent purposes," and leaves broad discretion to courts to assess whether abuse occurred, mentioning only fraud and unlawfulness, and commingling of assets as examples of abuse of the company, giving judges open-ended authority to disregard limited liability.

In a landmark decision, the Supreme Court of RS[18] clarified the application of Article 15 of the ZPDRS. The case concerned a municipality as the founder

[18] Supreme Court of RS (2019). Decision number 60 0 Ps 024805 19 Rev, from 2 October 2019. Available here: https://sudskapraksa.pravosudje.ba/case-law-documents/886/details. Accessed September 15, 2025.

of a public company, which had transferred immovable assets into the company's share capital but later attempted to withdraw and dispose of the same assets as if they were its own. The Court held that such conduct, disposing of company property as personal property, meets the statutory criteria of Article 15(1) ZPDRS, which establishes shareholder liability either when a company is misused for unlawful or fraudulent purposes, or when its assets are treated as personal property, effectively disregarding the company's separate legal personality. Importantly, the Court emphasized that these conditions are set alternatively rather than cumulatively, thereby lowering the threshold for establishing shareholder liability.[19]

The jurisprudence of courts in RS, much like that of their counterparts in the Federation of FBiH, demonstrates persistent uncertainty in the application of the doctrine of piercing the corporate veil. However, in RS, this can be explained by the fact that the previous law on companies, included managers in the definition of veil piercing. In a recent case concerning the recovery of approximately 3.8 million KM in unpaid debts, the Supreme Court of Republika Srpska[20] overruled the second-instance court because the appellate judges had wrongly extended liability under Article 15 of the ZPDRS to a defendant who was not a shareholder of the company. The dispute arose after the debtor company, K. LLC D. (later S. LLC D.), was liquidated and deleted from the commercial register, leaving the plaintiff unable to collect on enforceable judgments. The plaintiff alleged that the defendants had abused the company by transferring employees, assets, and business operations to a related company (K.P. LLC). While the Higher Commercial Court in Banja Luka (second instance) held that both defendants were personally liable under Article 15 ZPDRS, the Supreme Court clarified that veil piercing applies only to members or shareholders of the company. It confirmed liability for the first defendant, who was the sole shareholder and who authorized the transfer of business operations, but dismissed the claim against the second defendant, who, despite being connected through contracts and related-party transactions, was never a shareholder of the company. A similar inconsistency in the application of veil piercing can be observed in a recent judgment of the Supreme Court of the Republic of Srpska[21]. In this case, the first-instance court correctly

[19] Pušac (2024), p. 100.

[20] Supreme Court of Republika Srpska (2024). Decision No. 60 0 Ps 030404 23 Rev, from 15 February 2024. Available here: https://sudskapraksa.pravosudje.ba/case-law-documents/6495/details. Accessed September 17, 2025.

[21] Supreme Court of the Republic of Srpska (2024a). Judgment No. 80 0 P 099848 23 Rev. Available here: https://sudskapraksa.pravosudje.ba/case-law-documents/6703/details. Accessed January 28, 2026.

recognized that the shareholder's conduct, founding a new company at the same address, transferring employees and core assets, and extracting dividends while aware of pending creditor claims, constituted misuse of the corporate form under Article 15 ZPD. The appellate court, however, reversed the decision, reasoning that these actions were not expressly prohibited by law. Upon revision, the Supreme Court reinstated and expanded the liability of the shareholder, emphasizing that veil piercing operates as a corrective mechanism when the corporate form is used to evade legal obligations and harm creditors. The Court underscored that the decisive factor is not the formal legality of individual transactions, but their economic purpose and effect, particularly where corporate restructuring and dividend distribution render the company unable to satisfy existing or foreseeable claims. This decision therefore highlights both the corrective potential of Article 15 ZPD and the ongoing doctrinal uncertainty in its interpretation across judicial instances.

6.1.3 Piercing the Corporate Veil in BD

Article 7 of the ZPDBD, similarly to ZPDFBiH, emphasizes that a shareholder in a joint-stock company, a member of a limited liability company, and a limited partner in a limited partnership is liable for the company's obligations only up to the value of his/her contribution to the company's capital. However, limited liability is disregarded when:

1. they represent the company before it has been registered;
2. if they use the company to pursue personal goals that are not consistent with the goals of the company and the other owners as a whole;
3. if they manage the company's business or assets as if they were their own;
4. if they use the company to defraud company's creditors;
5. if they cause or influence the squandering or dissipation of the company's assets for their own benefit or for the benefit of third parties, or if they cause or influence the company to incur obligations even though they knew or ought to have known that the company would not be able to settle such obligations.

Similarly to ZPDFBiH the ZPDBD lists specific cases such as fraud, comingling of assets, pursuit of personal goals, undercapitalization, however, it includes the pre-incorporation phase as reason for veil piercing. This could be seen as questionable itself since the legal entity has no legal personality before incorporation within the court register.[22] This itself shows a limited understanding of the legislator for the doctrine, which is an even bigger issue than the interpretation of the provision by courts. It is therefore not surprising that in the limited number of judgments on piercing the corporate veil, courts do not always understand how the provision could be applied to a concrete case. For example, in a case brought before the Appellate court of BD[23], the first-instance court attempted to characterize piercing the corporate veil through the lens of contract law instead of corporate law. The first-instance court, after establishing that the defendant instrumentalized the company Bosnaplod LLC Šabac, concluded that the transaction structure amounted to a disguised contract within the meaning of Article 66(2) of the Law on Obligations[24]. By treating the triangular arrangement: plaintiff vs company vs defendant, as a simulation concealing the "real" sales contract between plaintiff and defendant, the court conflated the concepts of simulation and piercing the corporate veil.

6.1.4 The Similarities and Differences in Veil Piercing in BiH

Based on the definitions of veil piercing in company law legislation of all three jurisdictions, similarities and differences can be traced down and elaborated. Unfortunately, the lack of harmonization among company laws in all three jurisdictions results in differences how this doctrine is understood by courts and implemented in practice. This leads to unnecessary uncertainties for investors in BiH since rights and obligations of businesses differ based on their jurisdiction of incorporation. In FBiH, the ZPDFBiH sets out a list of specific abuse scenarios such as pursuing personal goals, misusing company assets, defrauding creditors,

---

[22] Grbo (2017), p. 25; Grbo & Davidović (2016), p. 7.

[23] Appellate court of BD (2015), p. 5. Case number 96 0 Ps 064332 15 Pž, from 24 July 2015. Case was delivered by Supreme court judge for the purposes of writing this dissertation. It cannot be retrieved online.

[24] Law on Obligations of FBiH ("Sl. list SFRJ", br. 29/1978, 39/1985, 45/1989—odluka USJ i 57/1989, "Sl. list RBiH", br. 2/1992, 13/1993 i 13/1994 i "Sl. novine FBiH", br. 29/2003 i 42/2011). Available here: https://www.paragraf.ba/propisi/fbih/zakon-o-obligacionim-odnosima.html. Accessed September 23, 2025. Article 66 of the Law on Obligations titled Simulated Contract, stipulates that (1) a simulated contract has no effect between the contracting parties. (2) However, if a simulated contract conceals another contract, that other contract shall be valid if the conditions for its legal validity are fulfilled. (3) The simulated nature of the contract cannot be invoked against a third party acting in good faith.

or knowingly overburdening the company, while the Supreme Court has interpreted these grounds cumulatively, requiring several elements to be established together, including abuse, personal gain, detriment to creditors, and a causal link. This represents a relatively structured but strict framework, although case law reveals persistent confusion between shareholder liability and director liability. By contrast, Article 15 of the ZPDRS adopts a broader, general clause, sanctioning abuse for unlawful or fraudulent purposes or commingling of assets, and, crucially, interprets these grounds as alternative rather than cumulative. This lowers the evidentiary threshold and grants courts wider discretion, making the RS regime the broadest in practice and most similar to the regime in Croatia. The BD provision in Article 7 of the ZPDBD mirrors the FBiH enumerated approach but peculiarly extends liability to the pre-incorporation phase, despite the absence of legal personality before registration. This comparison highlights that BiHs jurisdictions collectively reflect a spectrum of regulatory approaches, ranging from the broadest in RS, to the more structured and cumulative in FBiH and BD. However, conclusions on the doctrine cannot be derived only from its regulatory framework, but from caselaw and the application of the norm by the courts. The following Chapter will outline cases and identify a common denominator for joint and several liability of shareholders in cases of abuse within and of the company.

6.2 Relevant Case-Law

BiH, unlike Croatia, has a very limited number of judgments concerning the doctrine of piercing the corporate veil. In the official online case-law databases,[25] only eight decisions of the Supreme Courts of the Federation of BiH and RS are currently available. Several factors explain this scarcity. First, such cases are often difficult to identify, as they are not systematically distinguished in the CMS court filing system but rather subsumed under general debt recovery disputes. Second, even when properly classified as piercing-the-veil cases, many decisions remain undigitized and therefore inaccessible in the electronic archive maintained by the High Judicial and Prosecutorial Council of BiH (HJPC). This dissertation examines thirteen judgments from courts in the Federation of BiH, RS, and BD that directly address or apply the doctrine. The analysis also highlights systemic challenges in judicial practice: proceedings from the first-instance court to the Supreme Court often take more than six years, which in practice discourages

[25] Available here: https://sudskapraksa.pravosudje.ba. Accessed September 26, 2025.

litigation[26]. As a result, parties either settle following the first-instance judgment or, more commonly, refrain from initiating proceedings at all. For the purposes of this dissertation, all available judgments were analyzed, total of 3 judgments in BD, 4 judgments in RS, and 4 judgments in FBiH. All judgments are judgments issued by supreme courts of the entities and appellate courts of the BD.

6.2.1 Federation of BiH Cases

6.2.1.1 Hercegovačka banka vs Vitezit Cromen LLC[27] (51 0 Ps 108754 18 Rev)

The plaintiff, Hercegovačka banka (in liquidation), sued co-owners of Vitezit Cromen LLC Vitez, claiming repayment of outstanding debts based on a credit agreement. The Municipal court in Travnik recognized the claim, finding that the three co-owners (Defendant 1 with 90,7% ownership in the company, Defendant 2 with 6,1% ownership in the company, and Defendant 3 with 3,1% ownership in the company) decreased the company's assets due to mismanagement and shareholder interference. On appeal, the Cantonal Court in Travnik upheld the acquittals of Defendants 2 and 3, while confirming the Municipal Court's judgment with respect to Defendant 1. The court held that the plaintiff had failed to present sufficient evidence of abuse of company assets by Defendant 2, and that Defendant 3 had joined the company's ownership structure at a later stage, rendering it impossible for him to have caused harm to the creditors. In case of Defendant 1, the Cantonal court concluded that, as the majority shareholder, he "…was liable for the payment of the debt to the plaintiff because he unlawfully interfered with the company's assets and, on the basis of the director's decision from 2001, took over the company's means of operation and employees, as well as its entire documentation, while failing to maintain the company's analytical records and final accounts, which was his legal obligation, and thereby through his actions and omissions pierced the corporate veil of the company."[28] However, the Supreme Court of the Federation of BiH found that the appellate court

[26] USAID (2022), p. 36. Pending cases (backlog) were concentrated in a few courts at each instance. Sarajevo and Tuzla accounted for 85% of the pending appellate caseload, with most of it in Sarajevo. Publication available here: https://measurebih.com/uimages/JEI-BiH-2021-Report-50820corrected.pdf. Accessed September 23, 2025.

[27] Decision No. 51 0 Ps 108754 18 Rev, of March 7, 2019. This judgment is not available online. It is made available in hard copy by a Supreme court judge for the purposes of writing this dissertation.

[28] Supreme Court of the Federation of BiH (2019), p. 3.

incorrectly applied the law by failing to properly assess whether shareholder's conduct (Defendant 1) relating to transferring assets, failing to maintain accounting records, treating company property as personal property, satisfied the statutory criteria for veil piercing. The Supreme Court FBiH emphasized that such liability requires a proven causal link between shareholder misconduct and the company's inability to meet its obligations, which neither the Municipal court, nor the Cantonal court in regard to Defendant 1, established. The Supreme Court of FBiH annulled the appellate judgment and remanded the case for retrial, holding that the lower courts had not properly established the existence of the cumulative conditions for piercing the corporate veil under Article 5(2) ZPDFBiH.

Discussion

Some worthwhile observations regarding this case are: firstly, the first instance court did not consider it relevant whether the shareholders are majority or minority shareholders. Secondly, it was also deemed irrelevant by the first instance court that the second minority shareholder joined the ownership structure after the credit agreement was entered into by the company. Thirdly and most importantly, the Supreme Court of FBiH established that in order for piercing the corporate veil to be established by the court, there needs to be a consequence for the opposing party, arising from a causal link between the abusive conduct and the company's inability to satisfy its creditors. The court emphasized that abuse of the company may be either subjective or objective. Subjective misuse arises where the corporate form is employed to achieve goals that the shareholders could not otherwise attain individually. Liability based on fault corresponds to the general principles of the law of obligations and arises when the wrongdoer causes harm either intentionally or negligently. Fault requires that the impugned conduct be unlawful and comprises two elements: intent (dolus) and negligence. Intent represents the most severe form of fault and presupposes that the actor was aware of the consequences of his conduct and either desired their occurrence (direct intent) or reconciled himself with their occurrence (eventual intent).[29] The court therefore evaluates whether fault exists on the side of the shareholder, as a prerequisite for his liability, which is a concept more similar to Germany's piercing the corporate veil model, and way stricter than in Croatia. The Supreme Court did not find elements for veil piercing because the lower courts did not establish exactly what kind and how much property the company possessed at the time the credit was approved, what actions led to the reduction of the company's assets, when those actions occurred, who undertook them, and with what intent (i.e., whether there was intent to obstruct the plaintiff in collecting its

[29] Supreme Court of the Federation of BiH (2019), p. 4.

claim), nor whether a causal connection existed between specific actions and the company's inability to settle its debt.

6.2.1.2 D LLC vs Shareholder of BH D LLC[30] (65 0 P 180427 16 Rev)

The plaintiff, D LLC, entered into an agreement with the company BH D LLC, for the transport of frozen chicken from BiH to Hong Kong. The contracted transport was interrupted in Croatia and suspended by the defendant due to "company incorporation problems". [31] (Supreme Court of the Federation BiH, 2018) The plaintiff later learned that the defendant did not have an open transaction account for the company. The plaintiff sought compensation of costs incurred by organizing the transport to Hong Kong, in the total amount of EUR 10,350.97. Since the company was never fully incorporated, the plaintiff sued the sole shareholder of the company, asking the court to pierce the corporate veil. The lower courts rejected the claim (both municipal and cantonal courts), holding that the defendant had no passive legitimacy since obligations were those of the company, and not of the shareholder personally. However, the Supreme Court found that the lower courts failed to consider whether the defendant, as shareholder and director, knew the company could not perform obligations due to lack of registration and no open bank account.[32] (ibid.) The Supreme court ruled that evidence suggested that the defendant personally participated in contractual negotiations, continued business despite the company's incapacity, and thus may have used the company improperly to the detriment of the plaintiff. The Supreme Court annulled the appellate judgment and remanded the case for retrial, holding that the lower courts misapplied substantive law by not properly examining whether the conditions for piercing the corporate veil were met.

Discussion

The first-instance court, when rejecting the plaintiff's claim, found that there was no passive legitimacy of the defendant in relation to the company BH D. LLC as a legal entity, because the requirements for the exceptional liability of the defendant as a shareholder were not fulfilled. The appellate court upheld the first-instance

[30] Decision No. 65 0 P 180427 16 Rev, of October 30, 2018. This judgment is not available online. It was made available in hard copy by a Supreme court judge for the purposes of writing this dissertation.

[31] Supreme Court of the Federation BiH (2018), p. 2.

[32] Supreme Court of the Federation BiH (2018), p. 5.

court's view that the mere fact that BH D. LLC lacked a transaction account could not, by itself, establish the defendant's liability. It further reasoned that a company's non compliance with the law may only be confirmed through a final criminal con viction. According to the court, it had not been demonstrated that the defendant, as a shareholder, used the company to pursue personal objectives, treated its assets as his own, or employed the company as a vehicle for fraud or to the detriment of creditors. However, the Supreme Court did not agree with this stance, it elaborated that the very fact that the defendant acted as the director of the company in which he was a shareholder, concluding legal transactions on behalf of the company that did not have an open transaction account, must be assessed in relation to the defendant's personal liability, and not solely as the liability of the company as a legal entity. The defendant's knowledge that his company was not registered and lacked an open transaction account constitutes sufficient evidence to trigger the application of Article 5(2)(d) of ZPDFBiH, as it demonstrates that he assumed obligations despite knowing, or having a duty to know, that the company would be unable to perform them.

6.2.1.3 Šumsko privredno društvo Zeničko-dobojskog kantona" LLC Zavidovići vs "Krivaja" LLC Zavidovići u stečaju and Ferimpex LLC Zavidovići (43 0 Ps 073499 15 Rev)

The plaintiff claimed compensation of approx. 2,050,700 KM for unpaid wood deliveries made under contracts with Krivaja 1884 LLC Zavidovići, a newly established company created through restructuring agreements by the defendants with share capital of Krivaja LLC Zavidovići u stečaju od 30% and Ferimpex LLC Zavidovići of 70%. The issue arose because the newly established company was registered, later struck from the registry, and its assets and obligations were transferred multiple times between entities (IP Krivaja, Ferimpex, PD Krivaja 1884). The plaintiff argued that the defendants, as founders and participants in these restructuring processes, should be liable for the company's debts. The Supreme Court confirmed the lower courts' rulings: the defendants, as founders and shareholders of Krivaja 1884 LLC, were not personally liable for the company's debts.[33] The plaintiff's claim was dismissed due to lack of proof that the

[33] Supreme Court of the Federation of BiH (2016). Decision No. 43 0 Ps 073499 15 Rev, of April 12, 2016. This judgment is not available online. It is made available in hard copy by a Supreme court judge for the purposes of writing this dissertation.

statutory conditions for piercing the corporate veil (misuse, fraud, or unlawful reduction of company assets) were fulfilled.

Discussion

The first instance court (Municipal Court in Zenica), dismissed the plaintiff's claim reasoning that the plaintiff had no valid claim against the defendants personally because the contracts were concluded with the legal entity (Krivaja 1884 LLC), and founders are generally not liable for company debts. This was confirmed by the second instance court. The Supreme Court agreed. In its decision, it stated that the plaintiff did not prove abuse according to Article 5 of ZPDFBiH, and that the fact that Krivaja 1884 LLC was struck from the registry does not automatically create liability for the founders. This reasoning is interesting because the situation between this case and case D LLC vs Shareholder of BH D LLC is similar. The difference is that the Supreme Court in this case found that there was no proof of intentional misuse of the company form by the founders.

The collapse of Krivaja LLC Zavidovići, once a leading furniture and wood industry giant in BiH employing more than 10,000 workers, illustrates the intersection of failed privatization processes and the limitations of judicial doctrine on shareholder liability. The first major privatization attempt in 2008, through the joint venture Krivaja 1884 LLC (70% Ferimpex, 30% Federation government), collapsed within three years, culminating in protracted litigation in which the Federation BiH was ultimately ordered to pay approximately 12 million BAM in damages, while no counterclaim was filed against Ferimpex.[34] A second attempt in 2014, through Krivaja Mobel formed by a consortium of four small firms, likewise failed; the Privatization Revision Agency later concluded that the process amounted to an illegal privatization, as debts were shifted onto the new entity while valuable property was registered in the names of the private partners. Both ventures left workers without jobs, pensions, or entitlements, while the Federation budget absorbed tens of millions in losses. In this context, the 2016 Supreme Court judgment in the Krivaja 1884 case reaffirmed the principle of limited liability by dismissing the plaintiff's claim against the founders, holding that personal liability of shareholders cannot arise merely from a company's deletion from the register but only where statutory veil-piercing conditions, such as misuse, fraud, or personal enrichment, are established. Formally, the Court's reasoning was correct given the evidentiary record available, which did not demonstrate fraudulent conduct. Substantively, however, subsequent

[34] Gutić, (2024). News article "The Federation is paying millions in damages to private companies, while the prosecutor's offices remain silent." Available here: https://www.zurnal.info/clanak/the-federation-is-paying-millions-in-damages-to-private-companies-while-the-prosecutors-offices-remain-silent/27277.

findings of the Privatization Revision Agency revealed serious irregularities in the registration and operation of Krivaja 1884, suggesting that misuse of corporate form may indeed have occurred. Thus, the judgment, while legally consistent, appears materially unjust in retrospect, not because of judicial misapplication of doctrine, but because the plaintiff failed to provide the Court with the evidence necessary to pierce the corporate veil. Taking this into consideration, and through the veil piercing test as stipulated in Supreme Court judgment from 2019, if the case was tried today, the Court would be able to establish abuse of the company for unlawful or fraudulent purposes, due to proven irregularities of privatization, disposal of company assets as if they were personal assets, by selling off and transferring property of the company to other legal entities without legal ground, financial gain of the responsible person (shareholder), with people within the government directly profiting from contracts concluded with the defendant, detrimental consequences for the creditor, especially the workers who were left with no pay-out and jobs, and the causal link between the abusive conduct and the impossibility of satisfying the creditors claim. This situation resonates with the reasoning of the ECtHR in Mykhaylenky and Others v. Ukraine[35], where the Court held that the Statecould not evade its obligations under Article 6 and Article 1 of Protocol No. 1 ECHR by hiding behind the corporate personality of a State-owned enterprise. The ECtHR emphasized that when the State exercises dominant influence or control over a company, or when that company performs public functions or operates with public assets, the State remains internationally responsible for its acts and omissions, especially where those acts result in the non-enforcement of judicial awards or deprivation of property rights.

6.2.1.4 B LLC Sarajevo vs 3 A LLC and H.M. (managing director) (65 0 P 195188 11 Rev)

In its decision the Supreme Court of the Federation of BiH[36] reviewed a dispute brought by B. LLC Sarajevo against 3 A LLC Sarajevo and H.M. (managing director of 3 A LLC) concerning repayment of an 80,000 BAM credit. The lower courts had ordered the defendants to jointly compensate the plaintiff, who had repaid the credit on behalf of 3 A LLC under a surety agreement, holding both the company and its director personally liable. On revision, the Supreme Court

[35] ECtHR (2004). Judgment available here: https://hudoc.echr.coe.int/fre#{%22itemid%22:[%22001-67580%22]}. Accessed October 18, 2025.

[36] Supreme Court of the Federation of BiH (2012). Case 65 0 P 195188 11 Rev from July 12, 2012. Available here: https://sudskapraksa.pravosudje.ba/case-law-documents/1807/details. Accessed September 29, 2025.

confirmed liability of 3 A LLC, since the company had failed to repay its debt, but annulled the judgments against H.M., finding that his role as director did not in itself establish passive legitimacy for personal liability under Article 5 of ZPDFBiH. The Court emphasized that shareholders not directors, may only be held personally liable if they misuse the company to defraud or harm creditors. Assuming that the second defendant was a shareholder of the first defendant, the plaintiff did not prove that the second defendant used the company to the detriment of its creditors, and without establishing this fact, the Court established that there can be no liability of the second defendant for the obligations of the company. The plaintiff's mere statement that the second defendant used the company to harm its creditors, without appropriate evidence cannot serve as a basis for the appellate court's generalized conclusion that the second defendant had passive legitimization in this matter by reference to Article 5 ZPDFBiH.[37]

Discussion

This case illustrates how courts in the Federation of BiH often conflate shareholder liability with director liability. The confusion is reinforced by the widespread corporate practice in BiH, where many companies have a sole shareholder who also serves as the director. However, for piercing the corporate veil to be applicable, it is not enough that an individual acts as director; the individual must also hold shares in the company, and this fact must be proven by the plaintiff. The Supreme Court emphasized that using a company to the detriment of creditors requires clear evidence, which may include situations where the company has repeatedly failed to meet obligations toward the plaintiff or other creditors, or where the shareholder has been convicted in criminal proceedings for creditor fraud. This reasoning is particularly noteworthy, as it shows that the Court, similarly to judicial practice in Croatia, expressly values criminal convictions as probative evidence for establishing the conditions of veil piercing.

[37] Supreme Court of the Federation of BiH (2012), p. 3.

6.2.2 RS Cases

6.2.2.1 J.Đ. v. S.T. (80 0 P 099848 23 Rev)

In J.Đ. v. S.T.[38], the plaintiff was an injured employee of the company M.B. LLC K., who had secured two final judgments for work-injury damages and wages following an unlawful dismissal by director and sole shareholder of M.B. LLC K., the defendant in this case, S.T. In order to avoid payout of employee J.Đ., the shareholder of M.B. LLC K. incorporated a successor company (B.M. LLC K.) at the same address, transferred the entire workforce and core assets through an intra-group "asset sale" he executed on both sides, and extracted dividends from M.B. LLC in 2015 and 2016, leaving the debtor company illiquid and culminating in a no-asset bankruptcy on 17 February 2020. The first-instance court partially upheld the Article 15 claim, while the appellate court reversed, deeming the steps the shareholder undertook, not per se unlawful. Upon revision, the Supreme Court reinstated and broadened the award against S.T., holding that Article 15's exception to limited liability was met. The Court found that the defendant, as a shareholder, misused the company by diverting assets and operations and distributing dividends knowing or having to know of the plaintiff's claims, thereby causing the creditor's non-recovery. It emphasized the causal assessment required by Article 15, focusing less on the formal legality of each transaction and more on their purpose and effect, and awarded sums with default interest running from the filing of the Article 15 action.[39]

Discussion

This case illustrates that the absence of explicit, coherent legal standards and judicial practices concerning the doctrine of piercing the corporate veil, can pose challenges for the legal system of Bosnia and Herzegovina. The legal reasoning of the first instance and appellate court were conflicting. The appellate court stated that establishing a new company at the address of the previous one, engaging in the same business activity as the previous company, taking over the employees and assets of the previous company, by distributing dividends, and granting loans to pay the purchase price, are not prohibited by any legal provision.[40] This was overruled by

[38] Supreme Court RS (2024a).Case 80 0 P 099848 23 Rev from 2024, June 25. Available here: https://sudskapraksa.pravosudje.ba/case-law-documents/6703/details. Accessed October 3, 2025.

[39] Supreme Court RS (2024a), p. 8.

[40] Supreme Court RS (2024a), p. 6.

the Supreme Court who in its ruling defined "abuse" of the company. The Court stated that "It is considered that abuse exists if a member of the company:

1. uses the company to achieve a purpose that is otherwise prohibited to them;
2. uses the company's assets or disposes of them as if they were their personal property;
3. uses the company or its assets with the intention of harming the company's creditors; or
4. reduces the company's assets for the benefit of themselves or third parties, knowing or having reason to know that the company will not be able to meet its obligations."[41]

These are the exact reasons for veil-piercing defined in Article 5 of the ZPDFBiH. The Supreme Court stressed that regardless of whether the actions of the shareholder are not per se prohibited by law, the plaintiff rightly argued that it is essential to establish the purpose for which these actions by the shareholder were undertaken. For the Court, it was evident that the shareholder carried out these activities with the aim of avoiding the probable obligation of his company towards the plaintiff in order to gain benefit for himself. The actions of the shareholder were undertaken contrary to the interests of the company[42] and in bad faith[43], with the purpose of placing the company in a position where it could not fulfill its obligations toward its creditors, which constitutes an abuse of the company. According to Barbić[44], abuse of the company arises in situations in which a shareholder establishes a new company with the sole purpose of harming its creditors by transferring its assets to the new company, or when he establishes a new company with minimal assets and transfers its business operations to that company, so that the original company conducts business through the bank account of the new company. These situations are considered reasons for piercing the corporate veil, which was confirmed in this case too by the Supreme Court ruling. This case is also relevant in terms of determining the default interest on the total debt amount that was awarded to the plaintiff. The Court found that the default interest should be calculated from the date of filing the lawsuit in this case, until payment, because by filing the lawsuit the plaintiff called upon the defendant to be held liable on the basis of abuse of the

[41] Supreme Court RS (2024a), p. 7.

[42] Art. 31, ZPDRS.

[43] Art. 32, ZPDRS.

[44] Barbic (2009), p. 40.

company, and thus, in accordance with Article 324(2)[45] of the ZOORS, the claim became due at that time.

6.2.2.2 I. LLC D. v. A.T.B. G., and K. K. H. G.[46] (60 0 Ps 030404 23 Rev)

A short summary of the case was given under Sect. 6.1.2. (Piercing the Corporate Veil in RS) as example case for basic lack of knowledge courts demonstrate when applying Article 15 of the ZPDRS. The plaintiff, I. LLC D., had final judgments against K. LLC D. (later S. LLC), but could not collect after the debtor's workforce, assets, customers, and brand were shifted to a new company, K.P. LLC, followed by liquidation, bankruptcy without estate, and strike-off of the debtor company. The first-instance court, namely the District Commercial Court in Doboj[47], rejected the plaintiff's claim seeking to hold the first and second defendants jointly and severally liable for the payment of 3,801,520.49 BAM as compensation for damages allegedly caused by their dishonest conduct and abuse of the company's legal personality. The first instance court did state that there is no passive legitimization for the second defendant since he is not a shareholder of K. LLC D. In terms of the first defendant, the Court found that the plaintiff did not prove that the first defendant abused the company through the bankruptcy proceedings and thereby caused damage to the plaintiff. The Court also found that there was no causal link between the damage suffered by the plaintiff and the actions of the first defendant, mentioning Article 154(1) ZOORS[48] and not Article 15 ZPDRS, as legal grounds for his reasoning.

---

[45] Article 324(2) Law on Obligations of RS reads as follows: "If the time for performance has not been determined, the debtor is in default when the creditor calls upon him to perform the obligation, either orally or in writing, through an out-of-court notice or by initiating proceedings whose purpose is to achieve performance of the obligation."

[46] Supreme Court of Republika Srpska. (2024). Judgment No. 60 0 Ps 030404 23 Rev from February 2, 2024. Available here: https://sudskapraksa.pravosudje.ba/case-law-documents/6495/details. Accessed October 8, 2025.

[47] District Commercial Court in Doboj, case no. 60 0 Ps 030404 21 Ps, dated 28 February 2022.

[48] Article 154 (1) stipulates that: Whoever causes damage to another is obliged to compensate for it, unless they prove that the damage occurred without their fault. (2) For damage caused by an object or activity that presents an increased risk of harm to the environment, liability exists regardless of fault. (3) Liability regardless of fault also applies in other cases prescribed by law. Law available here: https://www.paragraf.ba/propisi/republika-srpska/zakon-o-obligacionim-odnosima.html. Accessed October 9, 2025.

The Appellate Commercial Court (second-instance court) referred to a criminal judgment of the Basic Court in Derventa[49], which found B.A. and S.S. (responsible persons within the legal entity) guilty and sentenced them to imprisonment. The criminal court found that B.A. and S.S. as responsible persons of the company K. LLC D., had intentionally transferred employees, business premises, machinery, and equipment to a connected company, K.P. LLC D., to obtain an unlawful financial benefit for that new company. This transfer effectively caused K. LLC D. to cease operations in 2016. On 19 January 2017, the workers of K. LLC D. formally became employees of K.P. LLC D., and payments were made selectively to certain creditors important to the new company's business, while public revenues and other obligations were withheld. These actions resulted in significant unlawful gain for K.P. LLC D. and large financial damage to the budget of RS and to the creditor I. LLC D. (the plaintiff in this case). Both accused (B.A. and S.S.) pleaded guilty, and the criminal court's decision was rendered based on their plea agreement. The second-instance court found that the opening of bankruptcy proceedings over the company against which the plaintiff held a claim, followed by the simultaneous takeover of that company's business operations through a new legal entity, K.P. LLC D., into which the entire business, management, employees, production facilities, and clients of the defunct company were transferred, this constituted an abuse of the company form for unlawful purposes within the meaning of Article 15 ZPDRS. According to the second-instance court, the first defendant, as the founder of the second defendant, together forming a corporate group engaged in PVC production and using the K. trademark protected before the World Intellectual Property Organization (WIPO), are connected persons within the meaning of Article 357 ZPDRS[50]. Consequently, the appellate court wrongly concluded that the defendants are jointly and severally liable for payment of the claimed amount. Even though the second defendant, K.K.H.G. later contracted with the debtor company in relation to leases, supply, loans, and arranged fiduciary/share transfers in the newly formed company, the Supreme Court RS (2024)[51] found that these were downstream transactions with a different company. The Court then concluded that personal liability attaches to the member who orchestrated the asset diversion (shareholder A.T.B.G) and

[49] Basic Court in Derventa. Case no. 84 0 K 054917 21 K, dated 11 October 2022.

[50] This article refers to the definition of affiliated companies as companies that: consist of two or more companies, in accordance with the law, that are connected to each other through: a) participation in share capital or partnership interests (companies connected by capital), b) contractual relationships (companies connected by contract), and c) both capital and contractual relationships (mixed connected companies).

[51] Supreme Court of Republika Srpska. (2024), p. 5.

shutdown of the debtor of I. LLC D., but not to a non-member business partner, even though he was a nominee shareholder.

Discussion

In this case the Supreme court of RS set a standard for veil piercing, identical to the one in the Federation BiH. For veil piercing to occur, the court determent the following cumulative conditions:

(1) that an act constituting abuse of the company has been committed;
(2) that at the time of abuse, the creditor had a claim against the company (which was due at the time of filing the lawsuit);
(3) the abuse was carried out by a member of the company; and
(4) there is a causal link between the member's conduct and the abuse.[52] (ibid. p. 7) The Court also listed modalities of abuse or fraudulent conduct by which owners or company managers harm creditors by disposing of company assets for their own or others' benefit.

As forms of abuse, the court listed:

a) mixing personal assets with company assets;
b) using company funds for personal expenses (e.g., to buy a house or a car);
c) transferring company assets to relatives or third parties; or
d) otherwise disposing of company property for personal gain, with the intention of defrauding creditors, or reducing the company's assets for personal or third-party benefit, knowing that the company will not be able to meet its obligations from the remaining assets. This again is a combination of elements of the veil piercing definition in Federation of BiH, with a more detailed explanation what actions could constitute commingling of assets.

The Nominee shareholder

This case is very relevant because it describes a nominee shareholder who was used to shield the second defendant from responsibility in this case, and with success. On 16 May 2018, the second defendant signed a trust agreement with a natural person (R.B. as the nominee or trustee), stating that R.B. would hold a share in K.P. LLC D. in his own name, but for the benefit and in the exclusive interest of the second defendant, K. K. H. G. R.B. was only a formal owner, while the second defendant was the true (beneficial) owner of the company share. On the same date,

[52] Supreme Court of Republika Srpska. (2024), p. 7.

they also signed a share purchase agreement: R.B. sold, and the second defendant bought, the entire share in K.P. LLC D. for a nominal value of 1.00 KM. The seller authorized the buyer (the second defendant) to register himself directly as the owner in the company's register and in the court registry, without any further consent. On 19 February 2020, they repeated both the trust agreement and share transfer, confirming again that R.B. was holding the shares for the second defendant's benefit and that the second defendant had the right to register ownership directly. D.S. LLC, was founded in 2015 by R.B. Later, in 2017, the company changed its name to K.P. LLC and appointed as directors the same individuals (A.B. and S.S.) who had managed K. LLC, the debtor company. Around the same time, all employees, production facilities, machinery, and equipment from K. LLC were transferred to the new company, K.P. LLC, which continued operating under the same trademark "K." and served the same customers. In essence, the entire business of K. LLC was moved to K.P. LLC, while K. LLC was left without assets and later went into liquidation and bankruptcy. This maneuver effectively allowed the defendants to continue the same business under a new legal entity, leaving the old one empty and unable to pay its creditors. K.K.H.G. was the nominee shareholder of K.P. LLC, but avoided responsibility because shares of K.P. LLC were held by R.B. instead of K.K.H.G., leaving the Supreme Court without the shareholder connection from which liability would arise. Interestingly, in a case before the Supreme Court of FBiH[53] the court found that a contract concluded between parties who acted in bad faith, because they knew or ought to have known that the contract's content and purpose were contrary to mandatory legal provisions, is null and void. The agreement on the sale of shares between R.B. and K.K.H.G. should have given the court evidence for suspicion in a case in which abuse of corporate form was determined. The contract was concluded to hide real ownership and avoid repayment of debt for the plaintiff. In the case before the Supreme Court of FBiH, the court held that the plaintiff was a bad faith contracting party, since he knew or, given the circumstances, could have known that the partnership agreement on the sale of shares was, in both its content and purpose, directly contrary to mandatory provisions. This is because the legal basis was unlawful[54], the subject matter of the obligation was unlawful (Art. 47 in conjunction with Art. 49 of the same Law), and the agreement was unlawful also in its purpose (motive or intent).[55]

[53] Supreme Court of FBiH (2018a), p. 4. Judgment No. 58 0 P 101552 16 Rev, from January 16, 2018, made available by attorney at law, Prof. Dr. Almir Gagula. Not available online.

[54] Art. 51 and 52 of the ZOOFBiH.

[55] In this case, the court held that the Partnership Agreement (*ugovor o ortakluku*) concluded on 10 January 2006 between T. Dž. and Ž. Dž. was null and void because it violated

6.2.2.3 Tk LLC B. vs V.M (Rev. 80 0 P 098942 20 Rev)

In this Supreme Court RS case[56] the court ruled that there has not been a violation of Article 15 ZPDRS and that V.M. as sole shareholder and director of the company M. LLC, cannot be held personally liable for the debt of the company towards the plaintiff. In prior civil proceedings, the plaintiff has sued the company M LLC and received an enforcement title over its real estate. M. LLC and V.M., as co-owners sold the property for 150,000 BAM to a minor. Since a mortgage had been registered on that property since 2010 in favor of a bank that issued a loan to M. LLC, with V.M. as a co-debtor, 70,755.68 BAM was paid directly to the bank to close the company's loan, 4,244.32 KM was transferred to M. LLC, and 75,000 KM was paid to V.M. for his personal co-ownership share. The company's debt to the bank was thus settled, and the mortgage was removed, and the new owner registered. The Court reasoned that the transaction was formally lawful, as the property was jointly owned by the company and its director, and each received proceeds according to their ownership share. The portion belonging to the company was used to repay a secured bank loan, which had priority over unsecured creditors, while the director's portion represented his personal asset, not company property. Because the plaintiff could not prove that the sale was fictitious, that the director used company assets for personal gain, or that there was a causal link between the sale and the company's insolvency, the

mandatory legal provisions and the public order. The purpose of the agreement was to establish a private security company ("E.S." LLC Mostar), an activity subject to strict licensing and oversight by the Ministry of Interior. At the time of the agreement, T. Dž. was a police inspector employed by the Ministry of Interior of the Herzegovina-Neretva Canton, while Ž. Dž. was under criminal prosecution, both circumstances that legally disqualified them from obtaining a license or acting as founders of a private security company. Despite the partnership agreement stating that the partners would hold equal shares (50% each), the company was registered in the court registry solely under the name of G. K., who was recorded as the sole founder (100% ownership) and the authorized representative without limitation. The court concluded that both parties acted in bad faith, knowing that the contract's purpose, object, and motive were contrary to mandatory provisions (Articles 47, 49, 51, and 52 of the ZOOFBiH). As such, the agreement was null and void, producing no legal effect, and the subsequent agreement on termination of the partnership was also invalid as it shared the legal fate of the original contract. Although the lower court initially recognized a right to restitution, the higher court rejected it, finding that the plaintiff had failed to prove the value of his alleged contributions and that no compensation could be granted for a nonexistent legal relationship.

[56] Supreme Court RS (2022). Judgement No. Rev. 80 0 P 098942 20 Rev, from January 27, 2022. Available here: https://sudskapraksa.pravosudje.ba/case-law-documents/4224/details. Accessed October 9, 2025.

Court held that the statutory conditions for piercing the corporate veil were not met.

Discussion

The property of the company was jointly owned: 50% by V.M. personally and 50% by M. LLC The mortgage (registered since 2010) gave the bank a superior claim to the property's value. Even if the plaintiff had tried to collect through enforcement, the bank would have been paid first, leaving nothing for unsecured creditors. Therefore, the Court reasoned that there was no causal link between the sale and the plaintiff's inability to collect the debt. Even though V.M. received 75,000 BAM from the sale of property, the Court viewed this as payment for his personal ownership share, not as siphoning company funds. It found no evidence that he diverted money belonging to the company or that he enriched himself at the expense of creditors. Since the funds from the company's portion were used to repay a secured bank debt, the Court found no fraudulent purpose and no causal link between V.M.'s conduct and the plaintiff's loss.

6.2.2.4 „L." LLC B.1 and „T." LLC B.1 v. JP Gradska toplana a.d. and Opština B.1 (60 0 Ps 024805 19 Rev)

This case concerns the liability of a local government (Opština B.1) as the founder of a public utility company (JP "Gradska toplana"), after the company became insolvent and its creditors ("L" LLC and "T" LLC) were unable to recover debts that had been confirmed by final court judgments. The creditors sued the municipality directly, claiming that it had abused the company's legal personality to evade payment and manipulated its assets to their detriment. The first-instance court held the municipality liable under Article 15 ZPDRS, finding that it had used the company for unlawful purposes and disposed of its property as if it were its own, thereby preventing creditors from enforcing their claims. The Court of Appeal, however, overturned that decision, reasoning that the company had never formally acquired ownership of the assets in the land registry, meaning that the municipality remained the legal owner and could therefore freely dispose of them. The Supreme Court of RS[57] disagreed and reinstated liability. It established that the municipality had initially transferred land, buildings, and heating infrastructure to the utility company as an in-kind capital contribution, increasing the

[57] Supreme Court of RS (2019). Judgment 60 0 Ps 024805 19 Rev, from October 2, 2019. Available here: https://sudskapraksa.pravosudje.ba/case-decisions/118-179538/details. Accessed October 12, 2025.

company's registered capital by almost 2 million KM (based on the 2009 decision and notarized transfer agreements in 2010 and 2012). Once these assets were contributed, they legally became property of the company, even if the transfers were not entered into the land register. Despite this, before the company's bankruptcy, the municipality unilaterally annulled the transfer agreements through an annex signed in 2013 and reclaimed the assets from the utility. It then reassigned them to another public company and later to a private operator, leaving the original company without any means to operate or to satisfy creditor claims. When the utility entered bankruptcy, its remaining assets were worth only 22,500.00 BAM, insufficient to cover even administrative costs. The Supreme Court held that this conduct amounted to abuse of the corporate form, because the founder treated the company's assets as its own, effectively disregarding its separate legal existence. The Court clarified that the conditions for veil-piercing are alternative, not cumulative: it is enough that the founder either uses the company for unlawful or fraudulent purposes or disposes of its assets as personal property. In conclusion, the veil was pierced because the municipality, as the company's founder, deliberately depleted the company's assets to avoid satisfying creditor claims, thus misusing the separate legal personality of the utility to achieve an unlawful and fraudulent outcome.

Discussion

This Supreme Court decision marked a turning point in the interpretation of Article 15 of the ZPDRS. The Court explicitly clarified that the conditions for veil-piercing are alternative, not cumulative, meaning that it suffices for a shareholder or founder to either (i) misuse the company for unlawful or fraudulent purposes or (ii) treat its assets as personal property, for personal liability to arise. Applying this reasoning, the Court pierced the veil where a municipality, as the founder of a public company, had reclaimed assets previously contributed to the company's capital and transferred them to another entity, thereby depleting the company's property and making it impossible for creditors to recover their claims. This constituted an evident abuse of the company's separate legal personality to achieve an unlawful objective. The Supreme Court stated that "For establishing the liability of shareholders or members of a company for unlawful disposition of the company's assets, it is not necessary to prove the existence of intent or purpose to defraud the company's creditors."[58]

[58] Supreme Court RS (2019) p. 5.

When comparing this case, to case Krivaja[59] they reveal differences in the judicial understanding of shareholder liability and corporate abuse in Federation of BiH and RS. The Krivaja judgment shows the early phase of judicial interpretation, formally correct but substantively narrow, where courts demanded direct proof of fraudulent intent. This decision, however, expanded the interpretative framework, recognizing that intentional asset withdrawal, misuse of corporate capital, and disregard for company independence can in themselves amount to unlawful abuse, even without explicit proof of deceitful intent. A similar case was tried before the European Court of Human Rights in Yershova v. Russia[60], where the Court found the State liable for the actions of a municipal enterprise that had been wound up under the direct control of local authorities. In that case, the municipal administration had not only decided to liquidate the company but had also transferred its assets to a newly created enterprise performing identical functions, thereby continuing the same public service under a different legal guise while evading existing debts. The ECtHR emphasized that the public nature of the company's functions and its complete dependence on the municipal administration demonstrated that the enterprise was an organ of the State for the purposes of the Convention. Consequently, the State was held responsible for the non-enforcement of judicial decisions awarding compensation to the applicant.

6.2.3 BD Cases

Three judgments by the Appellate Court of BD were kindly provided by a judge for the purposes of this dissertation. The reason why the analysis of the judgments is important to address the differences in the definition of veil piercing in BD as a specific jurisdiction.

6.2.3.1 Fructal Promet v. Bosnaplod Brčko (96 0 Ps 064332 15 Pž)

The case concerned a dispute between Fructal Promet, a sole proprietorship from Valjevo, Serbia, and Bosnaplod Brčko, a company based in BiH.[61] The claimant

[59] Šumsko privredno društvo Zeničko-dobojskog kantona" LLC Zavidovići vs "Krivaja" LLC Zavidovići u stečaju and Ferimpex LLC Zavidovići (2016, 43 0 Ps 073499 15 Rev).

[60] European Court of Human Rights (2011a), point 43. Judgement available here: https://hudoc.echr.coe.int/rus#{%22itemid%22:[%22001-98130%22]}. Accessed October, 18. 2025.

[61] Appelate Court of BD (2015), p. 2. Judgement 96 0 Ps 064332 15 Pž, from July 24, 2015. Judgment available only in hard copy.

sought payment of approximately 32,954 KM for deliveries of plums supplied in 2010, which had been received and used by Bosnaplod Brčko but never paid for in full. The defendant, Bosnaplod Brčko, argued that the deliveries were made not to it but to Bosnaplod LLC Šabac, a separate legal entity incorporated in Serbia, and therefore that any claim should have been directed against that company. The claimant responded that Bosnaplod Šabac was only a formal intermediary, established by defendant solely to facilitate customs clearance and export operations in Serbia, and that in substance, Bosnaplod Brčko was the real purchaser of the goods. The first-instance court found in favor of the claimant. It held that Bosnaplod Brčko was the actual buyer of the plums, while Bosnaplod Šabac was a mere façade used to disguise the true contracting party. The evidence showed that:

1. Bosnaplod Brčko was the sole founder and owner of Bosnaplod LLC Šabac;
2. The directors of the Serbian subsidiary were employees and later directors of the Bosnian company;
3. The goods were delivered directly to Bosnaplod Brčko's facilities in Bosnia;
4. The payments were handled in cash by employees of the Bosnian parent;
5. The bookkeeping of the Serbian company was done in Brčko, and transactions were recorded in Bosnaplod Brčko's accounts.[62]

The court therefore concluded that Bosnaplod Brčko had used the Serbian company merely as a *façade* to perform business it was not legally authorized to carry out directly in Serbia, and that it had managed the subsidiary's operations and assets as its own. These facts satisfied the conditions for piercing the corporate veil under Article 7(4)(3) of ZPDBD, which allows courts to disregard separate legal personality when a company is misused to evade obligations or cause damage. The Appellate Court of Brčko District confirmed this reasoning, rejecting the defendant's appeal. It held that the relationship between Bosnaplod Šabac existed only nominally. Consequently, the court affirmed that Bosnaplod Brčko was personally liable for the debt arising from the unpaid deliveries, as it had abused the legal form of its subsidiary to conceal its true contractual obligations.

Discussion

The Appellate Court of Brčko District in Fructal Promet v. Bosnaplod Brčko adopted a notably substantive and functional approach to the doctrine of piercing the corporate veil. Unlike courts in the Federation and the RS which generally require strong

[62] Appellate Court of BD (2015), p. 3.

evidence of fraudulent intent, personal enrichment, or direct creditor harm before disregarding corporate personality, the Brčko court focused primarily on economic reality and factual control. The court emphasized that the burden of proof lay with the claimant to establish that the defendant had managed the business or property of another company "as if it were his own."[63] Through testimony, accounting records, and documentary evidence, it was proven that Bosnaplod Brčko had (i) founded Bosnaplod LLC Šabac, (ii) appointed its own employees as directors of that company, (iii) conducted all trade directly through its own facilities and personnel, (iv) maintained Bosnaplod LLC Šabac accounts in Brčko, and (v) used the company merely to circumvent customs and foreign trade restrictions. These findings led the court to conclude that Bosnaplod Brčko had abused the separate legal personality and thus triggered veil piercing under Article 7(4)(3) ZPDBD. This reasoning demonstrates a more flexible and economically oriented interpretation of corporate abuse than typically seen in the entity-level courts. In RS, for instance, the Supreme Court has taken a strictly narrow view of Article 15 ZPDRS, requiring proof of subjective elements such as intent to defraud or deliberate harm to creditors (e.g., T.K. LLC v. V.M., 2019). Similarly, in the Federation of BiH, the courts have usually refused to pierce the veil absent clear evidence of fraudulent conduct or asset stripping, as illustrated in the Krivaja 1884 case.[64]

In contrast, the Brčko Appellate Court applied an objective standard: even if fraudulent intent could not be shown, the complete control and misuse of the subsidiary as a façade were sufficient to establish abuse. The court's focus was not on subjective culpability but on the functional misuse of legal form to conceal the real contracting party and evade commercial obligations.

6.2.3.2 Additional BD Cases

There are two more cases that were analyzed for the purpose of this dissertation; however, they were not relevant enough to be discussed in detail. The case BD v. Pegy LLC Brčko,[65] the Brčko District Government sought to enforce payment of a small debt (563.30 BAM) for waste collection services against "Pegy" LLC Brčko. During the enforcement procedure, the bailiff twice attempted to seize the debtor's movable property but found no assets, as the company no longer operated at its registered address. Following these failed attempts, the Basic Court of

[63] Appellate Court of BD (2015), p. 3.

[64] Supreme Court of FBiH (2016), p. 4.

[65] Appellate Court of Brčko District (2013), p. 2. Judgment No. 97 0 Ip 001353 13 Pž, from October 29, 2013.

Brčko District terminated the enforcement proceedings pursuant to Article 112(3) of the Law on Enforcement Procedure, which requires the court to discontinue execution if no attachable property is found after two attempts. The creditor (BD) objected, arguing that the enforcement should continue and that the assets of the company's founder, G.P., should also be seized, invoking Article 7 ZPDBD, which provides for shareholder liability in cases of misuse of the company form. The Appellate Court rejected the objection, holding that the founder was not a party to the enforcement proceedings and could not be treated as the debtor. The court reaffirmed the principle of limited liability, stating that shareholders of capital companies (LLC or JSC) are not personally liable for company debts beyond their contributions, except in specific cases of proven abuse (such as using the company to achieve personal goals, manage company assets as their own, or defraud creditors). Importantly, the court clarified that such findings of abuse must be established in a separate civil proceeding, not within the enforcement process itself.

In another case Š.D. v. Č.M.[66] (owner of Mesux LLC), the Appellate Court of Brčko District he plaintiff sought payment of 6,000.00 BAM from Č.M., the founder and director of Mesux LLC, for lumber delivered to the company. The claim was based on a written acknowledgment of debt signed by a company employee, not by Č.M. personally. Both the Basic and Appellate Courts rejected the claim, holding that the proper debtor was the company itself, not its founder. Applying Articles 7 and 340 of the ZPDBD, the Court reaffirmed the principle of limited liability, emphasizing that shareholders and founders are not personally responsible for company debts unless specific conditions for piercing the corporate veil, such as misuse of the company to defraud creditors or treating its assets as personal, are proven. Since the plaintiff presented no evidence of such abuse or any personal assumption of liability by Č.M., the Court found no grounds for shareholder liability and confirmed the dismissal of the claim.

6.2.4 Veil-piercing Factors

All cases can be compartmentalized under the veil piercing factors identified below. These factors were grouped after the case-law review identifying most relevant indicators for abuse of the corporate entity.

[66] Appellate Court of Brčko District (2017), p. 1. Judgment No. 96 0 P 097567 17 Gž, from September 27, 2017.

Seven courts out of those 10 cases overruled lower instance court decisions confirming the absence of coherent and harmonized judicial standards on piercing the corporate veil across BiH. All cases demonstrate that regular business activity that would not be considered as abuse, can be seen as abusive if it has detrimental consequences for the creditor.

6.2.4.1 Shareholder Abuse of Influence

Shareholder abuse of influence is identified in the following cases: Supreme Court of the Federation of BiH, 2016; Supreme Court of Republika Srpska, 2024a. This factor encompasses situations where majority shareholders, through their dominant control or decision-making power, abuse their influence over the company to the detriment of creditors or other stakeholders. Abuse of influence refers to the misuse of one's position to secure personal advantage or benefit that does not serve the interests of the company. In the framework of ZPD FBiH, Articles 32 and 36, establish the normative foundation of the fiduciary duties owed by individuals who occupy positions of special responsibility toward the company. Article 32 identifies such persons as (among others) members of limited liability companies possessing significant equity participation or exercising controlling influence. Article 36 complements this by articulating the duty to avoid conflicts of interest, which constitutes a core element of the broader fiduciary obligation of loyalty. This provision prohibits persons under Article 32 ZPDF-BiH from utilizing company property, confidential information, or their corporate position for personal or related-party benefit, and from appropriating business opportunities that rightfully belong to the company. Notably, the duty operates independently of whether the company was objectively capable of exploiting such assets or opportunities, thereby emphasizing the preventative and ethical dimension of corporate governance.[67] Typical examples of abuse include: interference in management decisions, extraction of company assets, or directing company operations for personal benefit. Courts acknowledged that dominant shareholders often interfere with company operations, divert assets, or obstruct creditor claims. However, only the Supreme Court of RS (2024a)[68] explicitly connected this conduct to personal liability, interpreting such abuse as an act contrary to the interests of the company and its creditors. The Federation courts, by contrast, continue to demand strict proof of fault and causality, thereby preserving the high threshold for lifting limited liability.

[67] Grbo (2016), p. 414.

[68] Supreme Court RS (2024a), p. 3.

6.2.4.2 Abuse of Corporate Form

This factor was identified in the following cases: Supreme Court of RS, 2024a; Supreme Court of RS, 2024; Supreme Court of the Federation of BiH, 2018; Supreme Court of the Federation of BiH, 2016; Appellate Court of BD, 2015. It refers to the use of the corporate form as a façade or sham to conceal real transactions, evade obligations, or continue business under new legal identities in order to avoid liability. Courts have pierced the veil when companies were used as fictitious intermediaries or newly created entities to perpetuate existing business while leaving creditors unpaid. Courts across all three jurisdictions recognized scenarios where the company was employed merely as a façade to conceal real transactions, evade registration obligations, or continue operations under a new name to avoid debts. The Appellate Court of Brčko District case[69] was pivotal in establishing an objective "economic reality" test, similar to the EU's Centros judgment, holding that factual control and substance prevail over formal legal structures.[70] RS jurisprudence expanded this doctrine[71] by explicitly defining abuse as establishing a new company or using an existing one for unlawful purposes or to harm creditors.

6.2.4.3 Comingling of Assets

Mixing personal and corporate property was identified as a key indicator of abuse, particularly in RS and FBiH jurisprudence. Courts treated actions such as the use of company assets for personal gain, transferring property to related parties, or failing to maintain accounting records as forms of commingling. However, the courts' treatment of this factor reveals inconsistencies: while the Supreme Court of the Federation of BiH viewed the failure to separate assets as indicative of potential abuse, Supreme Court RS (refused to pierce the veil, emphasizing formal ownership and legal title rather than economic reality.[72] The BD Appellate Court adopted a more functional approach, acknowledging that control and factual possession can outweigh formal ownership distinctions.[73] Commingling of assets occurs when shareholders or founders fail to maintain a separation between personal and corporate assets, using company funds for private purposes, transferring assets to related persons, or treating company property as their own. This factor

[69] Appellate Court of Brčko District (2015), p. 4.

[70] CJEU (1999), point 27.

[71] Supreme Court of RS (2024a, p. 4; 2024, p. 4).

[72] Supreme Court of the Federation of BiH (2019), p. 4.; Supreme Court RS (2022), p. 5.

[73] BD Appellate Court (2015), p. 3.

frequently coincides with inadequate bookkeeping and the absence of transparent financial reporting. In these situations the plaintiff needs to establish exactly what kind and how much property the company possessed at the time the selling of company property was approved, what actions led to the reduction of the company's assets, when those actions occurred, who undertook them, and with what intent (i.e., whether there was intent to obstruct the plaintiff in collecting its claim). The court needs to establish a causal connection between specific actions and the company's inability to settle its debt.[74]

6.2.4.4 Undercapitalization

Though less frequently invoked, undercapitalization appeared in RS case law 2024 and 2019, as a supplementary factor, especially were combined with asset diversion or deliberate depletion of company capital. The RS Supreme Court recognized that maintaining an entity without sufficient capital to meet foreseeable obligations can itself constitute an abuse of corporate personality, reflecting a deterrence-oriented approach aligned with comparative European practice. Undercapitalization involves establishing or maintaining a company without sufficient capital to meet foreseeable obligations or deliberately depleting its capital base to the detriment of creditors. The Criminal Codes of BiH (CCBiH)[75] recognizes this as reckless or negligent business conduct by the responsible person in a company. It is defined as such conduct that violates laws or regulations and causes significant financial harm to the company. If such misconduct leads to the compulsory liquidation or bankruptcy of the company, the punishment is imprisonment from six months to five years.[76]

6.2.4.5 Fraud

As established in Supreme Court of Republika Srpska, 2024a; Supreme Court of Republika Srpska, 2024; Supreme Court of the Federation of BiH, 2016, this factor is mostly present in situations where shareholders transfer employees, assets, clients, or operations to another company they control, thereby rendering the original debtor insolvent. The new entity effectively continues the same business while evading the old company's liabilities. This "tunnelling"[77] practice

---

[74] Supreme Court of the Federation of BiH (2019), p. 6.

[75] The Criminal Code of Bosnia and Herzegovina; Criminal Code of the Federation of Bosnia and Herzegovina; the Criminal Code of the Brčko District; Criminal Code of the Republic of Srpska.

[76] Art. 242 CCFBiH; Art. 251 CCRS; 236 CCBD; 246 CCBiH.

[77] Barbic, 2009, p. 40.

has been explicitly qualified as abuse in RS case law and indirectly observed in FBiH jurisprudence. This practice is overlooked in FBiH jurisprudence (as seen in Krivaja) but represents a distinct ground for piercing the corporate veil. The shareholders' personal liability for the company's obligations must be based on proven facts that the shareholder used the company to commit fraud or to harm their creditors.[78] Examples of such conduct include deliberately blocking the companies bank account to prevent the settlement of the company's debts, whereby obligations are incurred by one company while the benefits are realized by another company. This example is typical of companies within a corporate group, where the assets of one company are used for the needs of another.[79]

6.2.4.6 Use of the company for unlawful or criminal purposes

Established in Supreme Court of RS, 2024; Supreme Court of the Federation of BiH, 2018; Supreme Court of RS, 2019, this factor encompasses cases where the corporate form is used to commit or conceal criminal offenses such as fraud, tax evasion, or money laundering. RS courts have begun linking civil liability under company law with findings from criminal proceedings, treating the misuse of the corporate entity as proof for piercing the veil. Criminal convictions for asset diversion played a decisive role in establishing abuse under Article 15 ZPDRS. This convergence of legal regimes reflects an acknowledgment that the misuse of corporate structures cannot be addressed solely through private law doctrines but requires an integrated response.

6.3 Joint and Several Liability of Shareholders in the LLC

The principle of limited liability of shareholders is one of the foundational elements of company law in BiH. Both entity-level company laws and ZPDBD, preserve this principle as a rule, while providing only limited statutory pathways for extending shareholder liability. In contrast to Croatian company law, which expressly foresees joint and several liability of shareholders in a number of situations, the BiH legislative framework remains cautious and fault-based,

[78] Supreme Court of the Federation of BiH (2012), p. 4.

[79] Barbic, 2009, p. 36.

emphasizing diligence, loyalty, and the prevention of self-dealing rather than imposing broad secondary liability.[80]

The ZPDFBiH regulates the duties and potential liabilities of shareholders primarily through Article 32 ZPDFBiH[81], which identifies the persons with special duties toward the company. These include members with significant (at least 20%) or controlling (over 50%) shareholding, as well as members of management and supervisory bodies, proxies, and liquidators. These persons are required to perform their duties conscientiously and with the care of a prudent businessman (*pažnja dobrog privrednika*), acting reasonably and in the best interest of the company[82]. A shareholder or company member who acts in accordance with this standard of care is exonerated from liability for damage resulting from their decision, provided that it was made in good faith and on the basis of adequate information.[83] This rule mirrors the so-called business judgment rule in comparative company law, emphasizing subjective good faith and informed decision-making rather than the objective outcome of the decision. However, unlike the Croatian ZTDCRO, which explicitly foresees joint and several liability of shareholders in cases such as the appointment of ineligible managers or failure to pay contributions, the ZPDFBiH, nor the ZPDRS establish statutory joint liability among shareholders. The exception is the liability before formation of the company, however, at this stage, the company has not yet acquired legal personhood.

Under Article 69 of the Company Law (ZPDFBiH), members of the management board, other persons involved in preparing a reorganization plan, and auditors who reviewed and issued opinions for participating companies are jointly and unlimitedly liable for damages caused to the companies and their shareholders or members if they failed to act according to professional standards when determining exchange ratios during mergers, divisions, or transformations.

Article 128 ZPDRS restricts payments by limited liability companies to their members if such payments would reduce the company's net assets below its

[80] Trivun (2019), p. 60.

[81] The same provision is stipulated in the ZPDRS, article 31.

[82] Grbo (2016), p. 414. ZOOFBiH also defines this principle through Article 18 as requirement of the party to act with the degree of care that is required in legal transactions of the corresponding type (the diligence of a prudent businessman). In performing a professional activity, the party is required to act with increased diligence, in accordance with the rules of the profession and customary practices (the diligence of a good expert). In exercising its rights, he is to refrain from any conduct that would make it more difficult for the other party to fulfill its obligation.

[83] Vasiljević (2015), p. 124.

registered capital (adjusted for distributable reserves and legal obligations). If prohibited payments are made, members who received them, and directors who authorized them, are liable to return the amounts if they knew or should have known that the payments were unlawful. In Federation BiH, Article 350 of ZPDF-BiH only prescribes that the company's share capital cannot be reduced below the 1.0000,00 BAM threshold that is needed for its registration. It is however interesting that if the members decide to reduce the share capital of the company, the only thing they must do is submit the decision on the reduction of share capital to the registration court and publish it in the official Gazette of the Federation of BiH. This is how the company informs its creditors that it is prepared to settle its obligations or provide security for them.

Articles 132–134 ZPDRS regulate the competences and functioning of the general assembly of a limited liability company: the assembly approves financial statements and decides on profit distribution; it must be convened at least once a year (within six months after the end of the business year). Any member may request its convening. In RS, case law highlights that although abusive acts are often carried out by statutory representatives (directors), liability may still extend to company members (owners) if a causal link is proven between their enrichment and the director's misuse of authority. Since directors implement decisions made by the members, responsibility can be attributed to members under Article 152(1)(g) of the RS Company Law when abuse results from or benefits their decisions. Similarly, Articles 336—338 ZPDFBiH regulate the work of the limited liability companies' assembly. It may be convened by the management, a management member, the supervisory board or its member, or by shareholders holding at least 10% of the share capital. It must convene at least once a year and also when the company incurs a loss exceeding one-fifth of its share capital. Shareholders holding at least 10% of the capital may add items to the agenda within eight days of receiving the invitation. The assembly can decide if shareholders representing at least half of the share capital are present (quorum). If there is no quorum, a new meeting is held within 15 days, and decisions can then be made if at least one-fifth of the capital is represented. A shareholder who voted against a decision may challenge it before a competent court within 30 days of its adoption. These rules provide a transparent and straightforward way of shareholder involvement.

6.4 Criminal Shareholder Liability

With the EU integration process, former Yugoslav republics, including BiH and Croatia, reformed their laws to introduce derived corporate criminal liability. A company's liability stems from the criminal act of a natural person closely connected to it.[84] Criminal sanctions may also be imposed on the legal successor, provided that its governing bodies were aware, before the entity's dissolution, of the commission of the offence.[85] There are several relevant criminal cases tried before the Court of BiH related to corporate crime in which the court identified liability of the natural person but not the legal person who was used for the crime. In the case before the Appellate Court of the BD[86], the proceedings were conducted only against the natural person D.V., who acted as the authorized representative of the company Aurus Grupa LLC Sarajevo. The company itself was not prosecuted, but it was central to the fraud scheme. D.V. used Aurus Grupa's name and documents, including improperly issued promissory notes, to mislead representatives of Zeraa LLC Sarajevo and its subsidiary Bosnaplod LLC Brčko into delivering large quantities of wine worth 31,755.11 BAM, despite knowing that Aurus Grupa was insolvent and its accounts blocked. The court found that D.V. had acted with fraudulent intent from the outset, immediately reselling the goods below purchase price and retaining the money. Thus, while the corporate entity was the instrument of the crime, only its responsible person, D.V., was held criminally liable for fraud[87], and sentenced to a suspended six-month prison term with a three-year probation period. This case is a great example of a piercing the corporate veil case that could be tried before civil courts and in which the creditors could seek compensation from D.V. directly if he is also shareholder of the company.

In another case before the Appellate Court of BD[88], the court confirmed the conviction of N.B. for concealing and removing the business records of the company M. LLC Brčko[89], over which he was proven to be the real, de facto owner

---

[84] Gotovuša (2020), p. 177.

[85] Trivun & Silajdžić (2020), p. 32.

[86] Appellate Court of the BD (2021), p. 3.

[87] Art. 288 CC BD BiH.

[88] Appellate Court of BD (2021a), p. 4. Judgment No. No. 96 0 K 106916 21 Kž 2. Available here: https://sudskapraksa.pravosudje.ba/case-law-documents/6182/details. Accessed November 5, 2025.

[89] Art. 255(2) in connection with (1) KZ BD BiH.

despite another person (A.R.) being formally registered, thereby upholding a suspended sentence for falsifying or destroying commercial documentation, while dismissing the allegation of credit-related deception. The court relied on a "Agreement on regulating mutual relations"[90] (ibid. p. 4) concerning the establishment and operation of "M." LLC Brčko, which expressly provided that although A.R. would be registered in the court register as founder and director, the real and sole owner of the company was N.B. This clause, corroborated by the notarial founding act, bank signature specimen authorizing N.B. to operate the company's account, a power of attorney from A.R. to N.B., termination and employment documents, and N.B.'s own dealings (including removing/withholding company records), established that N.B. controlled the company and was responsible for concealing/withdrawing its business documentation, satisfying the elements of the records-offence. This judgment is relevant as it shows that shareholders use legal forms of conducting business (as is concluding contracts on holding shares in shares), however, sometimes those legal act have illegal consequences as seen in the case Supreme Court RS[91], in which the court found that regardless of whether the actions through which the abuse is achieved are prohibited by law, what matters is the purpose for which those actions were undertaken. If the purpose was to deceit creditors, then the court will lift the corporate veil. Since criminal liability is derived from the natural person, there are almost no cases in which the court convicted only the legal entity. However, the decision of the Court of BiH[92] proves a different approach taken by the Court. The Court of BiH acquitted the director (M.M.) of liability under Article 210(4) of the CCBiH while maintaining the conviction of the legal person L. LLC Kreševo under Articles 124(c) and 125 CCBiH. Although the company's internal acts (fictitious inventory write-downs and VAT misreporting) constituted tax fraud, the prosecution failed to prove that M.M. had knowledge of, or intentionally tolerated, the misconduct. The court therefore held that managerial oversight failure, without evidence of intent or conscious approval, does not constitute criminal liability. This reasoning confirms that BiH applies a derivative model of corporate liability, whereby the company's culpability derives from the unlawful acts of its agents, yet it remains autonomous from the conviction of any individual perpetrator. Under Article 125 KZ BiH, a company may be held liable even if the physical perpetrator is unidentified or unprosecuted. The Court of BiH thus draws a clear line between organizational

[90] Appellate Court of BD (2021a), p. 4.

[91] Supreme Court RS (2024a), p. 4.

[92] Court of BiH (2022), p. 3. Judgment available here: https://sudskapraksa.pravosudje.ba/case-law-documents/5461/details. Accessed January 28, 2026.

mismanagement and personal criminal intent, reflecting the principle of subjective culpability in criminal law. Only if the prosecution proves that the director consciously tolerated or directed the unlawful conduct can intent (*dolus eventualis*) be established. Otherwise, the omission may give rise to civil or administrative consequences but not criminal culpability. In German law, this distinction is doctrinally formalized. Under Article 130 of OWiG, a managing director may face an administrative fine for a breach of supervision duties. Oversight failures create corporate, not personal, criminal liability, unless the director's intent or deliberate indifference is proven. The Bosnian case thereby fits within a broader European trend that differentiates between corporate wrongdoing (as organizational fault) and the individual culpability of managers.

Sholars as Khanna have argued that holding a company responsible for wrongdoing through corporate civil liability through fines, damages, or injunctions, can achieve many of the same benefits that are usually associated with corporate criminal liability.[93] Germany regulates liability of corporations through OWiG, Croatia regulates corporate criminal liability through ZOPPO, while BiH includes it within its general criminal code and procedure. Differences arise in defining the link between the natural and legal person, the types of sanctions and security measures, penal policy, and the procedural rights of legal persons.[94] In Croatia, it is easier to establish corporate liability because the law clearly defines who qualifies as a "responsible person" (e.g. those managing or entrusted with company affairs). In BiH, the law requires proving that a natural person acted on behalf, in the interest, or for the benefit of the legal person, which is more difficult to establish due to vague criteria. In future reforms of this institute, BiH should introduce a register of sanctioned legal and natural persons, and similarly to Article 130 OWiG or Article 13 ZOPPO, introduce a specific failure-to-prevent offence, thereby closing the compliance gap while preserving the subjective element of criminal guilt, so that the responsible person within the legal entity is sanctioned adequately.

6.5 The Controlling Shareholder

When it comes to other laws that define ownership in business companies in BiH, the Law on the Prevention of Money Laundering and Financing of Terrorist Activities (AMLBiH), that was adopted in 2024 on the level of BiH which is

[93] Khanna (1995), p. 1478.

[94] Gotovuša (2020), p. 175.

largely aligned with Financial Action Task Force (FATF) recommendations,[95] and the definition of the beneficial owner is the same as in the AMLD Consolidated with the same indication of direct ownership amounting to 25%. Article 4 of the AMLBiH defines the beneficial owner as any natural person or persons who ultimately own or control the company and/or any natural person or persons on whose behalf a transaction is being conducted.

"The control is acquired through direct or indirect ownership of a sufficient percentage of shares, voting rights, or ownership interests in that entity, including through bearer shareholdings or through control by other means, and even includes a natural person who indirectly provides or secures funds for a company and has the right to significantly influence the decision-making of the company's management bodies when deciding on financing and business operations." (Art. 4(p), AMLBiH) There is no such definition in the company laws in BiH, and these issues should be harmonized with the *lex specialis*, which is the company law, similarly as we have seen in Croatia. Besides the differences in the percentages of direct ownership which should be harmonized with the law on companies in all jurisdictions in BiH, what is more important is the definition and acknowledgment of beneficial ownership. The AMLBiH (Art. 4) defines the beneficial owner as one or more natural persons who ultimately own or control the legal entity through direct or indirect ownership of a sufficient percentage of shares, voting rights, or ownership interests in that entity, including through bearer shares or by means of control through other mechanisms. By including beneficial owners in the definition of piercing the corporate veil in FBiH, RS, and BD, the court would have grounds to hold responsible shareholders who are hidden behind Trust Agreement. If the Article 15 of ZPDRS would have forseen nominee shareholders in the definition for piercing the corporate veil, the case Supreme court of RS from 2024, would have had a different outcome, since the nominee shareholder would have been held liable.

[95] OSCE (2024). News article available here: https://bih.osce.org/mission-to-bosnia-and-herzegovina/563310.

7 Towards a New Veil-Piercing Doctrine in Bosnia and Herzegovina

Non-payment of debts has become a common and socially tolerated practice in the domestic economy.[1] According to a report[2] from the Tax Administration of the Federation of BiH (TAFBiH) the number of active taxpayers is 95,354, whereas the number of passive taxpayers is 18,258. This situation is particularly alarming when viewed through the structure of limited liability companies out of 42,000 registered LLCs, only 29,608 are active, while nearly 12,000 (11,985) are classified as passive, that is, they have blocked bank accounts, no employees, or no business activity. Although such inactivity is not, in itself, a criminal offence, the ECtHR in Lekić v. Slovenia recognized that the existence of a large number of dormant companies can pose a serious public policy concern. In that case, Slovenia implemented the strike-off procedure under the FOCA to remove approximately 6,000 dormant companies, a figure representing only half of the number currently existing in the Federation of BiH.[3]. It is therefore evident that a coherent understanding and consistent judicial application of the doctrine of piercing the corporate veil could significantly contribute to enhancing corporate accountability and ensuring greater economic stability in BiH.

According to the most recent international governance indicators, BiH continues to exhibit systemic weaknesses in rule of law and institutional integrity. The 2024 Transparency International Corruption Perceptions Index (CPI) ranks

[1] Pušac (2024), p. 97.

[2] TAFBiH (2024), p. 14. Full report available: https://pufbih.ba/v1/public/upload/files/KORIGOVANI%20IZVJEŠTAJ%20O%20RADU%20PUFBiH%20za%202023_%20godinu.pdf. Accessed October 22, 2025.

[3] Data not available for RS.

L. Hasanovic, *Piercing the Corporate Veil: Shareholder Liability*,
Juridicum – Schriftenreihe zum Wirtschafts-, Unternehmens- und Bankrecht / Series on Business, Corporate and Banking Law,
https://doi.org/10.1007/978-3-658-52987-1_7

BiH 114th out of 180 countries, with a score of 33/100, its lowest score to date, placing it alongside Belarus as the second worst-ranked country in Europe.[4] (Transparency International, 2024) The World Justice Project's Rule of Law Index similarly ranks Bosnia and Herzegovina 71st of 142 globally and 7th of 15 regionally, underscoring persistent deficiencies in the enforcement of laws, judicial independence, and constraints on government power.[5] Complementing these findings, the 2025 V-Dem Report observes that almost all aspects of democracy are declining in more countries than they are improving, categorizing BiH as a lower-bound electoral democracy[6] with limited resilience to autocratization trends. Taken together, these indices reveal a pattern of institutional stagnation and erosion of democratic accountability, highlighting the urgent need for structural reforms that reinforce the rule of law, transparency, and corporate governance integrity as preconditions for sustainable economic development and EU integration. This data is important for policy considerations.

7.1 Analysis of Findings

The practical implementation of the piercing the corporate veil doctrine in BiH continues to be marked by significant conceptual and procedural inconsistencies across the FBiH, RS, and BD. Despite the existence of statutory provisions in Article 5 ZPD FBiH, Article 15 ZPD RS, and Article 7 ZPD BD, their judicial application remains fragmented, unpredictable, and often detached from comparative best practices.

A primary challenge concerns the ambiguity of passive legitimacy, that is, the uncertainty over which individuals fall within the scope of shareholder liability. Although the relevant provisions are directed exclusively at shareholders, courts, particularly at the lower instance, frequently extend liability to directors, thereby conflating the roles of ownership and management. This judicial expansion, while intended to address corporate abuse, lacks statutory grounding and undermines procedural clarity. In Croatia, by contrast, the codified doctrine in Article 10(3) and (4) ZTD clearly confines veil piercing to shareholders, while managerial misconduct is sanctioned under distinct provisions of company and criminal law.

---

[4] Transparency International (2024). Data available here: https://www.transparency.org/en/countries/bosnia-and-herzegovina.

[5] World Justice Project. (2023). Rule of Law Index 2023. Available here: https://worldjusticeproject.org.

[6] V-Dem Institute (2024), p. 16. Report available: https://v-dem.net/documents/61/v-dem-dr__2025_lowres_v2.pdf. Accessed November 2, 2025.

BiH courts have yet to achieve such conceptual separation, leading to overlapping and inconsistent jurisprudence.

A second challenge lies in the treatment of intent (*animus nocendi*) as a prerequisite for piercing. The divergence between FBiH and RS jurisprudence is particularly stark: FBiH courts generally require proof of an intentional act to harm creditors by shareholders, effectively narrowing the scope of Article 5 ZPD FBiH and making the doctrine almost inapplicable in practice. In contrast, RS courts adopt a more objective approach, recognizing liability based on the abuse of the corporate form regardless of proven intent. This latter model aligns with the Croatian approach, where liability arises from an objective abuse of limited liability under Article 10(4) ZTD, interpreted in light of the principles of good faith and prohibition of abuse of rights. In Germany, the question of intent remains central: under Article 826 BGB, creditors must prove deliberate immoral harm, a high threshold that reflects the strong constitutional protection of limited liability. The Trihotel and Gamma decisions narrowed this concept further, requiring proof of dolus (including *dolus eventualis*) and immoral conduct, excluding negligence. This stands in contrast to the Croatian and RS regimes, which more closely align with civil law's objective fault standards and may offer a more creditor-protective path for BiH's future doctrinal development.

The length and complexity of judicial proceedings further undermine the effectiveness of the doctrine in BiH. Cases involving shareholder liability typically last seven to eight years from the first instance to the Supreme Court. The lack of procedural efficiency discourages creditors from litigating, resulting in a dearth of appellate and supreme court jurisprudence necessary for doctrinal consolidation. Both Germany and Croatia have mitigated the procedural inefficiencies of veil-piercing litigation by integrating shareholder liability into established enforcement mechanisms. In Germany, insolvency administrators may pursue tort claims under Article 826 BGB against shareholders or controlling persons who deliberately cause moral and financial harm to creditors, thereby incorporating the concept of piercing the corporate veil within civil-law proceedings. Croatia, on the other hand, has institutionalized a more administrative approach. Under Article 30 GTA, tax authorities may directly impose shareholder liability for tax abuse without recourse to lengthy civil proceedings. This system allows Croatian public authorities to act swiftly against dormant or abusive companies, ensuring both creditor protection and fiscal discipline. In BiH, a similar administrative pathway is constitutionally precluded. The Constitutional Court of the Federation of BiH, in its decision U-14/10 of 9 March 2011, examined the constitutionality of Article 16 of the 2010 Amendments to the Law on the Tax Administration of the FBiH, which sought to introduce founder liability for corporate tax debts through administrative procedure. The amendment added the founder to the circle of persons jointly and severally liable for a company's unpaid tax obligations, thereby granting the Tax Administration authority to recover such debts directly from individuals. In its judgment from 2011, the Constitutional Court of FBiH held that this provision was inconsistent with the ZPD FBiH and violated Article II.A.2(1)(k) of the Constitution of the FBiH (right to property) and Article 1 of Protocol No. 1 to the ECHR. The Court reasoned that the Law on Tax Administration, being primarily organizational and procedural in nature, could not, without clear statutory criteria, expand the scope of personal property liability beyond that provided in company law. Because Article 5 of the ZPD FBiH does not envisage founder liability for tax debts, the legislative attempt to impose such responsibility was deemed to breach the principle of legal certainty and undermine constitutionally protected property rights. Consequently, unlike Croatia where administrative bodies may pierce the corporate veil in tax matters, BiH cannot constitutionally delegate this function to administrative authorities. Any extension of shareholder or founder liability must therefore occur within the judicial sphere and be grounded in the Law on Companies, not in tax or administrative legislation. For BiH, this means that reforms should aim not at administrative shortcuts but at clarifying the substantive criteria and procedural mechanisms for judicial application of Article 5 ZPD FBiH. This would strengthen creditor protection while remaining consistent with the principle of the rule of law and the constitutional guarantees of property and fair trial rights.

Another persistent obstacle involves indirect ownership structures and fiduciary shareholding, which enable concealment of beneficial ownership and frustrate efforts to establish liability. The absence of clear legal provisions addressing fiduciary arrangements allows individuals to avoid veil-piercing consequences by hiding behind nominal shareholders. Both Germany and Croatia offer instructive contrasts. Germany's GwG and Commercial Code define control and dominant influence as objective indicators of shareholder knowledge and power, lowering the evidentiary threshold for establishing intent in Article 826 BGB cases. Similarly, Croatia's AML framework and company law provisions rely on a 25% beneficial ownership threshold, providing an institutional link between transparency obligations and corporate liability. BiH's current regime lacks such harmonization, which weakens its ability to identify de facto controllers of companies engaged in abusive conduct.

A further difficulty lies in the fragmentation between company law and criminal law frameworks. The definition of the responsible person within the legal entity, in BiH criminal law remains inconsistent and often conflated with "director" or "beneficial owner." This incoherence complicates both prosecution and judicial reasoning. According to the 2024 Report of the TAFBIH, investigative units filed 35 criminal reports to prosecutors, estimating total tax evasion at 12,358,172.56 BAM, yet few of these cases resulted in individual accountability due to evidentiary ambiguities regarding corporate roles. Germany addresses this issue through the functional approach of Article 826 BGB, which extends liability beyond shareholders to any person, such as advisors or financiers, who knowingly contributes to fraudulent corporate activity. In contrast, Croatia's approach remains formalistic and limited to members, ensuring legal certainty but restricting flexibility. BiH's framework would benefit from harmonizing these perspectives, maintaining legal certainty while allowing liability to attach to any person who effectively exercises control and causes harm through corporate abuse.

To ensure coherence and prevent systemic abuse, BiH should develop a unified definition of "shareholder" and "controlling person" applicable across company, tax, and criminal law. Moreover, the introduction of administrative sanctions and fines for breaches of supervisory and reporting duties, similar to Germany's director liability regime or Croatia's administrative penalties for failure to maintain transparency, could create preventive incentives and relieve courts from over-relying on the veil-piercing doctrine.

Ultimately, the BiH experience illustrates that formal transposition of veil-piercing provisions without doctrinal and institutional integration leads to fragmentation and ineffectiveness. The comparative analysis of Germany and Croatia suggests that a sustainable reform should combine Croatia's codified objectivity with Germany's functional precision, thereby fostering a system that both preserves limited liability and ensures accountability for those who exploit it.

7.2 De Lege Ferenda Recommendations: Strengthening Corporate Governance and Accountability in BiH

Given the persistent challenges in corporate governance and the widespread presence of inactive or insolvent companies within BiH, legislative reform has become an imperative for enhancing transparency, accountability, and market integrity. The following *de lege ferenda* proposals aim to strengthen the company-law frameworks of the FBiH, RS, and BD, while ensuring consistency with EU standards and comparative developments in Germany and Croatia.

1. Deregistration of Inactive and Insolvent Companies
   It is proposed that companies which remain inactive or fail to initiate liquidation within a defined statutory period be subject to automatic deregistration from the business register. In such circumstances, members of the company should bear joint and several liability with their personal assets for any outstanding obligations incurred prior to deregistration.
   This mechanism, inspired by the Financial Operations of Companies Act (1999) would empower registry courts or commercial registries to remove dormant or insolvent entities *ex officio*. Such a measure would significantly improve the reliability of the corporate register, enhance creditor protection, and promote a healthier market environment by preventing the continued existence of legal entities used for fraudulent or tax-evasive purposes.
   However, in light of the Constitutional Court of the FBiH decision U-14/10 from 2011, any deregistration mechanism involving personal liability must incorporate judicial oversight and procedural guarantees consistent with Article 6(1) of the European Convention on Human Rights and Article II.A.2 of the Constitution of the FBiH. Legislative reform should therefore ensure that deregistration operates within the constitutional framework, balancing administrative efficiency with respect for the right to property and the principle of legal certainty.
2. Harmonization of Company Law with Anti-Money-Laundering Legislation
   ZPD on all three levels should be harmonized with the Law on the Prevention of Money Laundering and Financing of Terrorism, thereby ensuring coherence and transparency in the disclosure of ownership structures.
   In multi-member companies, the doctrine of piercing the corporate veil should be directed toward identifying shareholders exercising significant influence or control. The current ownership threshold of 20% should be raised to 25% to align with the beneficial-ownership standard under the EU's 5th Anti-Money-Laundering Directive (Directive (EU) 2018/843). Moreover, the legislation should expressly recognize indirect and fiduciary ownership, including trust-based and nominee arrangements, to ensure that ultimate beneficial owners cannot conceal their control through layered corporate structures.
   Such harmonization would enhance corporate transparency, facilitate cross-border regulatory cooperation, and strengthen the integrity of the business register. It would also address the current divergence between company law

and AML frameworks, a divergence which undermines effective identification of responsible persons and obstructs enforcement of corporate liability in BiH.

3. Establishment of a Register of Disqualified Directors
The duty of care forms a cornerstone of modern corporate governance. It imposes on directors and managers a legal and ethical obligation to act with diligence, competence, and loyalty toward the company and its stakeholders. This standard of behavior, rooted in both decision-making and supervisory processes, ensures that managerial actions are properly prepared, evidence-based, and directed toward the company's legitimate interests rather than personal gain.[7] Beyond its internal function, the duty of care serves as an instrument of public trust, reinforcing confidence among shareholders, employees, and the broader market.[8]
In line with comparative experience from Germany[9], the United Kingdom[10], and Croatia[11], Bosnia and Herzegovina should establish a Register of Disqualified Directors. This public register would contain individuals who have: seriously breached their fiduciary or statutory duties; caused harm to the company, its creditors, or shareholders; or engaged in conduct that demonstrates unfitness for managerial office.
Persons listed in the register would be prohibited from serving as directors, managers, or supervisory-board members in any legal entity for a specified period. Such a measure would strengthen corporate discipline, deter repeat misconduct, and reinforce a culture of ethical and responsible management. Additionally, shareholders should remain jointly liable for damages arising from breaches of their legal obligations, ensuring that both ownership and control are exercised in accordance with principles of good faith and accountability.
4. Automated electronic verification between the Tax Administration and the Court Register
Recent legislative developments in Croatia offer a compelling model for reforming the company registration framework in BiH. The 2023 Amendments to the ZTD, which entered into force on 1 January 2024, introduced a new Article 62.a under the title "Prohibition on Company Formation and

[7] Östberg (2022), p. 15.

[8] Sørensen (2022), p. 13.

[9] Art. 6(2) GmbHG.

[10] Company Directors Disqualification Act 1986.

[11] Court Register Act.

Appointment of Directors or Executive Managers by Persons with Outstanding Public Debts." This provision prohibits both legal and natural persons from founding or managing companies if they or their affiliated entities have unpaid public liabilities, such as taxes, social contributions, or unpaid wages.[12] Complementary amendments to the Court Register Act (ZSR) introduced Articles 40.a and 43(6–8), which modernized the registration procedure by replacing the founders' self-declaration of tax compliance with an automated electronic verification between the Tax Administration and the Court Register.[13] This reform eliminates the possibility of repeated company formation by tax debtors, enhances the integrity of the business register, and ensures that the corporate sector operates in compliance with fiscal and labor obligations. A similar mechanism should be introduced in BiH, adapted to its entity-level company laws and coordinated through a central business register. The adoption of provisions analogous to Article 62.a ZTD and Article 40.a ZSR would prevent individuals and legal entities with outstanding tax or contribution arrears from founding new companies or serving as directors, supervisory board members, or executive managers. The measure would directly address one of the most visible symptoms of regulatory failure in BiH, the ability of persons with significant public debts to repeatedly establish new companies, leaving unpaid obligations behind. For practical implementation, BiH authorities could establish an interoperable data exchange system between the Tax Administration, Pension and Health Funds, and the Business Court Registers, enabling real-time verification of tax compliance prior to company registration. This approach would not only reduce administrative burden but also strengthen fiscal discipline, corporate transparency, and public trust in the legal system. It would further align BiH with EU standards of responsible corporate governance and reflect the principle that participation in the market presupposes compliance with basic financial and social obligations. Such reform would also contribute to the stability of the corporate registry by preventing serial misuse of limited liability structures. Introducing clearly defined statutory preconditions for registration, combined with automated inter-institutional cooperation, would enhance both the integrity and credibility of BiH's company law framework.

[12] Brnabić (2019), p. 157.

[13] Barbić (2024), p. 140.

5. Policy Implications and Legislative Outlook
   The adoption of these measures would modernize BiH corporate framework and align it with the EU acquis, particularly within Chapter 6 (Company Law) and Chapter 23 (Judiciary and Fundamental Rights) of the accession negotiations. The combination of automatic deregistration, transparency in ownership, and director disqualification would enhance market confidence and reduce systemic risks associated with dormant or mismanaged entities.

   Ultimately, these proposals seek to achieve a balanced framework that preserves the principle of limited liability, safeguards individual rights, and promotes corporate responsibility in line with European standards of good governance and the rule of law.

8 Conclusion

This dissertation examined the doctrine of piercing the corporate veil in BiH through a comparative lens, juxtaposing the statutory and judicial frameworks of FBiH, RS, and BD with developments in Germany and Croatia, as well as relevant EU instruments touching company law, AML, taxation, and corporate governance. The central claim, that clearer, coherent, and consistently applied legal criteria for veil piercing enhance accountability, deter abuse of corporate form, and improve market integrity, has been broadly confirmed.

Empirically, BiH faces a pronounced enforcement deficit: large numbers of inactive or insolvent limited liability companies, widespread tolerance of non-payment, and prolonged litigation horizons. Doctrinally, the three BiH regimes diverge in the scope and construction of shareholder liability[1]: RS adopts a more objective, abuse-based approach; FBiH case law often imports a stringent "intent to harm" requirement that narrows creditor remedies; and BD blends enumerated scenarios with broader principles. This fragmentation produces uncertainty over passive legitimacy (shareholders vs. directors), proof standards (intent vs. objective abuse), and the interface with criminal and tax enforcement.

Comparative insights illuminate viable pathways but also constitutional limits. Germany's post-Trihotel/Gamma jurisprudence channels most shareholder external liability into the civil-tort paradigm of Article 826 BGB (intentional, immoral harm), preserving limited liability while sanctioning egregious conduct; director and insolvency-law remedies shoulder the bulk of creditor protection.

[1] ZPD FBiH art. 5; ZPD RS art. 15; ZPD BD art. 7.

L. Hasanovic, *Piercing the Corporate Veil: Shareholder Liability*,
Juridicum – Schriftenreihe zum Wirtschafts-, Unternehmens- und Bankrecht / Series on Business, Corporate and Banking Law,
https://doi.org/10.1007/978-3-658-52987-1_8

Croatia takes a codified, shareholder-focused route (ZTD Art. 10(3)–(4)), complemented by tax and registry tools (e.g., ZSR) and automated cross-checks, which lower enforcement frictions and align corporate transparency with fiscal compliance. However, the Constitutional Court of the Federation of BiH in its judgment from March 2011 has foreclosed Croatian-style administrative imposition of founder/shareholder liability via tax authorities, requiring that any extension of personal liability proceed through company-law criteria and judicial determination. In short, BiH reform must privilege judicial pathways, while modernizing the substance and procedure of shareholder liability in line with rule-of-law guarantees.

Normatively, the dissertation advances a calibrated reform model for BiH:

(i) sharpen and harmonize substantive veil-piercing criteria across FBiH/RS/BD toward an objective abuse-of-rights standard;

(ii) codify clearer rules on passive legitimacy (shareholders/controlling persons) while preserving distinct tracks for director and insolvency liability;

(iii) integrate AML-style beneficial-ownership definitions (with explicit recognition of fiduciary/indirect holdings) to close evidentiary gaps;

(iv) introduce a Register of Disqualified Directors with proportionate, judicially supervised consequences; and

(v) implement automated, pre-registration compliance verification between the tax administration and court registers, coupled with expedited judicial review to remain within U-14/10 constraints.

Taken together, these steps reconcile the protection of limited liability with credible accountability mechanisms and align BiH with EU-level expectations under Chaps. 6 and 23 of the acquis.

Substantively, the hypotheses are supported. H1 and H4 find confirmation in the German and Croatian evidence: legal clarity and a structured interface between civil and criminal liability increase accountability and deter misuse. H2 is borne out by BiH's inconsistent doctrine and cross-border exposure: the lack of harmonized standards correlates with higher abuse risk and regulatory arbitrage. H3 is validated in part: EU-driven transparency (beneficial ownership; digital formation) and procedural modernization, when transposed with constitutional care, can reduce misuse, though without doctrinal integration at the national level, gains remain limited. The broader governance context, weak rule of law, low CPI scores, and V-Dem's lower-bound electoral democracy classification, underscores that company-law reform, if pursued alone, is necessary but insufficient; institutional capacity and judicial specialization are equally decisive.

This dissertation makes several substantive contributions to the understanding and reform of shareholder liability and the doctrine of piercing the corporate veil in BiH. First, it provides a doctrinal synthesis by mapping the veil-piercing grounds across the legal frameworks of FBiH, RS, and the BD, and situating them in comparative perspective with the German tort-based and Croatian code-based models. This comparative analysis clarifies the available options for developing a BiH-specific and constitutionally sound doctrine of shareholder liability. Second, the research achieves constitutional constraint integration by operationalizing the Constitutional Court decision U-14/10 and proposing an enforcement architecture that enhances procedural speed and legal certainty while avoiding administrative overreach. Third, the dissertation offers a policy design contribution, formulating concrete and implementable reform measures, including harmonized definitions of control and beneficial ownership, the introduction of a register of disqualified directors, and interoperable links between tax administration and court registries under judicial supervision, that bridge the gap between legal principle and institutional practice. Nevertheless, the study is subject to certain limitations. It relies on reported judgments and administrative data, which may under-represent informal settlements and unreported jurisprudence. Furthermore, it does not include qualitative interviews with judges, insolvency practitioners, and registry officials that could have provided deeper insights into evidentiary standards and case-management dynamics.

Building upon the doctrinal and comparative findings of this dissertation, an avenue for future research lies in examining the role of artificial intelligence (AI) and digitalization in corporate monitoring and accountability. As business registration, financial reporting, and compliance processes increasingly move into digital environments, AI-driven tools could serve as an intelligent intermediary, or AI middleman, capable of observing, detecting, and flagging irregular corporate behavior in real time. Future studies could explore how machine-learning systems might identify early indicators of corporate misconduct, fraudulent asset transfers, or systematic non-payment, by analyzing large datasets drawn from tax administrations, company registries, and court databases. Research could also evaluate the ethical, legal, and data-protection implications of such predictive surveillance, as well as its compatibility with constitutional guarantees of privacy and due process. Integrating AI oversight mechanisms within the corporate-governance architecture of BiH could enhance transparency, improve enforcement capacity, and help mitigate the human and institutional limitations that currently hinder early detection of abuse. Investigating these possibilities would bridge the emerging field of AI-assisted regulatory governance with traditional company-law and corporate-liability frameworks, offering an innovative dimension to future doctrinal and policy development.

Literature

Books & Journal Articles

Achenbach, H. (2023). Der Allgemeine Teil des Ordnungswidrigkeitenrechts–Charakteristika im Vergleich mit dem Strafrecht. Albrecht, A. H.& Steinberg, G. in Der Allgemeine Teil des Wirtschaftsstrafrechts, Baden-Baden: *Nomos*, 2023. https://doi.org/10.5771/9783748942689

Achenbach, H. (2012). Haftung und Ahndung. Wider die Vertauschung zweier disparater Rechtsfolgemodelle. *Lorenz Schulz / Michael Reinhart / Oliver Sahan (Hrsg.), Festschrift für Imme Roxin, Heidelberg 2012. ISBN 978–3–8114–3628–2,* 3–11.

Adam, S., Vermeulen, G., & De Bondt, W. (2008). Corporate criminal liability and the EC/EU: bridging sovereignty paradigms for the sake of an area of freedom, security and justice. In La responsabilité pénale des personnes morales en Europe-Corporate Criminal Liability in Europe (p. 373–432). *La Charte.*

Akey, P., & Appel, I. (2021). The limits of limited liability: Evidence from industrial pollution. *The Journal of Finance*, *76*(1), 5–55.

Arlen, J., & Kraakman, R. (1997). Controlling corporate misconduct: An analysis of corporate liability regimes. *NYU Law Review, 72*(4), 687–779. https://nyulawreview.org/issues/volume-72-number-4/controlling-corporate-misconduct-an-analysis-of-corporate-liability-regimes/

Aronofsky, D. (1985). Piercing the Transnational Corporate Veil: Trends, Developments, and the Need for Widespread Adoption of Enterprise Analysis. *NCJ Int'l L. & Com. Reg.*, 10, 31.

Ayres, Ian. (1992). Making difference: the contractual contributions of Easterbrook and fischel. *University of Chicago Law Review*, 59(3), 1391–1420.

L. Hasanovic, *Piercing the Corporate Veil: Shareholder Liability*,
Juridicum – Schriftenreihe zum Wirtschafts-, Unternehmens- und Bankrecht / Series on Business, Corporate and Banking Law,
https://doi.org/10.1007/978-3-658-52987-1

Bainbridge, S. M. (2005). Abolishing llc veil piercing. *University of Illinois Law Review*, 2005(1), 77–106.
Bainbridge, S. M., & Henderson, M. T. (2016). Limited liability: a legal and economic analysis. *Edward Elgar Publishing.*
Banović, D., Gavrić, S., & Mariño, M. B. (2021). The political system of Bosnia and Herzegovina. *Cham: Springer International Publishing.*
Barber, D. H. (1980). Piercing the corporate veil. *Willamette Law Review*, *17*, 371.
Barbić, J. (2024). Zakon o trgovačkim društvima, Zakon o sudskom registru, Pravilnici, Zakoni, Uredbe EU: Pročišćeni tekstovi s uvodnim objašnjenjima i abecednim kazalima (9th ed.). *Zagreb: Organizator.*
Barbić, J. (2020). Pravo društava: Knjiga druga, Društva kapitala (Svezak II., 7. izmijenjeno i dopunjeno izdanje). *Zagreb: Organizator.*
Barbić, J. (2009). Odgovornost članova za obveze društva kapitala. *Računovodstvo, revizija i financije, 19*(1), 36–43.
Barbić, J. (2008). Pravo društava: Knjiga prva, Opći dio (3. izmijenjeno izdanje). *Zagreb: Organizator.*
Berger, B. (2025). International and domestic arbitration in Switzerland. Bern: *Stämpfli Verlag*, 2025 - 996 p. - ISBN: 9783727205101.
Berle, A. A. (1947). The theory of enterprise entity. *Columbia Law Review*, *47*(3), 343–358.
Bartolucci, M. A. (2024). The Implementation of Directive EU 2017/1371 (Known as the "PIF Directive") on the Fight Against Fraud to the Union's Financial Interests in Italian Law. *EuCLR European Criminal Law Review,* 14(1), 78–93.
Besson, S. (2010). Piercing the corporate veil: back on the right track. Multiparty arbitration, (VII), 147–160.
Biais, B., Mariotti, T., Rochet, J. C., & Villeneuve, S. (2010). Large risks, limited liability, and dynamic moral hazard. *Econometrica*, *78*(1), 73–118.
Birkmose, H. S., Neville, M., & Sørensen, K. E. (2019). Abuse of Companies: An Introduction. Abuse of Companies, Hanne S. Birkmose, Mette Neville & Karsten Engsig Sørensen (eds.), *Kluwer Law International*, 19–03.
Bittmann, F. (2011). Strafrecht und Gesellschaftsrecht. *Zeitschrift für Unternehmens- und Gesellschaftsrecht*, vol. 38, no. 6, 2009, pp. 931–980. https://doi.org/10.1515/ZGRE.2009.931.
Blackstone, W. (1809). Rights of persons (Vol. 1). A. Strahan.
Born, G. B. (2020). International commercial arbitration.(3rd Edition) *Kluwer Law International.*
Born, G. B. (2009). International commercial arbitration. *Kluwer Law International.*
Brnabić, R. (2010). Proboj pravne osobnosti i odgovornost za obveze. Doctoral dissertation, *Pravni fakultet u Zagrebu.*
Brnabić, R. (2019). Novine u pravu društava s ograničenom odgovornošću. In *54. savjetovanje "Računovodstvo, revizija i porezi u praksi"* (pp. 157–166). *Zagreb: Hrvatska zajednica računovođa i financijskih djelatnika.*
Brnabic, R., & Ivancev, M. (2017). Mixture of Properties and Legal Identities in the Corporate Law. *Economic and Social Development: Book of Proceedings*, 260–271.
Ceronja, P. (2022). Širenje učinaka arbitražne klauzule na treće putem proboja pravne osobnosti. *Zbornik Pravnog fakulteta u Zagrebu*, 72(1–2), 727–753.

Cheng, T. K. (2011). The Corporate Veil Doctrine Revisited: A Comparative Study of the English and the US Corporate Veil Doctrines. *BC Int'l & Comp. L. Rev.*, 34, 329.

Cheng-Han, T., Wang, J., & Hofmann, C. (2019). Piercing the Corporate Veil: Historical, Theoretical and Comparative Perspectives. *Berkeley Bus. LJ*, *16*, 140.

Choudhury, B., & Petrin, M. (2019). Criminal Law. In Corporate Duties to the Public (pp. 166–205). chapter, *Cambridge: Cambridge University Press.*

Coffee, J. C. Jr. (2020). Corporate crime and punishment: The crisis of underenforcement. *Berrett-Koehler Publishers.*

Deiser, G. F. (1909). The Juristic Person. III. *University of Pennsylvania Law Review and American Law Register*, *57*(5), 300–314.

Dewey, J. (1925). The historic background of corporate legal personality. *Yale LJ*, *35*, 655.

Dicey, A. V. (2019). *Lectures on the Relation between Law and Public Opinion during the 19th Century*. Jazzybee Verlag.

Dignam, A. (2000). Company law and the Human Rights Act 1998: Interesting times. *The Company Lawyer, 21*(5), 151.

Dhooge, LJ (2006). Human Rights for Transnational Corporations. Journal of Transnational Law & Policy, Vol. 16, Issue 2 (Spring 2007), pp. 197–250

Easterbrook, F. H., & Fischel, D. R. (1989). *Corporate contract*, the Columbia Law Review, 89(7), 1416–1448.

Easterbrook, F. H., & Fischel, D. R. (1985). Limited liability and the corporation *University of Chicago Law Review*, 52(1), 89–117.

Emberland, M. (2006). The human rights of companies: exploring the structure of ECHR protection. Oxford University Press.

Fama, E. F., & Jensen, M. C. (1983). Separation of ownership and control. *The journal of law and Economics*, *26*(2), 301–325.

Fleckner, A. M. (2016). Adam Smith on the Joint Stock Company. *Max Planck Institute for Tax Law and Public Finance Working Paper 2016 – 01.*

Fleischer, H., & Harzmeier, L. (2015). Zur Abdingbarkeit der Treuepflichten bei Personengesellschaft und GmbH. *Neue Zeitschrift für Gesellschaftsrecht*, 1289–1297.

Freeman, R. E., Wicks, A. C., & Parmar, B. (2004). Stakeholder theory and "the corporate objective revisited". *Organization science, 15*(3), 364–369.

Friedman, M. (2016). Capitalism and freedom. In *Democracy: a reader* (p. 344–349). *Columbia University Press.*

Friedman, M. (2007). The social responsibility of business is to increase its profits. In *Corporate ethics and corporate governance* (p. 173–178). *Berlin, Heidelberg: Springer Berlin Heidelberg.*

Gagula, A. (2020). Arbitrability of Shareholder Disputes in Bosnian Law. *Balkan Yearbook of European and International Law* 2019, 53–67.

Gelter, M., & Vicente, L. (2019). Abuse of Companies through Choice of Incorporation? *Fordham Law Legal Studies Research Paper.*

Gerner-Beuerle, C., & Schillig, M. A. (2019). Comparative company law. *Oxford University Press.*

Gerneth, N. (2022). Die Online-Grundung von Gesellschaften nach DiRUG und Digitalisierungsrichtlinie. *Freilaw: Freiburg L. Students J.*, 54.

Gevurtz, F. A. (2025). Do Courts Get It Right When Piercing The Corporate Veil? An Empirical Study. Available at SSRN: https://ssrn.com/abstract=5110762 or https://doi.org/10.2139/ssrn.5110762.

Gierke, O. von. (1913). *Das deutsche Genossenschaftsrecht* (Bd. 4: *Die Staats- und Korporationslehre der Neuzeit, durchgeführt bis zur Mitte des siebzehnten, für das Naturrecht bis zum Beginn des neunzehnten Jahrhunderts*). Weidmannsche Buchhandlung.

Gierke, O. von. (1887). Die Genossenschaftstheorie und die deutsche Rechtsprechung. *Weidmann, Berlin.*

Gierke, O. von. (1873). Das Deutsche Genossenschaftsrecht: Geschichte des Deutschen Körperschaftsbegriffs (Vol. 2). *Weidmann.*

Gierke, O. von. (1868). *Das deutsche Genossenschaftsrecht* (Bd. 1: *Rechtsgeschichte der deutschen Genossenschaft*). Berlin.

Gindis, D. (2009). From fictions and aggregates to real entities in the theory of the firm. *Journal of Institutional Economics*, *5*(1), 25–46.

Geis, Gilbert, & DiMento, Joseph F. C. (2002). Empirical evidence and the legal doctrine of corporate criminal liability. *American Journal of Criminal Law*, 29(3), 341–376.

Gotovuša, E. (2020). Criminal Liability of Legal Persons in Bosnia and Herzegovina and Croatia. *Regional Law Review*, 169.

Gray, Cheryl W.; Hanson, Rebecca J. (1993). Corporate governance in Central and Eastern Europe: lessons from advanced market economies (English). Policy, Research working papers; no. WPS 1182. Transition and macro - adjustment Washington, *D.C.: World Bank Group.*

Grbo, Z. (2024). Pravni okvir arbitraže u Bosni i Hercegovini – možemo (li) bez lex specialis? *Pravni zbornik: Journal for Legal Theory and Practice*, (1), pp. 71–94. Association of Jurists of Montenegro.

Grbo, Z. (2017). Uvod u pravo privrednih društava. Pravni fakultet Univerziteta u Sarajevu.

Grbo, Z. (2017a). Mehanizmi zaštite stranih investicija – slučaj Bosne i Hercegovine. *Godišnjak Pravnog Fakulteta u Sarajevu*, 60.

Grbo, Z. (2016). Režim posebnih dužnosti prema privrednom društvu u pravu Federacije Bosne i Hercegovine. *LIX*, 411.

Grbo, Z., Davidović, D. (2016). Pregled novih rješenja Zakona o privrednim društvima Federacije Bosne i Hercegovine. *Legal Thought/Pravna Misao.*

Grossman, S. J., & Hart, O. D. (1986). The costs and benefits of ownership: A theory of vertical and lateral integration. *Journal of political economy*, *94*(4), 691–719.

Gup, B. E., & Beekarry, N. (2009). Limited liability companies (LLCs) and financial crimes. *Journal of Money Laundering Control*, *12*(1), 7–18.

Habenicht, A. (2011). Praktische Aspekte einer Neuausrichtung der strafrechtlichen Organ- und Vertreterhaftung (§ 14 StGB). *Juristische Rundschau*, vol. 2011, no. 1, 2011, pp. 17–20. https://doi.org/10.1515/juru.2011.17

Hamill, S. P. (1998). The origins behind the limited liability company. *Ohio St. LJ*, *59*, 1459.

Harari, Y. N. (2014). Sapiens: A brief history of humankind. *Random House.*

Hasanovic, L. (2024). Expansion and Improvement of the Use of Digital Tools and Processes in Company Law. *YBL Fac. Sarajevo*, *67*, 209.

Henzler, J. (2009). Haftung der GmbH-Gesellschafter wegen Existenzvernichtung. *Nomos Verlagsgesellschaft GmbH & Co. KG.*

Hickman, E., Petrin, M. (2021) Trustworthy AI and corporate governance: the EU's ethics guidelines for trustworthy artificial intelligence from a company law perspective. *Eur Bus Organ Law Rev* 22:593 625. https://doi.org/10.1007/s40804-021-00224-0

Horwitz, M. J. (1992). The transformation of American law, 1870–1960: The crisis of legal orthodoxy. *Oxford University Press.*

Hutchison, A. (2014). The Whanganui river as a legal person. *Alternative Law Journal*, *39*(3), 179–182.

Imamović-Čizmić, K. (2017). Izazovi uvođenja procjene učinaka propisa – lekcije za Bosnu i Hercegovinu. *Godišnjak Pravnog Fakulteta u Sarajevu, 60.*

Jelinić, S., & Akšamović, D. (2009). O proboju pravne osobnosti. *Pravo u gospodarstvu, 48*(2), 544–574.

Jevremović, P. T. (2018). Arbitrability of corporate disputes regarding general meetings' decisions. *Pravo i privreda*, 56(4–6), 223–245.

Johnson, L. (2011). Law and legal theory in the history of corporate responsibility: corporate personhood. *Seattle UL Rev.*, *35*, 1135.

Jurić, D., & Braut Filipović, M. (2020). Limited Liability Companies in Croatia. *Central European journal of comparative law*, *1*(1), 69–85.

Kärki, A. T. (2020). Piercing the Corporate Veil in Finland–A Multijurisdictional Study Aimed at Developing the Finnish Piercing Doctrine.

Kersting, C. (2000). Die Vorgesellschaft im europäischen Gesellschaftsrecht: gemeinschaftsrechtliche Vorgaben und nationale Rechtsordnungen. *Sparkasse.* (ISSN 0038–6561), 2001–03–01

Khanna, V. S. (1995). Corporate criminal liability: What purpose does it serve. *Harvard Law Review*, *109*, 1477.

Kindhäuser, U., & Zimmermann, T. (2025). Strafrecht Allgemeiner Teil (12. Auflage.). *Nomos.*

Krawczyk-Giehsmann, A. (2020). Shareholders' Liability for Ruining a Company in Light of the CJEU's Judgment in Kornhaas. *European Business Organization Law Review*, *21*(2), 475–504.

Kryvoi, Y. (2010). Piercing the corporate veil in international arbitration. *Global Business Law Review*, *1*, 169.

Krendt, C. S., & Krendl, J. R. (1978). Piercing the corporate veil: focusing the inquiry. *Denver Law Journal*, *55*, 1.

Kuntz, T. (2018). Asset partitioning, limited liability and veil piercing: review essay on Bainbridge/Henderson, limited liability. *European Business Organization Law Review*, *19*, 439–463.

Kuntz, M. (2017). Conceptualising transnational corporate groups for international criminal law. *Nomos Verlagsgesellschaft GmbH & Co. KG.*

Lafarre, A. (2023). The proposed Corporate Sustainability Due Diligence Directive: corporate liability design for social harms. *European Business Law Review*, *34*(2).

Laufer, W. S. (2006). Corporate bodies and guilty minds: The failure of corporate criminal liability. *University of Chicago Press.*

Lee, I. B. (2017). Understanding Corporate Criminal Liability. In B. Choudhury & M. Petrin (Eds.), Understanding the Company: Corporate Governance and Theory (pp. 185–212). Chapter, *Cambridge: Cambridge University Press.*

Lepetić, J. (2015). Kompanijskopravni režim sukoba interesa–Dužnost lojalnosti. *Beograd: Pravni fakultet.*

Lopez, A. S. (1982). The Alter Ego Doctrine: Alternative Challenges to the Corporate Form. *UCLA Law Review, 30(1), 129–155.*

Macharashvili, N. (2023). Corporate Identity and Piercing the Corporate Veil: Comparative Perspectives from the United States, United Kingdom and Germany. Master Thesis. *University in Vienna.*

Machen Jr, A. W. (1911). Corporate personality. *Can. L. Times*, *31*, 565.

Macey, J. C. (2019). What corporate veil. *Michigan Law Review,* 117(6), 1195–1214.

Macey, J., & Mitts, J. (2014). Finding order in the morass: the three real justifications for piercing the corporate veil. *Cornell L. Rev.,* 100, 99.

Maitland, F. W. (1900). Corporation sole. *LQ Rev.*, *16*, 335.

Mark, G. A. (1987). The personification of the business corporation in American law. *U. Chi. L. Rev.*, *54*, 1441.

Matheson, J. H. (2008). The modern law of corporate groups: An empirical study of piercing the corporate veil in the parent-subsidiary context. *NCL Rev.* 87: 1091.

Matschernus, G. (2007). Die Durchgriffshaftung wegen Existenzvernichtung in der GmbH. *Nomos Verlagsgesellschaft mbH & Co. KG.* https://doi.org/10.5771/9783845200866

Meckling, W. H., & Jensen, M. C. (1976). Theory of the Firm. *Managerial behavior, agency costs and ownership structure*, *3*(4), 305–360.

Merkt, H., & Spindler, G. (2006). Direct liability of controlling parties (piercing the corporate veil) and related legal constellations. *Legal capital in Europe. De Gruyter Recht, Berlin*, 166–231.

Miller, S. K. (1998). Piercing the corporate veil among affiliated companies in the European Community and in the US: A comparative analysis of US, German, and UK veil-piercing approaches. *American Business Law Journal*, 36(1), 73–149.

Millon, D. (1990). Theories of the Corporation. *Washington and Lee University School of Law. Duke LJ, 201.*

Millon, D. (2006).Piercing the corporate veil, financial responsibility, and the limits of limited liability. *Emory Law Journal*, 56(5), 1305–1382.

Morel, S., Mathonet, C., Gounev, P., De Wispelaere, F., De Smedt, L., & Schuster, E. (2021). Letterbox companies: overview of the phenomenon and existing measures.

Munkholm, N. V. (2019). Abuse of companies and posting of workers. In Abuse of companies (pp. 343–368). *Wolters Kluwer.*

Neher, F. (2011). Innergesellschaftliche Haftung für die Verletzung von Sorgfaltspflichten und Durchgriffshaftung bei Kapitalgesellschaften. *Nomos Verlagsgesellschaft mbH & Co. KG.*

Neville, M. (2011). Shareholder Activism: The Suspicious Shareholder. *The European Financial Market in Transition, Hanne Birkmose, Mette Neville, Karsten Engsig Sørensen, eds., Kluwer Law International*, 10–17.

Nikolajev, A., (2020). Uvod u ekonomsku analizu prava, *Pravni fakultet – Univerzitet u Sarajevu.*

Obermaier, F., & Obermayer, B. (2024). The Panama Papers: A Political Earthquake and its Unfinished Legacy. *Brown Journal of World Affairs*, *31*(1).

Oh, P. B. (2010). Veil-piercing. *Tex. L. Rev.*, *89*, 81.

Osrečak, J. (2014). Poredbenopravni prikaz načela savjesnosti i poštenja. *Zagrebačka pravna revija, 3*(1), 53–77.
Ottolenghi, S. (1990). From peeping behind the corporate veil, to ignoring it completely. *The Modern Law Review, 53*(3), 338–353.
Örn, P. (2009). Piercing the Corporate Veil-a Law and Economics Analysis. Lund University Publications. Available here: https://lup.lub.lu.se/luur/download?func=downloadFile&recordOId=1563314&fileOId=1566244.
Östberg, J. (2022). The duty to act in the interest of the company. In H. S. Birkmose, M. Neville, & K. E. Sørensen (Eds.), *Instruments of EU corporate governance: Effecting changes in the management of companies in a changing world* (Vol. 19, pp. 15–37). Kluwer Law International BV.
Petričević, J. (2023). Proboj pravne osobnosti s posebnim osvrtom na komparativnu sudsku praksu. *Zagrebačka pravna revija, 12*(2), 241–290.
Phillips, M. J. (1993). Reappraising the real entity theory of the corporation. *Fla. St. UL Rev., 21*, 1061.
Pieth, M. (1997). International cooperation to combat corruption. *Corruption and the global economy*, 119–131.
Posner, R. A. (1975). The rights of creditors of affiliated corporations. *University of Chicago Law Review, 43(3), 499–526. 43, 499.*
Primorac, D. (2011). Liability of Legal Persons in Criminal Legislation Republic of Croatia and Bosnia and Herzegovina. *Collection Papers Actualities Civ. & Com. L. & Legal Prac.*, 292.
Pušac, J. (2024). Probijanje pravne ličnosti: aspekti doktrine, zakonodavstva i sudske prakse. *Annual of the Faculty of Law/Godišnjak Fakulteta Pravnih Nauka, 14*(14).
Pušac, J. (2024a). Značaj finansijskog forenzičnog veštačenja u sporovima zbog probijanja šravne ličnosti. *Economy & Market Communication Review/Časopis za Ekonomiju i Tržišne Komunikacije, 14*(1).
Rengier, R. (2025). *Strafrecht Allgemeiner Teil* (17., neu bearbeitete Auflage.). C.H. Beck.
Ribstein, L. E. (2005). Reverse Limited Liability and the Design of Business Associations. *Del. J. Corp. L., 30*, 199.
Ribstein, L. E. (1991). Limited liability and theories of the corporation. Maryland Law Review, 50(1), 80–130.
Röthel, L. (2020). Sittenwidrige Schädigung im Abgasskandal – Zur Deliktshaftung bei Dieselgate. *Juristische Ausbildung (JURA)*, 42(11), 1388–1393.
Röthel, A. (2021). Vorsätzliche sittenwidrige Schädigung (§ 826 BGB). *JURA-Juristische Ausbildung*, 43(3), 258–264.
Sahadžić, M., & Woelk, J. (2023). Federalizam u Bosni i Hercegovini,(a) simetrična „država blizanac". *Građani, устав, Europa, rječnik osnovnih ustavnih појмова у БиХ/Citizens, Constitution, Europe, Glossary of essential constitutional concepts in BiH*, 129–132.
Savigny, F. C. V. (1847). System der heutigen Römischen Rechts: vol. 6.
Schane, S. A. (1986). Corporation is a person: The language of a legal fiction. *Tul. L. Rev., 61*, 563.
Schmidt, K. (1994). Zur Durchgriffsfestigkeit der GmbH. Grenzen der Gesellschafter- und Geschäftsführerhaftung gegenüber Dritten nach dem BGH-Urteil vom 13. April 1994 – ZIP 1994, 867, ZIP 1994, 837–844

Schmidt, J. (2025). The Digitalisation Directive II–a Major Expansion and Upgrade of EU Business Registers. *European Company and Financial Law Review*, 21(5–6), 563–603.

Schmidt, J. (2021). DiRUG-RefE: Ein Digitalisierungs-Ruck für das deutsche Gesellschafts- und Registerrecht. *ZIP: Zeitschrift für Wirtschaftsrecht*, (3), 112–123.

Schneider, A. (2014). Corporate Criminal Liability and Conflicts of Jurisdiction. In: Brodowski, D., Espinoza de los Monteros de la Parra, M., Tiedemann, K., Vogel, J. (eds) Regulating Corporate Criminal Liability. *Springer,* Cham. https://doi.org/10.1007/978-3-319-05993-8_20.

Shavell, S. (1986). The judgment proof problem. *International review of law and economics*, *6*(1), 45–58.

Stiglitz, J. E., & Pieth, M. (2016). Overcoming the shadow economy, 1–24.

Smith, A. (2002). An Inquiry into the Nature and Causes of the Wealth of Nations. *Readings in economic sociology*, 6–17.

Sørensen, K. E. (2022). Managerial procedural rules. In H. S. Birkmose, M. Neville, & K. E. Sørensen (Eds.), *Instruments of EU corporate governance: Effecting changes in the management of companies in a changing world* (Vol. 19, Chapter 4). *Kluwer Law International BV.*

Sørensen, K. E. (2019). Free Movement in the EU and the Abuse of Companies. *Published in Abuse of Companies, edited by Hanne S. Birkmose, Mette Neville, Karsten Engsig Sørensen, Kluwer Law International*, 21–01.

Steffek, F. (2009). Der subjektive Tatbestand der Gesellschafterhaftung im Recht der GmbH—zugleich ein Beitrag zum Haftungsdurchgriff. *JuristenZeitung*, 77–85.

Stout, L. A. (2012). New Thinking on "Shareholder Primacy". *Accounting, Economics, and Law*, *2*(2).

Thompson, R. B. (1990). Piercing the corporate veil: an empirical study *Cornell Law Review*, 76(5), 1036–1074.

Tiedemann, K. (2012). Business-Related Criminal Law in Europe: A Critical Inventory. *U. Miami Int'l & Comp. L. Rev.*, *20*, 135.

Teichmann, C. (2019). The company law package–content and state of play. *European Company and Financial Law Review*, 16(1–2), 3–14.

Trivun, V. (2011). Fiducijarne dužnosti članova uprave dioničkog društva. U: Korporativno upravljanje, stanje i perspektive ekonomskog razvoja BiH. *Sarajevo: Revicon.* (p. 137–154).

Trivun, V. (2019). Odgovornost privrednih društava. *Ekonomski fakultet.*

Trivun, V., & Silajdžić, V. (2020). Krivična odgovornost privrednih društava. *Business Consultant/Poslovni Konsultant*, *12*(100).

Trivun, V. (2023). Kružne prevare i mjere za njihovo suzbijanje. *Business Consultant/ Poslovni Konsultant, 14(127).*

Uzun, H., Szewczyk, S. H., & Varma, R. (2004). Board composition and corporate fraud. *Financial Analysts Journal*, *60*(3), 33–43.

Van den Muijsenbergh, WH, & Rezai, S. (2012). Corporations and the European Convention on Human Rights. *Pacific McGeorge Global Business & Development Law Journal,* Vol. 25, Issue 1 (2012), pp. 43–68

Vasiljević, M. (2015). Kompanijsko pravo – Pravo privrednih društava. Beograd: *Udruženje pravnika u privredi Srbije.*
Vasiljević, M. (2020). Probijanje pravne ličnosti u kompanijskom pravu.
Wagner, G., & Kötz, H. (2021). *Deliktsrecht* (14., neu bearbeitete Auflage.). *Verlag Franz Vahlen.*
Wegner, K., Zimmermann, T., El-Ghazi, M. (2022). Vorschlag zur Einführung eines Gesetzes über das Aufspüren verdächtiger Vermögensgegenstande und über die selbständige Vermögenseinziehung (Vermögenseinziehungsgesetz). *KriPoZ 6.* https://kripoz.de/wp-content/uploads/2022/11/wegner-ladwig-zimmermann-el-ghazi-vorschlag-eines-vermoegenseinziehungsgesetzes.pdf
Wells, C. (2001). *Corporations and criminal responsibility.* Oxford University Press, USA.
Wells, J. T. (2017). *Corporate fraud handbook: Prevention and detection.* John Wiley & Sons.
Williams, C. C. (2015). Evaluating cross-national variations in envelope wage payments in East-Central Europe. *Economic and Industrial Democracy, 36*(2), 283–303.
Wodicka, J. M. (1993). Die Untreue zum Nachteil der GmbH bei vorheriger Zustimmung aller Gesellschafter.
Zimmermann, T., & Riegner, M. (2023). Prosecuting Corruption in Kenya, Uganda and South Africa. *Trier Institute for Money Laundering and Corruption Criminal Law (TrIGeKo).* https://trigeko.uni-trier.de/wp-content/uploads/2023/05/Corruption_in_Africa-Riegner_Zimmermann_2023.pdf.
Zimmermann, T. (2020). Vom Leid und Eigeninteresse künstlicher Rechtsträger: Juristische Personen als moralische Subjekte? In M. Bublitz, M. Bung, T. Grünewald, U. Magnus, G. Putzke, & M. Scheinfeld (Eds.), *Festschrift für Reinhard Merkel (pp. 295–315).* Duncker & Humblot.

Directives and Regulations

Council of Europe. Committee of Ministers. (1990). Liability of Enterprises for Offences: Recommendation No. R (88) 18 Adopted by the Committee of Ministers of the Council of Europe on 20 October 1988 and Explanatory Memorandum (Vol. 18). Council of Europe. https://rm.coe.int/16804c5d71.
Council of the European Union. (2018). Council Directive (EU) 2018/822 of 25 May 2018 amending Directive 2011/16/EU as regards mandatory automatic exchange of information in the field of taxation in relation to reportable cross-border arrangements. Official Journal of the European Union, L139, 1–13. https://eur-lex.europa.eu/legal-content/EN/TXT/?uri=CELEX:32018L0822
Council of Europe/European Court of Human Rights. (2020). Guide on Article 1 of Protocol No. 1 to the European Convention on Human Rights: Protection of property (Updated 31 August 2020). Strasbourg: Council of Europe. Retrieved from https://www.echr.coe.int/documents/guide_art_1_protocol_1_eng.pdf

European Parliament and Council. (2008). Directive 2008/99/EC of the European Parliament and of the Council of 19 November 2008 on the protection of the environment through criminal law. Official Journal of the European Union, L 328, 6.12.2008, 28–37.

European Parliament and Council of the European Union. (2009). *Directive 2009/102/EC of the European Parliament and of the Council of 16 September 2009 in the area of company law on single-member private limited liability companies (Codified version). Official Journal of the European Union*, L 258, 11–15.

European Parliament and Council. (2017). Directive (EU) 2017/1132 of the European Parliament and of the Council of 14 June 2017 relating to certain aspects of company law. Official Journal of the European Union, L 169, 46–127.

European Parliament and Council. (2017a). Directive (EU) 2017/1371 of the European Parliament and of the Council of 5 July 2017 on the fight against fraud to the Union's financial interests by means of criminal law. Official Journal of the European Union, L 198, 29.7.2017, 29–41.

European Parliament and Council. (2015). Directive (EU) 2015/849 on the prevention of the use of the financial system for the purposes of money laundering or terrorist financing, amending Regulation (EU) No 648/2012, and repealing Directive 2005/60/EC and Commission Directive 2006/70/EC. Official Journal of the European Union, L 141, 73–117. Amended by Directive (EU) 2018/843, Directive (EU) 2019/2177, Regulation (EU) 2023/1113, and Directive (EU) 2024/1640.

European Parliament and Council. (2018). Directive (EU) 2018/843 of the European Parliament and of the Council of 30 May 2018 amending Directive (EU) 2015/849 on the prevention of the use of the financial system for the purposes of money laundering or terrorist financing. Official Journal of the European Union, L 156, 43–74.

European Parliament and Council. (2019). Directive (EU) 2019/1151 of the European Parliament and of the Council of 20 June 2019 amending Directive (EU) 2017/1132 as regards the use of digital tools and processes in company law. Official Journal of the European Union, L 186, 80–104.

European Parliament and Council. (2024). Regulation (EU) 2024/1620 of the European Parliament and of the Council of 31 May 2024 establishing the Authority for Anti-Money Laundering and Countering the Financing of Terrorism and amending Regulations (EU) No 1093/2010, (EU) No 1094/2010 and (EU) No 1095/2010 *(OJ L, 2024/1620, 19.6.2024, ELI:* http://data.europa.eu/eli/reg/2024/1620/oj).).

Council Directive 2006/112/EC of 28 November 2006 on the common system of value-added tax (VAT Directive).

European Commission (2023). Proposal for a DIRECTIVE OF THE EUROPEAN PARLIAMENT AND OF THE COUNCIL amending Directives 2009/102/EC and (EU) 2017/1132 as regards further expanding and upgrading the use of digital tools and processes in company law. Brussels, 29.3.2023. COM(2023) 177 final.

Treaty on the Functioning of the European Union (TFEU), Articles 49–50 (freedom of establishment).

Bosnia and Herzegovina Legal Framework

Company Law of the Federation of Bosnia and Herzegovina (Official Gazette FBiH, No. 81/15 and 75/2021).
Company Law of Republika Srpska ("Official Gazette of RS", nos. 127/2008, 58/2009, 100/2011, 67/2013, 100/2017, 82/2019, and 17/2023)
Criminal Code of the Federation of Bosnia and Herzegovina ("Official Gazette of the Federation of BiH", nos. 36/2003, 21/2004 - corr., 69/2004, 18/2005, 42/2010, 42/2011, 59/2014, 76/2014, 46/2016, and 75/2017)
Criminal Code of Brčko District ("Official Gazette of Brčko District of BiH", nos. 19/2020 - consolidated text, 3/2024, and 14/2024)
Criminal Code of Republika Srpska ("Official Gazette of RS", nos. 67/17, 104/2018 - Constitutional Court decision, 15/21, 89/21, and 73/2023)
Law on Companies of Brčko District of Bosnia and Herzegovina – Consolidated Text ("Official Gazette of Brčko District of Bosnia and Herzegovina", nos. 49/11 and 01–02–815/20)
Law on Obligations of FBIH ("Sl. list SFRJ", br. 29/1978, 39/1985, 45/1989 - odluka USJ i 57/1989, "Sl. list RBiH", br. 2/1992, 13/1993 i 13/1994 i "Sl. novine FBiH", nos. 29/2003 i 42/2011)
Law on Obligations ("Official Gazette of SFRY" nos. 29/78, 39/85, 57/89 and "Official Gazette of the Republika Srpska" nos. 17/93, 3/96, 39/03, 74/04)
Law on the Prevention of Money Laundering and Financing of Terrorism (Official Gazette BiH, No. 13/24)
Law on the Tax Administration of the Federation of Bosnia and Herzegovina ('Official Gazette of the Federation of Bosnia and Herzegovina' nos. 33/02, 28/04, 57/09, 40/10, 29/11 – Constitutional Court decision, 27/12, 7/13, 71/14, 91/15 and 44/22)

Germany Legal Framework

Act on Regulatory Offences (Gesetz über Ordnungswidrigkeiten – OWiG). Gesetz über Ordnungswidrigkeiten in der Fassung der Bekanntmachung vom 19. Februar 1987 (BGBl. I S. 602), das zuletzt durch Artikel 10 des Gesetzes vom 12. Juli 2024 (BGBl. 2024 I Nr. 234) geändert worden ist.
BaFin - Acts - Money Laundering Act. Geldwäschegesetz vom 23. Juni 2017 (BGBl. I S. 1822), das zuletzt durch Artikel 8 des Gesetzes vom 27. Dezember 2024 (BGBl. 2024 I Nr. 438) geändert worden ist.
Civil Code in the version promulgated on 2 January 2002 (Federal Law Gazette (*Bundesgesetzblatt*) I page 42, 2909; 2003 I page 738), last amended by Article 1 of the Act of 10 August 2021 (Federal Law Gazette I p. 3515).
German Criminal Code (Strafgesetzbuch – StGB). Strafgesetzbuch in der Fassung der Bekanntmachung vom 13. November 1998 (BGBl. I S. 3322), das zuletzt durch Artikel 2 des Gesetzes vom 9. Januar 2026 (BGBl. 2026 I Nr. 3) geändert worden ist.

German Civil Code BGB. Bürgerliches Gesetzbuch in der Fassung der Bekanntmachung vom 2. Januar 2002 (BGBl. I S. 42, 2909; 2003 I S. 738), das zuletzt durch Artikel 4 des Gesetzes vom 22. Dezember 2025 (BGBl. 2025 I Nr. 364) geändert worden ist.

German Code of Criminal Procedure (Strafprozeßordnung – StPO). Strafprozeßordnung in der Fassung der Bekanntmachung vom 7. April 1987 (BGBl. I S. 1074, 1319), die zuletzt durch Artikel 3 des Gesetzes vom 11. Januar 2026 (BGBl. 2026 I Nr. 9) geändert worden ist.

German Commercial Code. Handelsgesetzbuch in der im Bundesgesetzblatt Teil III, Gliederungsnummer 4100–1, veröffentlichten bereinigten Fassung, das zuletzt durch Artikel 18 des Gesetzes vom 22. Dezember 2025 (BGBl. 2025 I Nr. 369) geändert worden ist.

Limited Liability Companies Act, as consolidated and published in the Federal Law Gazette III, Index No. 4123–1, as last amended by Article 9 of the Act of 22 February 2023 (Federal Law Gazette 2023 I No. 51)

Motive zu dem Entwurfe eines Bürgerlichen Gesetzbuches. (1888). *Band II* (zu §§ 704, 705 E I, p. 727). Berlin: Reichs-Justizamt.

Stock Corporation Act (Aktiengesetz – AktG). Aktiengesetz vom 6. September 1965 (BGBl. I S. 1089), das zuletzt durch Artikel 18 des Gesetzes vom 23. Oktober 2024 (BGBl. 2024 I Nr. 323) geändert worden ist

Croatia Legal Framework

Act on the Prevention of Money Laundering and Terrorist Financing. Official Gazette Nos. 108/2017, 39/2019, 151/2022.

Act on the Liability of Legal Persons for Criminal Offences. Official Gazette Nos. 151/2003, 110/2007, 45/2011, 143/2012, 114/2022, 114/2023.

Criminal Procedure Act. Official Gazette Nos. 152/2008, 76/2009, 80/2011, 91/2012, 143/2012, 56/2013, 145/2013, 152/2014, 70/2017, 126/2019, 126/2019, 80/2022, 36/2024, 72/2025.

Criminal Code of the Republic of Croatia. Official Gazette Nos. 125/2011, 144/2012, 56/2015, 61/2015, 101/2017, 118/2018, 126/2019, 84/2021, 114/2022, 114/2023, 36/2024.

Dayton Peace Accords, (1995). General Framework Agreement for Peace in Bosnia and Herzegovina. *Washington, DC*.

General Tax Act (*Opći poreski zakon*). Official Gazette Nos. br. 115/16., 106/18., 121/19., 32/20., 42/20., 114/22 and 114/24

Law Business Companies of Republic of Croatia (Zakon o trgovačkim društvima), Offcicial Gazette nr. 111/1993, 34/1999, 121/1999, 52/2000, 118/2003, 107/2007, 146/2008, 137/2009, 111/2012, 125/2011, 68/2013, 110/2015, 40/2019, 34/2022, 114/2022, 18/2023, 130/2023, 136/2024

Law on the Prevention of Money Laundering and Financing of Terrorist Activities. (*Zakon o sprečavanju pranja novca i finansiranju terorističkih aktivnosti*). Official Gazette of Bosnia and Herzegovina, No. 13/2024.

Law on Obligations (Zakon o obveznim odnosima). Official Gazette of the Republic of Croatia, Nos. 35/2005, 41/2008, 125/2011, 78/2015, 29/2018, 126/2021, 114/2022, 156/2022, 155/2023.

Dataset

Eurostat (2024). Business demography by legal form and NACE Rev. 2 activity. Data coverage 2015–2022. https://doi.org/10.2908/BD_L_FORM

Case Law

Appellate Court of the Brčko District of Bosnia and Herzegovina. (2021a). *Judgment No.* No. 96 0 K 106916 21 Kž.

Appellate Court of the Brčko District of Bosnia and Herzegovina. (2021). *Judgment No. 96 0 K 124261 21 Kž.*

Appellate Court of Brčko District of Bosnia and Herzegovina. (2017). Judgment No. 96 0 P 097567 17 Gž.

Appellate Court of Brčko District of Bosnia and Herzegovina. (2015). *Judgment No. 96 0 Ps 064332 15 Pž.*

Appellate Court of Brčko District of Bosnia and Herzegovina. (2013). Judgment No. 97 0 Ip 001353 13 Pž.

Atlas Maritime Co. SA v. Avalon Maritime Ltd. (The Coral Rose (No. 3)), (1991) 4 All E.R. 783 (C.A.).

Bundesgerichtshof. (1987). *BGHZ 101, 380, 388.*

Bundesgerichtshof. (2004). Judgment of 19 July 2004 – II ZR 217/03. Neue Juristische Wochenschrift (NJW), 2004, 2667–2669.

Bundesgerichtshof. (2005). Judgment of 14 November 2005 – II ZR 178/03. https://www.bundesgerichtshof.de/SharedDocs/Entscheidungen/DE/Zivilsenate/II_ZS/2003/II_ZR_178-03.pdf?__blob=publicationFile&v=1

Bundesgerichtshof. (2008, April 28). *BGH, Urteil vom 28. April 2008 – II ZR 264/06* (TRIHOTEL-Fall). Retrieved from https://juris.bundesgerichtshof.de

Bundesgerichtshof. (2010, October 19). VI ZR 248/08 (Judgment).

Bundesgerichtshof. (2014). Judgment of 11 February 2014 – XI ZR 170/13. Neue Juristische Wochenschrift (NJW), 2014, 1380.

Bundesgerichtshof. (2020a). Judgment of 25 May 2020 – VI ZR 252/19. *Neue Juristische Wochenschrift (NJW)*, 2020, 1962–1963.

Bundesgerichtshof. (2020b). Judgment of 28 July 2020 – VI ZR 397/19. *Neue Juristische Wochenschrift (NJW)*, 2020, 2798–2802.

Bundesgerichtshof. (2023a). *Judgment of 26 June 2023 – VIa ZR 335/21* (Volkswagen Passat EA 288).
Bundesgerichtshof. (2023b). *Judgment of 26 June 2023 – VIa ZR 533/21* (Audi SQ5 EA 896Gen2BiT).
Bundesgerichtshof. (2023c). *Judgment of 26 June 2023 – VIa ZR 1031/22* (Mercedes-Benz C 220 d OM 651).
Bundesgerichtshof. (2025). Judgment of 08 July 2025 – II ZR 165/23
Bundesgerichtshof. (2025a) Judgment of 3 April 2025 - *III ZR 23/24.*
Bundesgerichtshof. (2025b) Judgment of 2 April 2025 - VIa ZR 282/22.
Bundesgerichtshof. (2025c). Judgment of 2 January 2025 - *III ZR 284/20.*
Boyle Transport (Northern Ireland) Ltd v. R; Patrick Boyle and Mark Boyle v. R, (2016) EWCA Crim 19 (Eng. & Wales C.A. Crim. Div.).
Cantonal court in Sarajevo. (2010). Decision 09 0 P 008897 Gž from 24.11.2010.
Commercial Court in Varaždin. (2025). *Judgment, case no. P-23/2025–45.* Varaždin.
Constitutional Court of Bosnia and Herzegovina. (2023). *Decision on admissibility and merits in case no. U-2/23.* Sarajevo: Constitutional Court of BiH.
Constitutional Court of the Federation of Bosnia and Herzegovina. (2011). Decision Number U-14/10.
County Court in Pula-Pola. (2025). Decision Kž-400/2024–7.
County Court in Rijeka. (2025). Judgment, case no. Gž-338/2025–2. Rijeka.
County Court in Split. (2014). Judgment No. *Gž x-533/2013–2.*
Court of Bosnia and Herzegovina. (2022). Judgment No. S1 2 K 032246 21 K.
Court of Justice of the European Union. (2022). Judgment of the Court (Grand Chamber) in WM and Sovim SA v. Luxembourg Business Registers (Joined Cases C-37/20 and C-601/20). ECLI:EU:C:2022:912.
Court of Justice of the European Union (2015). Judgment Tipou A.E. v. Ipourgos Tipou Kai Meson Mazikis Enimerosis (C-81/09). Available at: https://eur-lex.europa.eu/legal-content/en/TXT/?uri=CELEX:62009CC0081.
Cour de cassation (1985) Judgment from 4 February 1085. Arrêt n° 84–91.581, rejet du pourvoi contre CA Paris, 9e chambre, 14 février 1984. Bulletin criminel 1985, n° 52. https://www.legifrance.gouv.fr/juri/id/JURITEXT000007064646/
Cour de cassation (2000) Judgment from 16 April 2000. *Société hôtelière Anne Y et al. v. Administrateurs judiciaires de la société SEAM et al.*, Nos. 96–15.827 & 96–15.828. https://www.legifrance.gouv.fr/juri/id/JURITEXT000007041397
Court of Appeal (England and Wales). (1991). *Atlas Maritime Co. SA v. Avalon Maritime Ltd. (The Coral Rose (No. 3)), (1991) 4 All E.R. 783 (C.A.).*
Court of Appeal (England and Wales), Civil Division. (2012). *VTB Capital Plc v. Nutritek International Corp, (2012) EWCA Civ 808, (2012) 2 C.L.C. 431, 460 (Eng. C.A.).*
Court of Justice of the European Union. (2010). Idrima Tipou AE v. Ipourgos Tipou Kai Meson Mazikis Enimerosis, Case C-81/09, ECLI:EU:C:2010:625.
Court of Justice of the European Union. (2019). Skatteministeriet v. T Danmark (C-116/16) and Y Denmark ApS (C-117/16), Judgment of the Grand Chamber, 26 February 2019, ECLI:EU:C:2019:135.
Court of Justice of the European Union. (2019a). N Luxembourg 1 and Others v. Skatteministeriet, Joined Cases C-115/16, C-118/16, C-119/16, and C-299/16, Judgment of 26 February 2019, ECLI:EU:C:2019:134.

Court of Justice of the European Union. (2000). Emsland-Stärke GmbH v. Hauptzollamt Hamburg-Jonas, Case C-110/99, ECLI:EU:C:2000:695

Court of Justice of the European Union. (1999). Centros Ltd v. Erhvervs- og Selskabsstyrelsen, Case C-212/97, ECLI:EU:C:1999:126.

European Court of Human Rights. (2013). Khodorkovskiy and Lebedev v. Russia (Applications Nos. 11082/06 and 13772/05, Judgment of 25 July 2013). Strasbourg: Council of Europe.

European Court of Human Rights. (2015). Ljubljanska banka v. Croatia (dec.), no. 29003/07.

European Court of Human Rights. (2018). Lekić v. Slovenia (Application No. 36480/07, Judgment of 11 December 2018.

European Court of Human Rights. (2000). *Comingersoll S.A. v. Portugal* (Application No. 35382/97). Strasbourg: Council of Europe.

European Court of Human Rights. (2020). Slovenia v. Croatia, no. 54155/16.

European Court of Human Rights. (2025). Radelić v. Croatia (Application Nos. 12432/22, Judgment of 13 May 2025). Strasbourg: Council of Europe.

European Court of Human Rights. (2004). *Mykhaylenky and Others v. Ukraine* (Applications nos. 35091/02, 35196/02, 35201/02, 35204/02, 35205/02, 35207/02, 35208/02, 35213/02, and 35217/02). Strasbourg: Council of Europe.

High Commercial Court of the Republic of Croatia. (2021, November 19). Decision Pž 1820/2020–3.

High Commercial Court of the Republic of Croatia. (2007, December 13). Decision Pž-1250/2004–5.

High Commercial Court of the Republic of Croatia. (2004, February 17). Decision Pž-6369/03.

High Commercial Court of the Republic of Croatia. (2003, April 15). Decision, Pž-1760/02.

High Commercial Court of the Republic of Croatia. (2003a, November 18). Decision Pž-636/03.

High Commercial Court of the Republic of Croatia. (2003b, September 23). Pž-1522/03.

High Court of Justice (England and Wales), Chancery Division. (1953). Re F.G. (Films) Ltd., (1953) 1 All E.R. 615 (Ch. D.).

High Court of Justice (England and Wales), Family Division. (2008). Faiza Ben Hashem v. Abdulhadi Ali Shayif, (2008) EWHC 2380 (Fam), (2009) 1 F.L.R. 115 (163) (Eng.).

Higher Regional Court of Stuttgart (2024). *Judgment from 30 January 2024. 12 U 285/21.*

International Chamber of Commerce. (1997). ICC Case No. 8385. Journal du Droit International, 124, 1061–1067.

International Centre for Settlement of Investment Disputes (ICSID). (2008). TSA Spectrum de Argentina S.A. v. Argentine Republic, Case No. ARB/05/5, 147 (Dec. 19, 2008)

International Centre for Settlement of Investment Disputes (ICSID). (2005). *Aguas del Tunari, S.A. v. Republic of Bolivia, ICSID Case No. ARB/02/3.*

International Centre for Settlement of Investment Disputes (ICSID). (2003). *Autopista Concesionada de Venezuela, C.A. v. Bolivarian Republic of Venezuela, ICSID Case No. ARB/00/5.*

Municipal court in Sarajevo. (2006). Decision number P-23/04 from 2.6.2006.
Oberlandesgericht Oldenburg. (2016). *Urteil vom 17.06.2016 – 6 U 22/16.*
Supreme Court of the Federation of Bosnia and Herzegovina. (2019). Decision case no. 51 0 Ps 108754 18 Rev.
Supreme Court of the Federation of Bosnia and Herzegovina. (2018). Decision No. 65 0 P 180427 16 Rev.
Supreme Court of the Federation of Bosnia and Herzegovina. (2018a). Decision No. 58 0 P 101552 16 Rev.
Supreme Court of the Federation of Bosnia and Herzegovina. (2016). Decision No. 43 0 Ps 073499 15 Rev.
Supreme Court of the Federation of Bosnia and Herzegovina. (2012). Decision case no. 65 0 P 195188 11 Rev.
Supreme Court of the Republic of Croatia. (2013). Decision Rev-666/2010–2.
Supreme Court of Republika Srpska. (2024). Judgment No. 60 0 Ps 030404 23 Rev. Banja Luka: Supreme Court of Republika Srpska.
Supreme Court of the Republic of Srpska. (2024a). Judgment No. 80 0 P 099848 23 Rev. Banja Luka: Supreme Court of Republika Srpska
Supreme Court of Republika Srpska. (2022). *Judgment Rev. 80 0 P 098942 20 Rev.* Banja Luka: Supreme Court of RS
Supreme Court of Republika Srpska. (2019). Judgment 60 0 Ps 024805 19 Rev.
Royal Courts of Justice. (2016). R v. Boyle Transport (Northern Ireland) Ltd, Patrick Boyle and Mark Boyle (2016) EWCA Crim 19. Judgment from 25 February 2016.
Reichsgericht. (1904). *RGZ 57, 239, 241.*
Texas Supreme Court. (1986). *Castleberry v. Branscum*, 721 S.W.2d 270 (Tex.).
UK Supreme Court. (2013, June 12). *Prest v. Petrodel Resources Ltd. and others, (2013) UKSC 34.*

Internet Sources

European Parliament. (2023). *Company law.* Fact Sheets on the European Union. https://www.europarl.europa.eu/factsheets/en/sheet/35/company-law
Gutić, A. (2024). *The Federation is paying millions in damages to private companies, while the prosecutor's offices remain silent.* Žurnal. https://www.zurnal.info/clanak/the-federation-is-paying-millions-in-damages-to-private-companies-while-the-prosecutors-offices-remain-silent/27277
Transparency International. (2024). Corruption Perceptions Index 2024. https://transparency.org
World Justice Project. (2023). Rule of Law Index 2023. https://worldjusticeproject.org

Publications

FATF (2025). Terrorism & Proliferation, FATF, Paris, France, www.fatf-gafi.org/en/publications/Fatfrecommendations/Fatf-recommendations.html.

FATF (2022). Anti-money laundering and counter-terrorist financing measures Germany. Mutual Evaluation Report 2022. Available here: https://www.fatf-gafi.org/content/dam/fatf-gafi/mer/Mutual-Evaluation-Report-Germany-2022.pdf.coredownload.inline.pdf.

FATF (2024b). Anti-money laundering and counter-terrorist financing measures Croatia. 2nd Enhanced Follow-up Report &Technical Compliance Re-Rating. Available here https://rm.coe.int/moneyval-2024-18-hr-5thround-2ndenhfur/1680b2bbbc.

FATF (2024a). Anti-money laundering and counter-terrorist financing measures Bosnia and Herzegovina. Fifth Round Mutual Evaluation Report. Available here: https://www.fatf-gafi.org/content/dam/fatf-gafi/fsrb-mer/MONEYVAL-MER-Bosnia%20and%20Herzegovina.pdf.coredownload.inline.pdF

G20. (2013, September 6). G20 Leaders' Declaration: St. Petersburg Summit. Retrieved from https://www.g20.org

OECD. (2025). OECD Benchmark Definition of Foreign Direct Investment (Fifth Edition). OECD Publishing. https://doi.org/10.1787/7f05c0a3-en

OECD. (2022). Better Regulation Practices across the European Union 2022, OECD Publishing, Paris, https://doi.org/10.1787/6e4b095d-en.

OSCE. (2024). *OSCE welcomes the adoption of the Law on Preventing Money Laundering and Terrorist Financing*. OSCE Mission to Bosnia and Herzegovina.

Tax Authority of Federation of Bosnia and Herzegovina (2024). *Annual report for the period 1 January – 31 December 2023* (No. 13/07–12–2–361–12/23). Sarajevo.

USAID. (2022). *Judicial effectiveness index of Bosnia and Herzegovina: 2021 report*. Prepared under the USAID Bosnia and Herzegovina Monitoring and Evaluation Support Activity II (MEASURE II), Contract Number AID-167-I-17–00004; Task Order Number 72016819F00001. USAID/Bosnia and Herzegovina.

V-Dem Institute. (2024). Democracy Report 2024: Autocratization in progress. University of Gothenburg.

World Bank. (2022). Legal Persons and Arrangements ML Risk Assessment Tool: With Guidance on Assessing Risks Related to Beneficial Ownership Transparency. National Money Laundering / Terrorist Financing (ML/TF) Risk Assessment Toolkit;. © World Bank. http://hdl.handle.net/10986/37701 License: *CC BY 3.0 IGO*

FSC
www.fsc.org
MIX
Papier | Fördert gute Waldnutzung
FSC® C083411

Kolibri 360 GmbH
Ferdinand-Jühlke-Straße 7
99095 Erfurt, Deutschland
produktsicherheit@kolibri360.de